The Catholic Digest Christmas Book

Edited by

Father Kenneth Ryan

CARILLON CB BOOKS

2413   4-10-92

THE CATHOLIC DIGEST CHRISTMAS BOOK

A CARILLON BOOK

ISBN: 0-89310-026-9

Library of Congress Catalog Card Number: 77-82809

Copyright ©1977 by Carillon Books

Printed in the United States of America

CARILLON BOOKS is a division of
Catholic Digest
2115 Summit Ave.
St. Paul, Minnesota 55105
U.S.A.

TABLE OF CONTENTS

iv

INTRODUCTION

A book about Christmas should certainly be religious, must be joyful, but of course can be in no way original. The customs and the emotions connected with the feast are timeless and to most persons variations are perversions of the eternal and blessed story. Yet, this same old story, in the case of Christmas, never loses its charm. There are other seasons of the year for sorrow and Christmas has no touch of any emotion but joy in it. It must be because we all like to be joyful, no matter how modern we feel.

People of these modern times pride themselves on bringing ever fresh novelties into their lives, but even in so up-to-the-minute a business as television, repetition has become the secret of success. A new series can just about break even between production costs and income; it is only when the reruns begin and further production costs stop that substantial profit is made. The spiritual profits of observing Christmas have been rolling in for years, even though it is only the youngest child who is hearing its story for the first time. This kind of profit can be made a constant income by again reading about, and again reverently observing, the holy feast of Christmas.

—Kenneth Ryan, editor

Chapter I
This Was God's Love

The Child, the Mother, the angels, the shepherds, the stable-cave, the Star and the Magi are chapters in the story of the Birth at Bethlehem

"What Child Is This?"—John Cardinal Wright answers here the question asked in the famous Christmas carol. Thomas Merton picks up the theme and points out what Christ's answer was to the question. Fulton Sheen tells us of the meaning of the Mother in the Christmas story; Daniel-Rops discusses the angels; Father Richard Murphy, the shepherds; Kay Sullivan, the Magi and their Star.

Denis O'Shea and Father Filas describe the place of the birth of the Child and the home and daily life of the Holy Family.

These are the elements of the "basic" Christmas story and even a book concerned with all the other aspects of the ancient feast should begin with them.

WHAT CHILD IS THIS?[1]

The true Christian welcomes all children into the world
By John Cardinal Wright

During the Advent season I kept remembering the opening
words of one of the loveliest of all Christmas hymns:

> *What Child is this, who laid to rest,*
> *On Mary's lap is sleeping?*
> *Whom angels greet with anthem sweet,*
> *While shepherds watch are keeping?*

Whenever a baby is born, any baby, anywhere, normal people
look on the child with wonder and hope. Minds with any ray of
faith find themselves reflecting on the providence of God; hearts
with hopes that this child may be somehow an instrument of
that providence. Even people disillusioned by their neighbors
and disappointed in themselves gaze on a newborn baby with
the beginnings of refreshed hope. They ask: What blessings
may this child bring? Who may he prove to be? What child is
this?

Christians have always felt this way about babies; so have
civilized people generally. Powerful natural feelings as well as
prayerful supernatural hopes are behind the passion with which
good people sing the lines of the Christmas liturgy: "A Child is
born to us, and a Son is given to us . . . ."

But in some "undeveloped" civilizations the coming of a baby
is, we are told, no longer a source of joy. No commentary on a
society is more dismal. And no commentary on some
"progressive" civilizations is more damning than that they often
cynically question the joy and wonder that should greet the
coming of a baby.

In heathenized societies of our day people are being taught to
dread the coming of a child. When conceived, babies are
disposed of in a slaughter of the innocents more horrendous than
Herod's, because more scientifically planned, approved, and
executed. In some areas of Western Society the attitude toward
babies is not so different. A mass-circulation magazine once

3

featured on its cover two symptomatic articles: "The Great
Fall-Out Shelter Panic" and "Birth Control: World Problem."
There, it seems, are the twin dreads of a neurotic civilization:
bombs and babies!

What insane line of thought is this? Perhaps meditation at
Christmas on the question with which we began—What Child
is This?— will help remind us of the providence of God. Perhaps
such Christian thought about babies will hasten second thoughts,
more rational and religious thoughts, about bombs as well.

The ancients described war in a compact phrase which meant
"that which is hateful to mothers." People who think in terms
of babies do not think in terms of bombs. People who welcome
babies are impatient with the immorality that leads to bombs.
.Their belief in God's providence gives them the courage both
to have babies and to reject bombs.

Such people may have heartbreaking problems. But they
would be incapable of seriously comparing the problems of
bombs and babies. They have too much intellectual dignity
and spiritual serenity to talk so perversely.

In the midst of all the panic about bombs and babies, I
received a Christmas card from a devout Christian, a convert to
Catholicism. He and his wife sent their friends this Christmas
message in the form of a prayerful meditation:

"Suppose the dreadful holocaust will come, and there is only
a moment left before all is dark and still on earth. What would
you have me do, Lord, while waiting for the final, fateful hour?
Surely, You would not have me cringe in fear before any evil,
or flaunt your truths to beg or barter my precious soul for even
a sweet moment more of life upon this planet."

"Dearest Lord, grant me the strength and courage to be
unafraid; to resist until the final moment and shed my blood if
need be, nourished by the faith that sent the martyrs gayly
singing to their deaths. Dearest Lord, if this be the final hour,
let me not hesitate to the very last to do your will. To bear
witness to your truths. To honor your great commandment to
love all your creatures. To help the less fortunate of any skin
or race or creed in any land. To share to the last crust with
him who has no bread. To oppose injustice, exploitation, greed.

To care for my neglected and oppressed neighbor wherever he may be. To spend myself in more ways still, and sacrifice in Christian charity, even when it may involve the least of your creatures half a world away. To be in truth my brother's keeper, true to the innate conscience of my being, created man in your image. To pray until the last for my friend and my foe alike. And on my knees never to give up hope that evil will succumb at last to good. And faced with awful danger, to live each blessed day so that, come what may, I shall not fear the end."

These are the thoughts and the courage of one whose mind and heart have been transformed by the coming of the Baby born at Christmas. What Child is this who teaches still, as centuries ago He taught the martyrs, a faith so luminous, a hope so courageous, a charity so inspired? What Child is this?

> *This, this, is Christ the King,*
> *Whom shepherds guard and angels sing;*
> *Haste, haste, to bring Him laud:*
> *The Babe, the Son of Mary!*

CHRISTMAS DISCOVERY[2]

A knowledge of identity
By Thomas Merton

It is a terrible thing that no one of us should realize what it means that there has been a Christmas in our world.

Yet some of us will, perhaps, say, "We know what it is all about. Christ is born."

"So Christ is born! And what does that mean?"

"It means we are redeemed; it means we are saved."

"Is that all?"

"Christ is born! We are going to go to heaven!" And I say to you, it is a terrible thing that none of us should be able to realize what it means, that there has been a Christmas in our world.

Is this something that happens in every man's childhood? It happened in mine. Yours too, I suppose. One day (which was almost certainly not Christmas) without any apparent reason or occasion, you suddenly became conscious of who you were. Your identity came out like an image on a negative, and it was real with a new and unfamiliar kind of reality that was more real than anything you knew.

It was something you felt to be too important to tell anybody, so important that it was impossible to explain.

You had discovered you were a person. You knew who you were.

There was once conceived a Man to whom this happened at the first second when He came into existence.

A human soul, a will capable of unimaginably great love and a mind wide enough to take an infinity; a soul, mind, and will, which had a moment before been nothing, had not existed, came into being because in the heart of a girl an almost unspoken assent was given to a movement of great grace.

And in the fraction of a second in which this soul, in its flesh, began to exist, the man who was so conceived was at once awake and saw, not vaguely, not in mystery, not with surmise or question, but saw clearly and fully, and without being dazzled or

6

frightened—saw who He was.

He saw who He was, because when He awoke out of nothingness He was gazing, with His whole intellect into the face of the infinite truth who was at the same time his Father and himself.

This Man, who had never before existed, and had just begun to exist, saw, realized, fully grasped the meaning, not of the words "I exist, I am myself," but:

"I am God!"

MOTHER MEANS LOVE[3]

Through all evolution there could never be a human mother until love came into the world
By Fulton J. Sheen

It took a long time in God's plan to make a mother. In lower forms of life, such as the amoeba, motherhood is only a fission, or splitting, as the young life breaks off from the parent cell. Land crabs take care to push their eggs into the water, but then abandon them. No real motherhood here, for the young never see their mothers, nor do the mothers care for the young.

This universe of ours is full of orphans; the young that are begotten are completely forgotten. Almost all fruit is orphaned; it lives in independent existence from the tree.

In the insect world, butterflies show mother instinct to the extent of hatching eggs under a leaf, where they are least exposed. In the animal world hens show a motherly concern for their young; indeed, the Lord used them as an example.

How often have I been ready to
gather thy children together,
As a hen gathers her chickens under
her wings;
And thou didst refuse it!

No boy who ever gathered eggs from the barnyard or a crib, as I did when I was a boy, will ever forget the wrath of a cackling, setting hen. You begin to know what an "old hen" is, when you go about gathering eggs.

As we go up nature's ladder, there is an increasing unity of mother and offspring, until finally, in the higher species, we find that mothers carry the young within them. Despite all this cosmic evolution, however, there could never be a human mother until love came into the world.

If a mother is to be made, what is begotten must come from a free act of the will. The woman freely submits to the love of a man, not like the earth to the seed, but rather in an active surrender: two human beings who are freely united in soul freely unite in body. One might almost say that the generation begins in the mind and soul with love and completes itself in the body.

All love tends to an incarnation, even God's. Generation, then, is not a push from below but a gift from above. The child is the incarnation of the mutual love of a husband and a wife.

When a mother conceives the young life within her through a free act of love, she has a kind of love different from what any man has for a neighbor. A mother's love during the time she is a flesh-and-blood ciborium is a perfect example of love which hardly knows a separation between herself and her child. Motherhood thus becomes a kind of priesthood. She brings God to man by preparing the flesh in which the soul will be implanted; she brings man to God in offering the newborn child back again to the Creator.

Mothers in the animal kingdom care only for a body; mothers in the spiritual kingdom must care also for a soul, a mind, and a heart. The soul comes from God and must go back again to Him. God sets the target, the parents are the bow, and their vocation is to shoot the arrow straight.

It does not take long in the animal order to generate and develop the brain of a monkey, because the monkey brain does not have very much to do. But it takes a long time to develop the mind of a child, to inculcate ideals, virtues of purity, honesty, patriotism, and piety.

8

Animals can quickly leave their parents, because they have no eternal destiny. But humanity is under a compulsory educational act, and to fulfill this, there must be domesticity.

The home is the schoolhouse for affection wherein a mother completes the work that was begun when the child was conceived. Motherhood then turns into mother craft, as biology hands the work over to ethics. A tiny baby needs much mother care to become all that God destined it to be.

A mother must love each offspring as if it were the only one in all the world. This means recognizing that human beings are not just individuals, but persons. In the animal order there are *individuals;* in the human order there are *persons.*

The difference between an individual and a person is this: individuals are replaceable, and persons are not. You go to buy oranges in a store and say, "No, this one is bad. Give me another." But you cannot say that about children. A child is a person, unique, incommunicable, irreplaceable—that is why a mother sorrows so much when one is lost. It is a person and an immortal soul that has departed.

God, who became Man, pre-existed His own Mother, as an artist pre-exists his own painting. On one occasion, Whistler was complimented for the beautiful painting of his mother. His answer was, "You know how it is. One tries to make one's mommy as nice as one can." There is no reason to feel that Christ would do otherwise.

That every mother might understand that the interior generation is born of love, she, the ideal mother, conceived because she submitted herself to the Love of God. One day there came an angel who descended over the plains of Israel. Passing by the daughters of great kings of the East, he came to a woman who was kneeling in prayer, and said, "Hail, full of grace." These were not words; they were the Word, and "the Word was made Flesh, and dwelt amongst us."

And she, the Mother, was overshadowed by the Spirit of Love and bore within herself the Guest who was really the Host of the World. This was the greatest love that the world ever knew—the Love that came down into a woman and ended in an Incarnation.

This Mother gave further example to all mothers by caring both for the body and the soul of her Son. She cared for His body, for she wrapped Him in swaddling clothes and laid Him in a manger. She cared for His soul and His mind, for He was subject to her. This Child, who was subject to His Mother, was also the Creator of the world. Every mother, when she picks up the young life that has been born to her, looks up to the heavens to thank God for the gift which made the world young again. But here was a Mother who did not look up. She looked down to heaven, for this was heaven in her arms.

She gave the example of the worth of personality to all mothers; for, like every mother, she gave her Child a name. Since this Child was unique, it was fitting that He be given a name that would describe His mission. This Child came not to save people from insecurity, not to make them rich and powerful, but to save them from their sins. Hence He was given the name of Jesus, which means Saviour. It was a name before which the heavens and the earth trembled, and before which our knees bow.

If any one of us could have made our own mother, we would have made her the most beautiful woman in the world. As God pre-existed His own Mother somewhat in the way that an artist pre-exists his work, we can understand why she should be the Madonna of the World.

THE CAVE OF BETHLEHEM[4]

"Here, of the Virgin Mary, Jesus Christ was born"
By Denis O'Shea

St. Luke states in his Gospel that Mary laid her newly born Son "in a manger; because there was no room for them in the inn." A manger implies that the shelter found by Joseph was some kind of stable. In what part of Bethlehem was it? This stable is popularly supposed to have been in a cave in the fields outside the town. But it is almost certain that the stable formed part of the inn. It was a cellar, something like the basement of a modern hotel. You can find such cellars still, as at Khan Djoub-Yousef, a truly ancient caravanserai. The principal part of the khan is a large court surrounded by walls against which leans a covered gallery. The traveler leads his donkey or camel, the shepherd his sheep, and the herdsman drives his cattle across the floor of the open court and then down a passage to the underground caves, where he stables them for the night. When the gate of the inn is closed, the watchman takes up his station, and all is secure for the night.

The keeper had refused Mary and Joseph admission to the inn itself but he allowed them to take shelter in one of these stables. Down there, they could give him no trouble. A gratuity from Joseph may have helped to gain them admission. Or maybe the keeper was a humane man with a wife and children of his own.

However, the fact is certain that they were permitted to go to the stable. With feelings of inexpressible relief they saw the keeper stand aside and allow them to enter the gate. Barely glancing at the crowded alcoves around, they picked their way across the littered floor, through the bales of merchandise. Under the archway in the back wall of the khan a flight of steps led down to an underground passage.

They paused at the top of the steps until Mary unpacked their lamp and filled it with oil. Joseph had no trouble in obtaining a light at the cooking fire in the nearest alcove. He put the lamp in her hand and she led the way down the slippery, unclean steps.

11

He followed her with the donkey.

When they reached the passage below, they moved along, seeking an unoccupied stable. The caves must have been fairly full on that cold winter night. They saw camels chewing the cud, donkeys tethered to the mangers, and sheep and cattle from beyond the Jordan and the Negeb. No owner would expose his beasts to the weather in the unroofed courtyard above. Mary went slowly along past the mouth of each cave, lamp in hand.

They were fortunate enough to find one stable untenanted save by a solitary ox. They stepped in, Mary holding the lamp high above her head, and looked about. What did they see by its light? Just a rude cave. It was 40 feet long from east to west, 16 feet wide, and 10 feet high. There was neither window nor door. There was no furniture except the manger, and the floor was far from clean. Though the rock walls were cold they were dry, and there was a stone roof overhead. But in Mary's eyes the stable had a supreme advantage. It afforded a privacy unobtainable in the human habitations above, and the Holy Couple sought privacy rather than a place to sleep.

The Evangelist does not state that the Saviour was born in a cave. His mention of the manger naturally indicates a stable of some sort, but he does not use the word "cave." How, then, do we know that the Saviour was born in this cave? The tradition of the first and second centuries has supplemented the Gospel on the point, and that tells us that the manger was in a cave, a fact of inestimable interest.

St. Justin Martyr wrote down the tradition as he heard it, and he was a native of Palestine. He was born at Neapolis, the ancient Sichem, within forty miles of Bethlehem, early in the second century, and was thus a member of the generation that succeeded the Apostles. He is a witness to the belief of the early Christians who lived at Bethlehem itself. He wrote, "Since Joseph could not find any lodging in the village, he took up his quarters in a certain cave near the village and it was while they were there that Mary gave birth to the Christ and laid Him in a Manger."

In the next century the erudite Origen founded a school of

Christian studies in Caesarea, and visited the holy places. He states that everyone knew the cave in which the Lord was born. He wrote, "With respect to the Birth of Jesus in Bethlehem, if anyone desires, after the prophecy of Micheas and after the history recorded in the Gospels by the Disciples of Jesus, to have additional evidence from other sources, let him know that, in conformity with the narrative in the Gospel regarding his Birth, there is shown at Bethlehem the cave where He was born, and the manger in the cave where He was wrapped in swaddling clothes. And this sight is greatly talked of in surrounding places, even among the enemies of the faith, it being said that in this cave was born that Jesus who is worshipped and reverenced by the Christians."

Few of the holy places of Palestine have in their favor such an ancient and authentic tradition as the Cave of Bethlehem. In 132 A.D. the Emperor Hadrian attempted to desecrate the holy places by building over them shrines to the pagan gods. Fortunately, this action served to mark them for future generations. St. Jerome, the greatest Scriptural scholar of all, lived in Bethlehem for 34 years, from 386 to 420. He wrote, "From the time of Hadrian to the reign of Constantine, a period of 180 years, the spot which had witnessed the Resurrection was occupied by a figure of Jupiter; while on the rock where the Cross had stood, a marble statue of Venus was set up by the heathen and became an object of worship. The original persecutors, indeed, supposed that by polluting our holy places they would deprive us of our faith in the Passion and in the Resurrection. Even my own Bethlehem, as it now is, that most venerable spot in the whole world of which the psalmist sings, 'The truth hath sprung out of the earth,' was overshadowed by a grove of Tammuz, that is, of Adonis; and in the very cave where the infant Christ had uttered his earliest cry, lamentation was made for the paramour of Venus."

But in the year 330, St. Helena Augusta indignantly pulled down the temple of Adonis, and erected in its place the Church of the Nativity. Eusebius, the historian, who was a personal friend of Emperor Constantine, wrote of Constantine's mother, St. Helena, "For without delay, she dedicated two churches to

13

the God whom she adored, one at the cave which had been the scene of the Saviour's birth, the other on the mount of His Ascension. For He who was 'God with us' had submitted to be born in a cave of the earth, and the place of His Nativity was called Bethlehem by the Hebrews. Accordingly the pious empress honored with rare memorials the scene of her travail who bore this heavenly Child, and beautified the sacred cave with all possible splendor."

That Church of St. Helena, the Basilica of the Nativity, still stands, although it has suffered much through the centuries both from ravages and restoration. The holy cave is in the crypt below the floor of the sanctuary. The roof of the cave was removed to give place to the supports needed to sustain the weight of the building above. Nowadays two flights lead down to it, one of sixteen steps and the other of thirteen. The original walls and floors remain, now protected by slabs of marble. Into this marble is set a silver star with the inscription in Latin, "Here of the Virgin Mary, Jesus Christ was born."

The limestone caves of Palestine have figured largely in the history of the country. It was to one of them that Lot and his daughters fled upon the destruction of Sodom and Gomorrah. Abraham bought a cave in Hebron as a burial place for Sara and, in the course of time, Abraham himself, Isaac and Rebecca, Jacob and Lia were buried there too.

When David fled from the jealousy of Saul, he and his men lived first in the caves of Adullam, and afterwards in the caves of Engaddi. As a boy in Bethlehem he would, of course, have been familiar with the caves of the district. Did the future king ever visit the cave in which the Son of David would be born long afterwards?

It was in a cave of Horeb that the prophet Elias hid from the wrath of Queen Jezebel. To the present day there are caves under houses in Nazareth and Bethlehem. During most of his 34 years in Bethlehem, St. Jerome lived and studied in a cave close to that cave which was the cradle of the Christian faith. He wrote, "I, too, miserable sinner that I am, have been accounted worthy to kiss the manger in which the travailing

Virgin gave birth to the infant Lord."

It seems clear from the remarks of Origen, quoted above, that the manger was still in the cave when he visited it. St. Jerome saw it too, for he spoke of his privilege of kissing it. Apparently it was later removed, for he wrote sadly, "Alas! Through a feeling of veneration for Christ, we have taken away the manger of clay to substitute for it one of silver. But how much more precious to me is that which has been removed. Silver and gold are the goods of the gentiles; this crèche of clay is of much more value for the Christian faith."

What was the nature of the manger? From St. Jerome's description it does not seem to have been made of wood, but of potter's clay. In Palestine this is cheaper, more abundant, and easier to work. The manger was a kind of trough in which fodder was placed. Unfortunately, it was stored away so safely in the troubled times that now it cannot be found. But some relics of the manger remain. In the year 640 the Arab armies of the Caliph Omar were in Palestine and had captured Jerusalem. The long night of Moslem rule had fallen upon the Holy Land. During the reign of Pope Theodore I (642-649), a native of Jerusalem, some relics from the cave were brought to Rome for safety. These were five boards of sycamore wood that had been the supports of the manger. They are preserved in St. Mary Major, and are now enclosed in an urn of silver and crystal, surmounted by a gilt figure of the Holy Child.

What was in the manger? Not hay, for this, as we understand it, was not made in Palestine. It is customary in Bible lands now to cut or pull grass and other fodder plants, and give them to livestock. Women, with large back loads of such fodder, or donkeys similarly laden, may be seen any morning at the gates or in the market places of the cities.

Large areas are sown in barley, vetch, clover, madick and other forage plants, to be cut and given to domestic animals in the spring and early summer. It is clear that it was also the custom in Bible days to cut grass for this purpose. But it is not customary to dry such cut grasses to be stored up as winter fodder, and there is no evidence that the Hebrews had such a custom. In fact, it would be out of place, as the winter is their season of green grass. Stall-fed animals have cut-grass mixed with their barley.

Barley straw was the usual provender used in the stables of Solomon. "Will the wild ass bray when he hath grass? Or will the ox low when he standeth before a full manger?" asks Job. The Hebrew *teben* is the same as the Arabic *tibn,* which is the straw of wheat and barley cut by the threshing machine into pieces from one half to two inches long, and more or less split and torn, and mixed with chaff. It is the universal accompaniment to the provender of domestic herbiverous animals. It is usually mixed with barley, and takes the place of hay.

Tradition has it that there were an ox and an ass in the cave. Isaias had said, "The ox knoweth his owner, and the ass his master's crib." It has been suggested that this text has given rise to the tradition, that the cave was a stable, the natural place for such animals. The ass belonged to Joseph, the ox to some other traveler. One of the old Latin hymns *(De Nativitate Domini)* sings of the ox and the ass as warming the newly born Saviour with their breath. In Christian art, from the sixth century to the sixteenth, there is no picture of the cave without these two animals.

THE VIRGIN BIRTH[5]

**"And she brought forth her first-born Son, and wrapped Him
in swaddling clothes, and laid Him in a manger"**
By Denis O'Shea

Mary must have shivered as she stepped into the darkness of
the underground stable. At every step she had to hold up her
white tunic, lest it be soiled. She held the lamp while Joseph
cleared a space near the door, away from the beasts at the back.

The discomforts of the cave were real enough, but they were
not intolerable. Joseph made up a bed of straw for her near
the entrance, but she would not have to lie upon bare straw.
Mary had been expecting to be confined in Bethlehem, so she
came provided with the necessities. Her foresight extended
even to swaddling clothes. Joseph unpacked their belongings
from the saddlebags, and laid them out on the manger.

The very poor people of the time had no proper beds at all.
They simply lay on the floor, wrapped in their large outer
mantles. The mantle was the poor man's cloak by day and his
coverlet by night. The Law commanded that when a mantle was
put in pledge for a loan, it should always be returned to its
owner by sunset, lest he lack bedclothes for the night. But
Mary and Joseph were not so poor as to be compelled to pawn
their garments.

Over the straw, Mary spread out the quilted caparison cloth
as a mattress; the stuffed saddle served as a pillow. From her
wallet, she produced a change of linen, a spare tunic, the long,
white-sleeved undergarment reaching to the feet. Her goatskin
cloak would make a warm coverlet. By contemporary standards,
Mary had a good bed in the cave and was comfortable enough.

The pious people of the period, encouraged by the Pharisees
and rabbis, were sticklers for purifications. Indeed, the rabbis
had drawn up an elaborate code on the practice. It was strictly
forbidden to eat with unwashed hands. Mary and Joseph dared
not disregard the precept lest they be excommunicated and cast
out of the synagogue. On their journey, they carried the vessels
for washing hands before meals and feet before retiring. These,

called the *tesht* and *ibreeq,* were of either metal or earthenware. The *ibreeq* is a water jug, with a spout, from which the water is poured on the hands or feet, held over the basin. *Tesht* and *ibreeq* could be wrapped in a towel and carried in the saddlebags.

The mire of unpaved roads in the East has to be seen to be believed, and as neither stockings nor socks were worn in sandals or open shoes, foot washing was necessary before going to bed. For the convenience of the guests at the wedding of Cana, "there were set there six water pots of stone, according to the manner of the purifying of the Jews, containing two or three measures apiece." No inn would lack such facilities, for no pious guest would break bread without first washing his hands. So Joseph could fill his ewer with fresh water and provide Mary with an adequate supply even in the cave.

The cave was dark, for it had no window. Its sole illumination was the feeble light coming from the passage from the outside. Anyone using the stable had to bring his lamp with him. A niche in the rocky wall provided a place for the lamps, as it does in the stone huts of the very poor to this day. Here Mary put the lamp, and in its light saw grotesque shadows cast on the wall by the heads of the animals.

The cave was dirty, cold, and dark, but she was clean, warm, and provided with a lamp. She was grateful when she could lie down on a good bed. The presence of the animals was inevitable, and she would not resent it. Furthermore, the warmth of their bodies took the chill off the air.

Mary and Joseph said their night prayers together as usual. When Joseph rose to retire, the eloquent look with which Mary thanked him brought balm to his harassed heart. Outside in the passage, he continued his prayers, but in silence, for he did not wish to attract attention by voice or movement. He sat down cross-legged, and waited with Oriental patience. He would not sleep, lest Mary should call. He was young, healthy, and warm in his heavy cloak, so a cold and wakeful night had no terrors for him. Overhead, noise and movement gradually ceased. The only sound was the slow munching of the contented animals.

At midnight, the silence was broken by the cry of a Baby.

"And it came to pass that when they were there her days were accomplished, that she should be delivered. And she brought forth her firstborn Son, and wrapped Him in swaddling clothes, and laid Him in a manger, because there was no room for them in the inn."

There was no nurse present. "No midwife assisted at His birth," declared St. Jerome. "With her own hands she wrapped Him in swaddling clothes, herself both mother and midwife." Not even St. Joseph is mentioned as being present at the birth. The canonical Gospel gives the impression that the Mother was able to attend to the care of her Babe immediately, and the Church Fathers have concluded that the birth was without pain, as befitted the Virgin-Mother. Surely, the immaculate Mother of God was exempt from the curse pronounced upon errant Eve: "In sorrow shalt thou bring forth children."

St. Cyprian says, "Instead of purple and king's linen, swaddling bands and folded garments are got together; the Mother is the midwife; to her beloved Offspring she proffers devoted homage; she clasps, embraces, kisses and offers Him her breast, the whole occupation full of delight: there is no pain, none of nature's offensiveness in her confinement." Bossuet contends, "He comes forth like a shaft of light, like a ray of the sun; his Mother wonders to see Him appear all at once; this confinement is as free of cries as it is of pain and force; miraculously conceived, He is born more miraculously still, and the saints have found his being born even more truly wonderful than his being conceived of a virgin!"

Mary was able to rise from her bed to attend to the wants of her Child. With her own hands she wrapped Him up in swaddling clothes.

What are swaddling clothes? They are still in use in the East, and are very different from the little dresses or baby robes with sleeves in which Western infants are clothed. The Eastern infant was laid upon a square of cloth, spread diagonally. The upper corner was folded back to leave the head free, and the three other corners were folded over to enclose the whole body, including arms and legs. Then swaddling bands proper, rather like bandages, were wound outside the napkin, and tied.

19

The custom may have survived from early nomadic days, when the people dwelt in the wilderness, for the bandaging not only kept the baby warm and protected its spine, but enabled the mother to carry it more easily. Of course, the swaddling bands had to be unloosed in attending to the child's needs, but it was usually kept confined in them until it began to use its limbs. During this period, its skin was dusted with powdered myrtle leaves to prevent chafing, and any tender places were rubbed with olive oil.

Swaddling bands were usually of plain linen or cotton, but well-to-do people used embroidered stuffs. Mary was neither poor nor neglectful, and was skilled in spinning and weaving, having been educated in the Temple. Probably the swaddling clothes made by her own hands were of good linen tastefully embroidered. To this day, the mothers of Bethlehem bind up their babies with linen strings with long fringes, by means of which they can carry them upon their backs or even hang them up out of the way!

It was the custom to wash the newly-born infant in water and to rub it with salt to make the limbs supple, and then to wrap it up in the linen napkin tied with swaddling bands.

"Joseph!" When Mary called his name, he came into the cave, anxious, hoping, wondering. In the dim lamp light, he saw her kneeling by the manger, and he saw the white bundle in her arms. She turned her head at the sound of his steps, and he saw that her eyes outshone the stars. One glimpse of that radiant face assured him that all was well. Humbly he thanked the Holy One: "Blessed be his Name." Another step, and he was bending over her shoulder, and he saw Christ the Lord wrapped in swaddling clothes and laid in the manger; and falling down, he adored Him.

Beyond them, the heads of the animals loomed grotesquely, and their warm breaths rose up in the chill air. "The ox knoweth his master, and the ass, the stable of his Lord." The patient beasts of burden, the humble friends of man, had a place at the birth of the Lord of men and animals. But, after Mary his Mother, it was Joseph, her husband, guardian, and best friend, who had the honor of being the first to adore the Son of God made Man.

The Saviour was not only conceived in virginity, but also born in virginity. Mary retained her integrity in the birth of her Son. It was a miracle, of course, a special intervention of God in the laws of nature, "because no word shall be impossible with God." As Christ in his risen Body will one day pass out of the sealed, stone tomb without opening it, so now He leaves the womb of his Mother and enters the world without depriving her of her virginity.

St. Gregory of Nyssa wrote, "Although coming in the form of man, yet He is not subject in everything to the law of man's nature. While his being born of a woman tells of human nature, virginity becoming capable of childbirth betokens something above man's nature. Of Him, then, his Mother's burden was light, the birth immaculate, the delivery without pain, the nativity without defilement. For as she, who by her guilt engrafted death into her nature, was condemned to bring forth pain, it was fitting that she who brought Life into the world would accomplish her delivery with joy."

The pangs of childbirth, the sorrows of errant Mother Eve, were not for the immaculate Virgin Mother. Thus all Christians confess "the Blessed Mary ever virgin." She alone is so blessed among women as to wear the crowns of maidenhood and motherhood, the double crown which no other daughter of Eve has ever worn or ever will wear.

The Nicene Creed, in its own stately fashion, states the doctrine for all Christians. "I believe in one God, the Father Almighty, Maker of heaven and earth, and of all things visible and invisible. And in one Lord Jesus Christ, the only-begotten Son of God, born of the Father before all ages. God of God; Light of Light; true God of true God; begotten, not made; being of one substance with the Father, by whom all things were made. Who, for us men, and for our salvation, came down from heaven, and was incarnate by the Holy Ghost of the Virgin Mary, and was made man."

The Baby born in the cave is God, the Second Person of the most august Trinity, the Maker of heaven and earth, omnipotent, eternal, immense, and immutable. The Child is divine. "A mass

21

of legend and literature," wrote the inimitable G. K. Chesterton, "has repeated and rung the changes on that single paradox; that the hands that made the sun and stars were too small to reach the huge heads of the cattle. Upon this paradox all the literature of our faith is founded."

Some seven centuries before Christ's coming, Isaias had expressed the same paradox. "For a child is born to us, and a son is given to us, and the government is upon his shoulder: and his name shall be called Wonderful, Counsellor, God the Mighty, the Father of the world to come, the Prince of Peace." St. Paul, too, expresses the paradox. "But when the fullness of the time was come, God who made the world out of nothing is born of a woman, for of her He deigned to take his human nature."

It is incredible, but it is true, and Jesus Christ was born in the stable of Bethlehem. Look, Christian, at Christ; look at God in the cave. Look at the wretched hole, the beasts, and the dirt. Look at the grave man, bent in wondering awe over Mother and Child, the faithful guardian of both. Look at the lovely girl-mother, with a light in her eyes that never shone in woman's eyes before. Look at the Infant, look at Christ, the Lord wrapped in swaddling clothes and laid in a manger. Look, Christian, and adore your Creator, your Redeemer, and your Judge.

WHY IN A CAVE?[6]

Poverty and privacy were the reasons
By Giuseppe Ricciotti

The journey must have been very tiring for Mary. The roads
of the region were not yet the fine, well-kept highways built by
the Romans, masters of the art, but were so poor the camel and
donkey caravans could barely manage them. At that particular
time, with the confused traffic occasioned by the census, they
must have been more crowded than usual and much more
uncomfortable. Our travelers may have had at best a donkey
to carry their provisions and other baggage, one of the same
tribe of donkey which can still be seen in Palestine trudging
ahead of a line of camels or following a group of foot travelers.
The three or four necessary stopovers were perhaps spent in the
homes of friends or more probably in the public inns, where,
with the other travelers, they slept on the ground among the
camels and donkeys.

When they arrived at Bethlehem conditions were even worse.
The little village was spilling over with people crowded into all
the available lodgings, and the caravansary to begin with. The
caravansary of those days was substantially the same as the
modern khan of Palestine, that is, a moderate-sized space enclosed
by a rather high wall with only one entrance. Along one or more
sides of this wall ran a colonnade, which was sometimes
partitioned off at one point to form a large room with one or
two smaller ones beside it. This was the whole "inn"; the
animals were bedded down under the open sky and the travelers
took shelter in the portico or in the large chamber, if there was
room; otherwise they bedded down with the animals. The
smaller rooms, if there were any, were reserved for those who
could pay for such luxury. And there in the midst of men and
animals, some haggled and bargained while others prayed; some
sang while others slept; a man might be born and another die,
all amidst filth and stench with which the encampments of
traveling Bedouins in Palestine reek even today.

Luke tells us that when Mary and Joseph arrived in Bethlehem

23

"there was no room for them in the inn." This phrase is more studied than it may seem at first. If Luke had meant merely that not another person could fit into the caravansary, it would have been enough to say "there was no room"; instead he adds "for them," which is an implicit reference to the fact that Mary was soon to give birth to her Son. This may seem a subtlety, but it is not. In Bethlehem Joseph undoubtedly had acquaintances or even relatives from whom he might have requested hospitality; though the village was crowded, some little corner could always be found for two such humble persons. When hundreds of thousands poured into Jerusalem for the Pasch, the capital was jammed to overflowing, and yet all managed somehow to find a place to stay. But naturally, at such times, even the poor little private houses, usually only one ground-floor room, were as crowded as the inns and just as public, as far as the occupants and their actions were concerned. Hence it is easy to understand why Luke specifies that there was no "room *for them*"; since her time was near, Mary was seeking privacy most of all.

"And it came to pass while they were there, that the days for her to be delivered were fulfilled. And she brought forth her first-born Son, and wrapped Him in swaddling clothes, and laid Him in a manger." Mention is made only of the "manger" but, given the customs of the time, this clearly enough denotes a stable, which in those days meant a grotto or small cave cut into the side of one of the little hills near by. Such caves are still to be seen near settlements in Palestine, and they are still so used. The stable which Mary and Joseph found was perhaps already partially occupied by animals; it may have been dark and filthy, but it was somewhat removed from the village and therefore quiet and private.

Hence, when the two arrived in Bethlehem and saw the crowds, they made the best of the hospitality offered by the lonely hillside cave. There they decided to stay until they completed the formalities of registration and the Child was born. Joseph probably prepared some little corner in the place which seemed more comfortable and not quite so dirty. He perhaps made a bed of clean straw, took from the knapsack their provisions and other necessities, and arranged them on the manger attached to the wall.

Other comforts and conveniences were not to be had then in Palestine by two such travelers in their humble station, who had besides segregated themselves of their own will in a cave intended for animals.

In short, poverty and purity were the reasons why Jesus was born in a stable, the poverty of His legal father, who did not have enough money to secure a private room among so many competitors, and the purity of His Mother, who wished to surround His birth with reverent privacy.

Among the archaeological relics we have today of the life of Jesus, the stable is the one which has in its favor the oldest and most authoritative testimonies outside the Gospels. Justin Martyr, a Palestinian by birth, gives us in the second century the following precious evidence, "Thus the Child was born in Bethlehem: because Joseph had no place in that village to lodge, he lodged in a certain cave near the village and then, while they were yet there, Mary gave birth to Christ and placed Him in a manger." Origen testifies in the first part of the third century to the cave and the manger, citing a tradition widely known "in those places and even among those not of the faith." On the basis of that tradition Constantine in 325 ordered built on the spot a splendid basilica, which was respected by the Persian invaders of 614, and is still standing today.

When Jesus was born, Mary "wrapped Him in swaddling clothes and laid Him in a manger." In these words our physician-Evangelist, with his usual delicacy, is telling us clearly enough that the birth took place without the usual assistance of other persons. The Mother herself takes care of the newborn Infant, wraps Him up and lays Him in the manger.

Now, Bethlehem was and still is on the edge of a plain, abandoned, uncultivated, which can be used only for pasturing flocks. A few sheep owned by the habitants of the village were gathered at night into the surrounding caves and stables, but the large flocks remained always out on the heath with some shepherd to guard them. Night and day, summer and winter, those numerous beasts with their few guardians formed a community apart that lived on and from the plain. The shepherds had the very worst reputation among the Scribes and Pharisees, for since they led a nomadic life on the plains where water was not abundant, they were dirty, smelly, ignorant of all the most fundamental prescriptions regarding the washing of hands, the purity of utensils and the choice of foods, and hence more than any others they constituted that "people of the land" who, from the viewpoint of the Pharisees, deserved only most cordial contempt. They were, besides, all reputed to be thieves, and others were warned not to buy wool or milk from them because they might be stolen goods.

On the other hand, it was not wise to insist too much that they return to the observance of "tradition" or to try to persuade them to wash their hands well and rinse their dishes thoroughly before eating. They were tough characters who promptly and fearlessly used their clubs to bash in the heads of the wolves that came bothering their flocks, and they would not have hesitated to do the same for the Scribes and Pharisees who came bothering their consciences. Hence the despised and pugnacious rustics were excluded from the law courts, and their testimony, like that of the thieves and extortioners, was not admitted in a trial.

"And there were shepherds in the same district living in the fields and keeping watch over their flock by night. And behold, an angel of the Lord stood over them, and the glory of God shone round about them, and they feared exceedingly. And the angel said to them: Do not be afraid, for behold, I bring you good tidings of great joy, which shall be to all the people. For there has been born to you today in the town of David a Saviour, who is Christ the Lord. And this shall be a sign unto you: you will find the Infant wrapped in swaddling clothes and lying in a manger. And suddenly there was with the angel a multitude of the heavenly host, praising God and saying:

"Glory to God in the highest
and peace on earth among men
of good will!"

This episode follows immediately after the account of the Nativity, and it is undoubtedly the narrator's intention to show that only a few hours elapsed between the two. Hence Jesus was born at night, and the vision of the shepherds also occurred at night.

The shepherds understood from the angel that the Messias had been born. They were rough, untutored men, it is true, who did not know anything about the vast doctrine of the Pharisees; but as simple Israelites of the old school they did know of the Messias promised their people by the prophets, and they had probably talked of Him often during the long night watches over their flocks. Now the angel had given them a sign by which to recognize Him; they would find a Child wrapped in swaddling clothes and lying in a manger. Perhaps the angel had even pointed in the direction of the cave where they were to find Him. Hence these shepherds were still on familiar ground. Whenever possible they also took refuge in those caves against the heavy rains or the intense cold. More than one of them, perhaps, had sheltered his wife in one while she gave birth to her baby and had laid his own newborn child in a manger. And now they heard from one who could not deceive that the Messias Himself shared their humble circumstances. They went therefore "with haste," says Luke, the haste prompted by joyous familiarity, while they would have perhaps been slow to set out for the court of Herod had the Messias been born there instead.

They reached the cave, and they found Mary and Joseph and the Infant. And they wondered. And being lordly in spirit, however poor of purse, they asked for nothing whatever and went back to their sheep. But now they felt a great need of glorifying and praising God and of telling others in the vicinity what had happened.

THROUGH THE SPEECH OF ANGELS[7]

Matthew and Luke learned of heavenly messengers from Mary
By Henri Daniel-Rops

We know about the supernatural events attending the birth of Christ only from St. Luke and St. Matthew. The two other evangelists say nothing about them. Moreover, in Matthew and Luke these events appear as prefaces, easily detached. Nevertheless, tradition treats them as part of the Gospels. Even heretics like Cerintus and Carpocrates, or pagans like Colnes, who attacked the dogma of the Incarnation, did not question their truth.

Everything seems to indicate the two "evangelists of the childhood" had a personal source of information. It could only have been Mary, for she alone was familiar with many of the events related. St. Luke says that she did not speak to others about them.

Girls were betrothed in Israel at fourteen or fifteen. There was nothing to distinguish Mary from the village girls of Nazareth. Her name, *Mirya,* was from the Scriptures, and meant Beloved of God. It was usually distorted into *Miriam* or *Mariam,* which meant Good Lady. She was betrothed to a man much older than herself, a cabinetmaker and carpenter named Joseph.

A miraculous event broke the quiet monotony of her simple life, the appearance of an angel. Every Jewish child, brought up on the Scriptures, knew that supernatural beings often intervened in the lives of men. Nevertheless, she had been extremely excited. The strange presence (a human form, a white bird, or simply light?) had paused in front of her. Mary had heard its voice saying, "The Holy Spirit will come upon thee, and the power of the Most High will overshadow thee. Thus this holy offspring of thine shall be known for the Son of God."

We should visualize this delightful scene in the bare kitchen of one of those mud-fronted cavelike houses still to be seen in the little village in Galilee.

Mary had replied with total acquiescence, "Behold the hand-

maid of the Lord; be it done unto me according to thy word."
This sentence is the foundation of the great devotion which the
Church has always had for the Virgin Mary. Mary said Yes, and
the greatest of all mysteries was accomplished: God's
Incarnation in human nature.

Miraculous though it was, the event accomplished through
Mary raised some delicate problems. Mary was betrothed to
Joseph. According to modern law, marriage alone constitutes
the final bond. Jewish law clearly distinguished betrothal from
marriage, but in practice the two states tended to become
confused. For a year, in the case of virgins, the betrothed
woman was placed "under the law" of her future husband.
Theoretically, relations between the two were not allowed, but
the Talmud recognizes that they did in fact often exist.
A child born in these circumstances was regarded as legitimate;
that is why the woman had to observe strict faithfulness. If she
aroused suspicion, she had to undergo the dreadful "test of
bitter water." The woman accused of adultery had to drink a
potion prepared by the priests, and was judged innocent or
guilty according to its effect upon her. The apocryphal Gospel
of St. James, which was widely read in the early days of the
Church, says that Mary herself was subjected to this. If the
woman was convicted she had to suffer the penalty laid down
in Deuteronomy for unfaithful wives, stoning.

When Joseph showed surprise at her pregnancy, an angel came
to speak to him. "Joseph," said the angel, "do not be afraid to
take thy wife Mary to thyself, for it is by the power of the Holy
Ghost that she has conceived this Child; and she will bear a Son,
whom thou shalt call Jesus."

Joseph in his turn surrendered to a supernatural statement.
He kept her, married her, and was to act towards her and her
child as a foster father, a disinterested protector. There is
something both sublime and touching about St. Joseph, this
generous man "whose mere name," said Claudel, "makes
superior people smile."

As the end of Mary's term approached, a census was decreed
by Rome. The order obliged many of the inhabitants of Judaea
to make a journey. In accordance with customs still familiar in

the Moslem world, everyone had to be registered at the place where his clan originated. Even today an Arab can tell that exact spot. Mary and Joseph both belonged to the royal house of David, though by different lines of descent. So they had to be registered in the place of origin of the Ben Davids.

The place was known; it was indicated quite clearly in Scripture: Bethlehem. It was there that, ten centuries earlier, Ruth the Moabite, who had come to glean in this foreign land, had won the heart of the generous Boaz. From these two, through their son Obed, the "tree of Jesse" had sprung. Its supreme flower was to be Jesus Christ. A verse in the Prophet Micheas clearly confirmed the prediction: "Bethlehem-Ephrata! Least do they reckon thee among all the clans of Judaea? Nay, it is from thee I look to find a prince that shall rule over Israel. Whence comes he? From the first beginning, from ages untold!"

At Bethlehem, the bustle of the census had brought too many visitors. Everything was full, inns, private houses, even the great Khan of Canaan at the gates of the township.

St. Luke's Gospel says that when the child was born Mary laid him in a manger, a receptacle for fodder, indicating that the event took place in a stable.

An extremely ancient tradition, enshrined in the apocryphal gospels and confirmed by Fathers of the Church such as St. Justin, martyr, asserts that the birth was in a cave used to shelter sheep and cattle. Many such caves are still to be seen in the hills of Judaea. Legendary traditions speak of an ox and an ass as the only witnesses, a detail which would confirm the prophecy of Habacuc in the Septuagint version, "You will manifest yourself between two animals" (the Hebrew has "in the midst of the years"). As for the star which we are accustomed to hang above our Christmas cribs, that comes from the false gospels; no doubt it is supposed to be the one which, according to the true Gospel, later guided the Wise Men on their way.

One can dispense with these sentimental details. The event in itself is too extraordinary to need embellishment. The Christian paradox is already there. The Child of the manger was to be stronger than any human power.

Again an angel spoke, now to the shepherds on the hills: the

Child wrapped in swaddling clothes in the manger was the Lord, the Saviour. A whole choir of angels took up the news, "Glory to God in high heaven, and peace on earth to men that are God's friends."

We can leave the historians to debate on what precise date the event took place, and to decide whether it was December 25, where a tradition dating from the fourth century places it, or in March or May as others have thought. The essential point is that the event, the greatest in the whole of history, took place unknown to anyone except a few humble shepherds and the angels, in the hush of "silence" mentioned by the Christmas liturgy, the silence of the world which alone makes it possible for the call of God to be heard.

SHEPHERDS OF BETHLEHEM [8]

**They have their place in the history of salvation;
their occupation became the Lord's office**
By Richard Murphy, O.P.

A mile to the east of Bethlehem stands a shrine marking the field where, one night, shepherds were watching their flocks. Angels appeared to them, announcing "good news of great joy to all the people. For there has been born to you today a Saviour who is Christ the Lord." The shepherds hurried to Bethlehem, the town of David, and there "found the Infant in swaddling clothes lying in a manger."

Their names are not known, but they were the first to be told of the astonishing development in God's scheme of salvation: the birth of the Saviour.

Much has changed in the Holy Land since our Lord lived there. The land, depending on which side of the uneasy border you happen to be on, is now called Jordan or Israel. Cities on both sides have grown and become half-modernized. As one walks through the old bazaars, or through the modern stores, the weird melodies of the Near East are broadcast, and sometimes the even weirder music of the West.

Many things have remained as they were. The Sea of Galilee and the Dead Sea are unchanged. The Jordan hurries along as before. The flowers of the field still have a moment of beauty. Fig and olive and palm trees are, as they were in Jesus' day, graceful, fruitful, and in this land of fierce sun, welcome shade. The Bedouins continue to live in their black goat-hair tents on the edge of the desert. Sheikhs, looking like Abrahams, bring the desert with them as they move through the crowds. And camel caravans, arriving or setting out on journeys deep in the desert, grumble and groan and glide their way as though the world were still young.

Of all living beings, two things which have changed least are the shepherd and his sheep. Palestinian sheep have always had wide, fat tails. They are valuable animals. Their fleece is woven into cloth, and their hides become sandals and sheepskin coats. They provide milk and cheese and mutton, and if a big enough occasion arises, rams' horns serve as flasks or as trumpets. Thus the sheep was the ideal victim in Old Testament sacrifices.

On sheep depended the economy of ancient Israel, and the size of a man's flock was an index of his wealth and importance. Smaller flocks of sheep and goats were looked after by the owner's younger children, but for the larger herds professional shepherds were hired. Shepherds knew their charges well and invented names for them: that ewe was called Gimpy, this ram Crooked Horn. And, what is just as important, the sheep also knew their shepherd.

Shepherds in Palestine, even today, lead their flocks into a sheepfold at night. It may be only a makeshift affair, a cave, or an area marked out by a fence of thorns to keep the animals from wandering off. By night the enclosure is filled with hundreds of sheep, one like another. But the shepherds have no problem finding their own.

In the morning each shepherd takes his turn at the entrance to the sheepfold and gives his own peculiar call, which is a succession of animal-like sounds. The sheep instantly rise and make their way towards their own shepherd. Once he has counted them, he moves off; the sheep fan out behind him in a V-formation. Let him quicken his pace and put a few yards between himself and the sheep, or turn a corner and be momentarily hidden from them, and the sheep will rush to catch up with him. He is their shepherd, and their place is with him. They know him as their companion, leader, defender, and provider.

Artists often depict the shepherd's life as idyllic and peaceful. In reality there is nothing romantic about it; it is a grim struggle for existence. The valley of Jezreel (the east end of the plain of Esdraelon) and the coastal areas have the only good soil in Palestine. The rest of the country is too hilly, stony, and dry for extensive agriculture. This land supports its human population and their flocks of sheep and goats grudgingly. Sheep searching for grass just out of safe reach tumble into ravines. There were lions (mentioned more than 100 times in the Bible, but now extinct in the Holy Land), and still are bears, wolves, jackals, and foxes. The worst enemy is man—when he becomes thief and robber. Biblical, Babylonian, and Hittite codes of law all held the shepherd responsible for the loss of sheep, unless he could prove it was not due to his neglect.

Palestine has never had much grazing land and water. So the situation the shepherd faced was often critical. His sheep had a limited endurance, and could not be hurried or driven too far. He had to watch the weaker ones, seek out strays, and know first aid. Clearly he lived for his sheep, and his sheep either lived or died, depending on him.

The shepherd carried a crooked staff for pulling or prodding. From his belt hung a weighted club and a sling. The sling could be used with great accuracy, as David showed Goliath. Modern shepherds no longer carry slings, but they are pitchers. One day, not far from the Herodium, near Bethlehem, I watched a young shepherd keep his flock together by throwing stones; he could "turn" the sheep which had begun to stray from the main flock by bouncing stones near it. Without a word being spoken, he and I proceeded to engage in a friendly throwing match. My best efforts (and I was then fairly close to my baseball days) fell far short of his.

Everyone loves the familiar words of Psalm 22, "The Lord is my shepherd, I shall not want." God is directly addressed as Shepherd only four times in the Old Testament, but there is no doubt that He is Israel's Shepherd. He is repeatedly reminded of that fact: "We are your people, the sheep of your pasture," "He made us, his we are, his people, the flock He tends." "Like a shepherd He feeds his flock," Isaiah writes, "in his arms He gathers the lambs, carrying them in his bosom and leading the ewes with care."

Israel's kings, as those in Egypt, Persia, and Babylonia, were thought of as shepherds of their people. But not all of them measured up to the ideal, and Jeremiah raised up his voice, inveighing in the Lord's name against "bad shepherds, [who] rebelled against Me." The Lord, therefore, will "appoint shepherds for the," and one of these will be the "righteous Branch of David."

The image of shepherd and sheep was often on Jesus' lips. One beautiful parable dealt with the shepherd who left the 99 sheep in the desert and went seeking the one that was lost. Jesus declared that He was "sent to the lost sheep of Israel," that He was one who came "to save what was lost." He had "compassion on the crowds, for they were bewildered and dejected like sheep without a shepherd." He referred to his disciples affectionately as his "little flock," and encouraged them not to be afraid. He adapted Zechariah's words: "You will all desert Me, for the Scriptures say, 'I will strike the Shepherd and the sheep will be scattered.'" And his description of the judgment as being a separation of sheep from goats extends the shepherd motif to the end of the world.

The supreme expression of the great truth of the Christian revelation comes in the tenth chapter of St. John's Gospel. Jesus is the Good Shepherd, and He will lay down his life for his sheep. One can understand that a shepherd ought to risk life and limb in caring for his sheep, but that he should carry his devotion to the point of willingly laying down his life for them is startling. If the shepherd loses his life, who will tend the sheep? Would it not be better to lose an occasional sheep than to lose the shepherd? The vicarious death of the Good Shepherd far surpasses all the symbolism of the ordinary shepherd figure. By dying He does more for his sheep than others can do while alive. He dies that his sheep "might have life, and have it more abundantly."

"When the sun comes into a room it seems to put out the fire," Ronald Knox once said. When Christ came, shadow yielded to substance. He does all that the shepherds did, but infinitely better. He defends his flock from enemies. He feeds his flock with his own Body and Blood. He knows his sheep from within, where, with the Father and the Holy Spirit, He has taken up his abode. He loves the sheep and loses none.

The early Christians depicted Christ as the Good Shepherd on the walls of the catacombs. Leaders of the early Christian community were, in their turn, looked upon as shepherds of the flock. Peter received a solemn commission to "feed my lambs, feed my sheep." Bishops were urged by Paul to "tend the flock of God" and to exercise authority over it. And St. Peter assures his readers that when the Prince of the shepherds appears, they "will receive the unfading crown of glory."

Thus there is place even for the shepherds in the history of salvation. They are the little ones, the humble poor who depend on God completely, not only for social justice but for the blessings of rain and grass, and life itself. Their vocation was a marvelous foreshadowing of the eternal vocation of that divine Infant who, by his death and resurrection, was to show Himself the Good Shepherd and Saviour of all men.

PSALM 22

The Lord is my Shepherd, I shall not want:
He gives me rest in green pastures. He leads me to waters of peace:
He refreshes my soul, He guides me by right paths for his Name's sake:
Though I walk through a death-dark valley, I fear no harm,
For You are with me, your rod and your staff reassure me.
You spread a table before me, in the sight of my enemies:
You perfume my head with oil, my cup brims over:
Yes, goodness and mercy will follow me all the days of my life,
and I shall dwell in the house of the Lord forever.

THE STAR THE MAGI SAW[9]

It is only one of many mysteries in the story of the mysterious Wise Men
By Kay Sullivan

A well-loved carol celebrates one of the most dramatic, and most controversial, episodes of the Christmas story.

> *We three Kings of Orient are,*
> *Bearing gifts we traverse afar,*
> *Field and fountain, moor and mountain,*
> *Following yonder star.*

The Magi, their star, and their journey have been the subject of conjecture and exploration down through the centuries. Historians have investigated their origin and their beliefs. Geographers have attempted to trace their perilous route over "moor and mountain." Astronomers have produced charts on the movements of the planets and stars as far back as 2,000 years to establish just what the Magi saw in the heavens.

On canvas, great artists have speculated on the size, shape, dress, and bearing of the kingly figures. And storytellers have wrapped the event in a tapestry of legend. They have supplemented the Biblical record with fiction that is often mistaken for fact.

The one authentic account of the Wise Men comes from St. Matthew, the only Evangelist to tell their story. St. Luke dwells on other aspects of the Nativity, St. John and St. Mark begin their Gospels with the public life of Christ.

Matthew really tells us very little about the colorful trio from the Orient. He describes them merely as wise men from the East who had seen a star. He tells how they journeyed to Jerusalem, where they stopped to speak to King Herod.

Herod, after consulting with his high priests, sent the Magi on to Bethlehem. He asked them to inform him where they found the Child. Instead, after paying their homage to the Child, they went home by a new route. An angel had warned them. That is all Matthew has to say.

As for the star that led the Magi forth—that radiant,

celestial symbol which has brought light to the hearts of men for almost 2,000 years—Matthew writes only "and behold, the star that they had seen in the East went before them, until it came and stood over the place where the Child was."

Matthew's terse pen has not kept others from surrounding the Wise Men and their starry beacon with a flotilla of detail.

Our present conception of the Magi is not necessarily accurate. I say this with due respect to all the parents, teachers, and youthful performers who will be busy this Yuletide dyeing sheets purple, gluing on crepe-paper beards, and winding Turkish-towel turbans.

First, the Wise Men were not kings in the royal sense of the word, but were high priests. Second, more than three of them probably made the trek to Bethlehem, though Melchior, Caspar, and Balthasar are mentioned most often. Third, no one is sure that these are the right names.

Official historians of the early Church agree that the Wise Men were of the sacred caste of Medes or Persians. They were dignified, scholarly men. They followed the teachings of Zoroaster, who had founded his religion some 1,000 years before the birth of Christ.

They were not magicians, although Magi is the root word of *magic*. Zoroaster forbade sorcery, but his followers put a great deal of emphasis on the interpretation of dreams and the stars. Their high priests were competent astronomers. They regarded the movements of the planets as portents they could not afford to overlook.

The Gospel omits any mention of the number of Wise Men who followed the star. There has never been a certain tradition in that regard. Some of the early Fathers speak of three, influenced no doubt by the three gifts to the infant of gold, frankincense, and myrrh reported by Matthew.

In the Orient, tradition favors twelve Wise Men. Early Christian art is far from being a consistent witness. Various masterpieces depict two, three, and four. A rare vase, preserved since antiquity, bears a Nativity scene showing no fewer than eight.

The Magi's names are as uncertain as their number. Among

37

the Latins, from the seventh century on, Caspar, Melchior, and Balthasar were the names most frequently mentioned.

These are not quite the tongue-twisters that other peoples have bestowed. For example, the Syrians called them Larvandad, Hormisdas, and Gushnasaph. The Armenians singled out Kagba and Badadilma. In Hebrew, they were called Magalath, Galgalath, and Tharath; in Greek, Appelius, Amerius, and Damascus.

To compound the confusion, Caspar (he's the beardless youth who has the frankincense) can spell his name with a *C, K,* or *G,* depending on the mood of the scribe.

Legend has it that the Magi represented the three families descended from Noe, but that is strictly apocryphal.

Another legend which must be punctured, exciting as it is to ponder, is the one that says the Magi saw the star, mounted their camels, and reached Bethlehem within the next few days.

East of Palestine only ancient Media, Persia, Assyria, and Babylonia had a Magian priesthood at the time of the birth of Christ. From any one of these to Jerusalem was a distance of at least 1,000 miles. In that era, such distances would have taken anywhere from three to twelve months by camel. Besides travel time, there were probably many weeks of preparation. The Magi could scarcely have reached Jerusalem until a year or more had elapsed from the time of the appearance of the star.

They probably crossed the Syrian desert, journeyed on to Damascus, then southward, keeping the Sea of Galilee and the Jordan to their west until they got to Jericho. And they didn't meet snow or a single fir tree en route. Just desert sand and palms.

Legend and the customs of many lands have combined to furnish us with the picture long cherished of the Magi arriving at Bethlehem. Gray-bearded Melchior, eldest of the trio, bears the gift of gold; Caspar, the frankincense. And Balthasar, the dark-skinned Moor, bears an urn of the mysterious balm called myrrh. Together, they bow low to enter the humble, straw-filled stable and kneel to adore their newborn King. Lowing cattle, woolly lambs, awe-stricken shepherds, and angels witness their arrival.

That beautiful scene never fails to stir even the most indifferent heart. The great painters of the Renaissance envisioned it time and again.

Historians who have carefully studied the circumstances of the Magi's visit think they did not arrive in Bethlehem until after the Presentation of the Child in the Temple. Their reasons include the length of the journey from the East, and the fact that the Gospel itself says that no sooner had the Magi departed than the angel bade Joseph take the Child and his mother into Egypt.

They conclude that once Herod realized that the Magi were not returning to his palace to tell him where the Child was, he would take drastic measures, ordering the slaughter of all children. With such a command in force, it would be out of the question for Joseph and Mary to take the Child to the temple.

Alert Bible students counter with the fact that Luke says the Holy Family returned to Galilee after the Presentation. The theorists reply that it is perfectly logical to assume that this return was only a brief visit, and that the Holy Family came back again to Bethlehem. If so, the Magi could have visited the Child, not in a stable but in a house, and not immediately after his birth but a year or more later.

In fact, many historians are convinced that the Magi reached Jerusalem as much as two years after Christ was born. They point out that Herod asked the Magi what date it was on which they first saw the star, and then gave orders to kill all male children who were two years or under. Still, Herod was insecure enough to distrust the Magi. He may have thought they had deliberately given him a wrong date.

Art and archaeology of the early centuries support the belief that the Magi arrived at least a year after the Nativity. Only one monument has been discovered that represents the Child still in the crib while the Magi adore. All other early art shows Him resting on Mary's knee or depicts Him as fairly well-grown.

One thing that makes it almost impossible to discuss with accuracy the comings and goings of the Magi is that calendar systems don't agree. Our era does not actually date from the year of the birth of Christ. It is generally thought that He was born between the years we now know as 8 B.C. and 4 B.C. The strongest likelihood is 7 B.C. or 6 B.C.

Did the Magi really see a star? True, the Scriptures say "star," but in those days anything in the sky was a star. The planets were "wandering stars." The comets were "hairy stars." Meteors were called, as they still are, "shooting" or "falling stars."

Since the Magi were the leading astronomers of their time, it would have taken an extraordinary phenomenon to make them leave their homes.

It could not have been a comet, since comets pursue well-regulated orbits, controlled by the same laws that hold the earth on its path. They have been tabulated for centuries. Halley's comet, for example, has been observed at intervals of about seventy-six years. It was seen in 1910, and will return in 1986. There are definite records of its appearance in 11 B.C. But this would have been too early for it to be the star of Bethlehem. The next recorded comet, one seen in China in 4 B.C. would have been too late.

Nor is it likely that the star of Bethlehem was a meteor. Meteors revolve around the sun in regulated paths until the path of the earth crosses their route. The collision causes the meteor to fall through the atmosphere with speeds of seven to forty-five miles a second, glowing brilliantly all the while. Sometimes they survive their swift flights to descend to the earth's surface in a stone-and-metal mass.

The star of Bethlehem did not rush through the air, shooting off sparks like a meteor. It remained steadfast in the skies, ever beckoning the Magi forward.

It could not have been a planet, or a fixed star. The position of a fixed star in the heavens varies at the most one degree a day. No fixed star could have so moved before the Wise Men as to lead them over a 1,000-mile journey. It could not have disappeared, reappeared, and stood still in the skies as the Magi's star did.

Johann Kepler, renowned seventeenth century German astronomer, made a special study of the star of Bethlehem. His conclusions are classic. Indeed, New York City's famous

Hayden planetarium gives an annual Christmas lecture about the star of Bethlehem based chiefly on Kepler's discoveries.

In Prague, in 1603, Herr Kepler was studying one of the rare conjunctions of Jupiter and Saturn (these slowest-moving of the planets meet only about every twenty years) when he sighted a tremendously brilliant star nearby. It was a nova, a star that suddenly increases in brilliance for no known reason, then gradually burns out. Kepler's nova lasted for almost a year before it disappeared.

He checked to see if there could have been a conjunction of Jupiter and Saturn near the time of Christ's birth. He found that the same conditions had existed in the heavens during 7 B.C. as when he had spotted his bright star in Prague. He concluded that the star of Bethlehem could have been a nova, and that it could have shone forth, day and night, for as long as two years.

"The conjunction of Jupiter and Saturn was definitely a harbinger of the miraculous star of Bethlehem," Kepler wrote in 1614. "But that unexpected star was not of the ordinary run of nova. By a miracle, it moved in the lower layer of the atmosphere."

Kepler was not the only one to believe that there is no natural explanation for the star the Magi saw. In the fifth century, St. John Chrysostom said, "God called the Magi by means of their customary pursuits and showed them a great and extraordinary star, so as to astonish them by the size and beauty of its appearance and the way it traveled. Think it not unworthy of God to have called the Magi by a star. He did so to raise them to better things. When He had brought them and guided them and set them before the manger, He no longer addressed them by a star but through an angel."

Tradition has it that after they returned home, the Magi were baptized by St. Thomas and worked unceasingly to spread the faith. Cologne cathedral contains what are said to be their remains. These relics were discovered in Persia and brought to Constantinople by St. Helena. They were transferred to Milan in the fifth century and to Cologne in 1163.

It does not matter that astronomers have never been able to do more than set the stage for the appearance of the star of

Bethlehem, that they have been unable to fix its position with their astrolabes and sextants. Nor does it matter that traditions vary on the number of Magi and the circumstances of their journey.

What does matter is that mankind's conception of them is ever inspiring. Every year, the world kneels joyfully again with them to adore the Babe of Bethlehem, drawn to his side by the beckoning light of faith.

WHEN OUR LORD WAS A BOY [10]

There were years to be lived between Bethlehem and Calvary
By Francis L. Filas, S.J.

In the usual white Christmas scene Palestine's climate is not pictured correctly. Snow falls there rarely during the winter, and even then it melts within a few hours. The winter months, November through March, should more properly be called the rainy season. The average temperature of the coldest month, January, is only 46°.

Bethlehem was about eighty miles south of Nazareth. It was a hamlet with a population of no more than 2000. About three days were required for Joseph and Mary to complete the trip from Nazareth. Judging from the ordinary modes of travel of common folk in Palestine, Mary probably rode on an ass while Joseph walked alongside, leading the animal. They probably had no servant. Their road first descended into the Plain of Esdraelon, then began to rise more and more, passing through frequent towns that alternated with farm country. Finally, about five or six miles south of Jerusalem the two travelers reached their journey's end.

The inn in which "there was no room for them" was no more than a small caravansary or khan. Vastly dissimilar to our modern hotels, the khan consisted of a courtyard for the animals, surrounded by alcoves in which the travelers spent the night. The entire enclosure was made safe against robbers by a high fence, with a gate that was strongly barred at nightfall.

Mary and Joseph were not turned away by a hardhearted inn-keeper, greedy for money from richer patrons. That idea arose from the medieval legends and miracle plays of Europe. It contradicts the traditional hospitality found all over the East. The real reason was simply the fact that other travelers were living in the inn. Joseph therefore led his wife to the only available refuge, a cave hollowed into the rock and used as a shelter by the shepherds of the vicinity. Such grottoes have served and still serve as a common place of refuge for man and beast on rainy, chilly nights.

What circumstances prevented Joseph from getting adequate shelter? Many theories have been advanced by scholars who have spent long years in studying every possible clue ranging from the climate of the Holy Land to the minutest detail of Holy Scripture. Perhaps Joseph tried to get shelter better than the temporary home he acquired when he first came to Bethlehem; we do not know. But this seems certain: Mary's time was suddenly shortened by the direct providence of God so that Jesus Christ by his own choice would come into the world in poor circumstances, a lesson of detachment to all men of all time.

Evidently Jesus was born during the night, for "there were shepherds in the same district living in the fields and keeping watch over their flock by night." The weather may have been cool and raw, but not cold or snowy. Otherwise, the shepherds would have taken their flocks to some cave or other enclosure for shelter. Although tradition disagrees on the exact date of the first Christmas, it is rather uniform in holding that our Lord came into the world during the rainy (winter) season.

"And behold, an angel of the Lord stood by (the shepherds), and said to them, 'Do not be afraid, for behold, I bring you good news of great joy which shall be to all the people; for there has been born to you today in the town of David a Saviour who is Christ the Lord. And this shall be a sign to you: you will find an Infant wrapped in swaddling clothes and lying in a manger.'

And suddenly there was with the angel a multitude of the heavenly host praising God and saying, 'Glory to God in the highest, and peace on earth among men of good will.' And it came to pass, when the angels had departed from them into heaven, that the shepherds were saying to one another, 'Let us go over to Bethlehem and see this thing that has come to pass, which the Lord has made known to us.' So they went with haste, and they found Mary and Joseph, and the Babe lying in the manger. And when they had seen, they understood what had been told them concerning this Child. And all who heard marveled at the things told them by the shepherds. But Mary kept in mind all these words, pondering them in her heart. And the shepherds returned, glorifying and praising God for all that they had heard and seen, even as it was spoken to them."

Thus does St. Luke draw the curtain over the Christmas scene he has described in inimitable words, a scene whose richness painters and poets and preachers have never been able to exhaust. It is the first appearance of the Holy Family before men: "Mary and Joseph, and the Babe lying in the manger." Mutual love shines forth in the faces of this earthly trinity: loving respect in the face of Joseph, loving adoration in the face of Mary, loving generosity in the face of the eternal God-with-us.

On their return to Nazareth the Holy Family took up a life like that of their neighbors. The usual meals were two: a midday dinner and an evening supper, which was the large meal of the day. Breakfast was too scanty to be called a meal. It was no more than a cup of milk, a piece of butter, or a few baked cakes with olive oil. Wooden spoons might have been used, but more likely the Holy Family ate with their hands.

Bread was the staff of life, and was made of barley, various kinds of wheat, or lentils. Mary baked bread each day, although she could have purchased it from the town baker. She formed it into flat circular cakes about an inch thick and nine inches across. To bake it, she placed fuel in a clay-lined hole in the ground or an earthen or stone jar about three feet high. Baking was done on the outside of this portable oven or on the hot bottom of the clay hole, after the embers were taken out.

In preparing her bread our Lady did not use new leaven each day but kept a portion of the old dough from day to day with which to start fermentation in a new batch.

The rest of the diet of the Holy Family was made up largely of vegetable foods. Olives and olive oil, butter, milk, cheese, eggs, and stewed fruit helped out this menu. Meat appeared on the table rarely and then it was mutton or beef.

Relish consisted of onions, garlic, or leeks. For the equivalent of our present-day dessert, figs, and mulberries, pistachio nuts, almonds, and pomegranates were available. Grapes were served either fresh or sun-dried as pressed cakes of raisins. Cucumbers were an ever-popular vegetable.

Mary's ordinary way of cooking food was to boil it, but she occasionally roasted meat and broiled the fish from Lake Genesareth much as her Son was to do for His Apostles after His Resurrection, years later. Often on the menu, this fish was considered quite a delicacy in Galilee, and was eaten pickled or dried. In preparing grain our Lady parched or roasted it. Lentils and beans were boiled into a delicious pottage, often with meat, and seasoned with mint, anise, cumin or mustard.

For sweetening Mary used wild honey instead of sugar. The salt she bought was either rock salt from the shores of the Dead Sea or that evaporated from the water of the Mediterranean.

The two beverages on the table at Nazareth were goat's milk and wine. The butter made from the milk was sometimes solid, sometimes merely semifluid heavy cream, sometimes the thick curds from sour milk. Our Lady did the churning herself by jerking a skin of milk back and forth or by beating the container with a stick. The wine was kept in large goatskins in the cool cellar of the house. From these it was drawn off into smaller goatskin "bottles" for use at the table.

Jesus and Joseph had three types of garments. In a climate as mild as that of Palestine no more were necessary. The innermost garment next to the body resembled our modern nightshirt and was called a sheet or sindon. During strenuous labor other clothing was taken off to permit freedom of action. Thus, for example, when some of the Apostles were fishing "naked" on the Lake of Galilee at the time Jesus appeared to them, they

45

were actually clad in this undergarment. In other words, to wear only this sindon was to be in a state of undress.

Over the sindon Jesus and Joseph wore the tunic, a sort of dressing gown open down the front. This made up the usual indoor costume at home or in the shop. A wide sash or girdle at the waist and rather billowy long sleeves gave the garment pleasing lines. For freedom in walking, the ankle-length shirt was slit about a foot from the bottom on each side. White with brown or red stripes was a favorite color, but blue was common.

The third and outermost article of clothing was the cloak. Joseph and Jesus wore the cloak outdoors for protection against cold and rain, or as a covering during sleep. When made of fleece it was especially warm; cotton and woolen cloth were more usual. It was sleeveless and opened in front, but it reached almost to the ground. Either this cloak or the tunic was the valuable "seamless garment" for which the soldiers cast lots when Christ was crucified.

For headdress Jesus and Joseph wound a sort of long kerchief into a turban. Another kerchief covered the neck and shoulders for protection against the blazing sun. In Nazareth as in all the Orient it was considered disrespectful to pass anyone bareheaded, so they must have worn the turban almost always.

They were bearded and wore their hair long, as paintings universally show them. Two locks, ringlets, dropped from their temples as a vestige of the Old Hebrew tradition whereby the Israelites were distinguished from idolatrous peoples who cut their locks as an offering to their gods.

For foot covering the Holy Family used sandals during the summer and shoes during the rainy season. The ordinary sandal consisted of a wood or leather sole with thongs attached, to be strapped around the instep. Shoes were made of coarse material and protected the entire foot. Socks were seldom if ever worn. Since footwear was prescribed strictly for outdoor use, it was always left at the house door.

Mary's dress resembled the attire of her menfolk rather closely. Her distinctive mark was a veil and (for outdoor use) a mantle or great shawl. Judging from the colors usually favored, she wore a red dress with a blue mantle and a large white veil covering her whole body when she traveled in public. Her hair fell in long tresses, probably left unbraided, as it was considered more modest to wear it that way.

Palestinian houses followed a rather uniform pattern. Like the present-day houses at Bethlehem, that of the Holy Family was probably built of rough-hewn limestone blocks cemented with limestone mortar. It had at least one upper room, built above a lower room at street level, and reached by outside stone stairs. The dimensions of the rooms would be about fifteen by twelve, and six feet high.

The lower room at Nazareth may well have been St. Joseph's workshop, extending back as a cave into the hill rising directly behind the house. Artisans like St. Joseph worked in the street outside their shops. The shops themselves were merely places to keep equipment.

The living room of the Holy Family (the upper chamber) was windowless and simply furnished. Its only light came through the doorway. There was no fireplace or chimney, but a hearth placed near the door provided a spot for cooking where the smoke could easily escape. On a ledge running around the wall the gaily colored mats which were spread on the floor at night were rolled up during the day.

A large lamp hanging from a center beam shed a dim light at night. It resembled a saucer but had a neck for the cloth wick that rested in the supply of olive oil. Underneath this lamp was a painted table and a few chairs. Here the three took their quiet meal.

The roof of their house was flat, a cemented or earthen surface overlaid on the beams that spanned the side walls. It was reached by the outside stairway. During the cool evenings of the summer, Jesus, Mary, and Joseph retired to it for conversation and quiet prayer. They used the roof much as we use a front porch or veranda.

Joseph's position as carpenter placed him in the respectable middle class of artisans. Judging from his occupation, he was not desperately poor, nor on the contrary could he be called wealthy. His tools were the hammer, saw, ax, plane, chisel, and bow drill. Working in wood, he was a general handyman for making plows, milking tubs, winnowing fans, yokes, forks, and household furniture. Joseph on many occasions did not receive pay for each article as he fashioned it. Instead, he agreed under a sort of "blanket-contract" barter system to look after the farm implements of his neighbors in so far as was necessary. In return for these services he received produce from his various customers at harvest time.

One feature in particular of the Holy Family's daily life stands out. Jesus, Mary, and Joseph lived a genuinely "human" life, using the good things of this earth as was proper. There was no puritanical refusal on their part to accept the blessings of God's creation as if these gifts were evil in themselves. Rather, the bounty of nature gave them opportunity to praise and thank the eternal Father for what He saw fit to bestow on them.

THE INFANT WARRIOR [11]

Christians, know your dignity
By R. L. Bruckberger

When the liturgy presents the birth of Jesus Christ, it uses part of a poem from the Book of Wisdom: "For when peaceful stillness compassed everything and the night in its swift course was half spent, your all-powerful Word from heaven's throne bounded."

In the poem is a description of the night when the Angel of Death struck down all the first born of Egypt, both man and beast, sparing Israel. After the dreadful punishment Pharaoh allowed Israel to march out of the Egyptian concentration camp.

The Christian liturgy takes the Egyptian captivity as a metaphor for the prison of sin, and retains the imagery of liberation. The text of the poem in Wisdom identifies the Angel of Death and Liberation with the very Word of God.

It seems too warlike for use at Christmas: "A fierce warrior, into the doomed land, bearing the sharp sword of your inexorable decrees. And as He alighted, He filled every place with death; He still reached to heaven, while He stood upon the earth."

But the peace of Christmas is a victorious peace. It is the assurance that the enemy of man and of God will be liquidated, and that the days of his reign are numbered. This tiny Baby, bedded in a manger, is a warrior, already victorious, who will raise to its pinnacle the glory of God; He will extend his domain farther than the domain of the angels, beyond annihilation and death, even to the re-creation of the universe. For the poem continues, "For all creation . . . was being made over anew . . . that your children might be preserved unharmed."

The true spirit of Christianity is a spirit of conquest and victory, but for 300 years Christians have been apologizing for their own existence. They should instead feel themselves to be a responsible part of the universe, as the poet feels himself a responsible part of the universe, of the flowers, the wild animals, trees, mountains, dawn, rain and lightning. They are integral parts of the universe through the birth, the death, and the resurrection of Jesus Christ. That is what Catholicism means, but only poets can feel it.

By becoming the Son of Man, the all-powerful Word of God subjugated the whole of sensible nature to men of good will. All men of good will can henceforth traverse dryshod the Red Sea of sin, of suffering, and of death. The benediction promised Abraham is no longer limited to his race; it extends to infinity in space and time, to every point where there is a man of good will.

Christ Himself spoke of the mystery of human birth on the eve of his death, as though, for Him, birth and death had the same meaning; liberation. "A woman about to give birth has sorrow, because her hour has come. But when she has brought forth the child, she no longer remembers the anguish for her joy that a man is born into the world."

We Christians believe that our temporal life is the gestation period for eternity and that death is our birth into eternal life. We also believe that there is the possibility of miscarriage, that life may not come successfully to term and that failure in our life here below can bring also failure in death, that is, our real birth into eternal life.

Birth is an escape from the mother's womb. But for Jesus, temporal birth raises more questions than it answers. Like every human destiny, that of Jesus is made up of decisive thresholds that must be crossed. For every man there is the threshold of birth and the threshold of death. For Jesus there are two more, conception and bodily resurrection.

For an ordinary man, conception is not a threshold; he begins to exist absolutely. For Jesus, conception is a threshold, the passage into temporal existence in the womb of a woman. His birth (like ours) is a new threshold, from the womb into existence beneath the sun. His death (like ours) is a threshold though his dead human body never ceased to be united hypostatically with the divine person and his cadaver was that person. Finally, for Jesus there is one more threshold, the threshold of bodily resurrection; He is the first to have crossed it, but the door has remained open behind Him for us all.

Thus from threshold to threshold Christ's destiny proceeds from eternity to eternity. This is what He himself says to Nicodemus: "And no one has ascended into heaven except Him who has descended from heaven; the Son of Man who is in heaven." Strange words, if one considers that He who spoke them was a man among men, seated face to face with another man, on a night like any other night beneath the obscure skies of Galilee. By becoming a man, Jesus did not immerse himself in time, He drew time into his own eternity.

In passing through birth and death, an animal goes from nothingness to nothingness. In passing through birth and death, man goes from nothingness to eternity. In passing through birth and death, Jesus goes from eternity to eternity.

This is why the liturgy for Christmas celebrates at once the eternal birth of Christ in the bosom of his Father and the temporal birth of Christ from the womb of the Virgin Mary.

Jesus Christ is youth itself, perpetually welling forth. In Him eternity swallows up the whole of time. Each event of his life has the new, unexpected character of lightning flashing down from heaven and instantaneously returning. For every man, natural birth is the end of a period of maturation of nine months, it is the fruit that detaches itself naturally from the tree. The birth of Jesus is that too, but is above all the appearance in our shadowy miserable world of the sweetness and the smile of God: "The goodness and kindness of God our Saviour appeared." Each man's death comes by accident or through exhaustion of the body's vigor. Jesus' death is a violent accident that puts an end to his temporal life, but it also is an offering in which Jesus, at once priest and victim, freely immolates Himself at the will of his Father in expiation of our sins. Born of a woman, He has human weakness and vulnerability; born of God, He revives himself and assumes once more the authority of his place at the right hand of his Father. But this time He conquers it not only as a divine person but as a man among men. And this is the prodigious reversal. If Jesus Christ was not God, He could not heal and save our human nature, and if He were not man, could not serve as our example.

When Pope St. Leo wished to define for the faithful the significance of Christmas, he gave an urgent exhortation which has not lost timeliness: "Christians, be on your guard, be conscious of your dignity. You have been made participants in the divine nature. Do not, through your conduct, fall once more to the level of your former decadence."

The optimism of the humanist and of the philosophy of enlightenment has been destroyed in the experience of two world wars. Because in the horrors of war the nature of man revealed itself as even more disquieting than had been imagined, we are witnesses to a vast plot to defame humanity and particularly the image of God in man. Since the beginning of the last war, literature, motion pictures, and even philosophy, not to mention political and economic theories, have been trying to convince us that we emerge from nothingness and return to nothingness after a life in which our motives of action hardly rise above appetite and instinct.

May Christians recapture contempt toward images of human nature that are so false and so degrading. And may the light of Christmas, rising on our night, put them to flight.

51

Chapter II
With Answering Charity

*The coming of Christ to save the world
was the greatest demonstration of love that the
world was ever to know. It was and will
always be the greatest because it was divine,
an act of God Himself. That love is now
part of the general consciousness of mankind,
if we are to judge from the common, ordinary,
down-to-earth goodness in people that shows
up chiefly at Christmas time. Everyone who
knows the story of Christ's love tries to
show that he has learned the lesson by some
act of kindness to his fellow man. Children
usually learn the lesson early, as they do
in the first story of this chapter; that they
retain the lesson throughout their lives is
proved by the host of Christmas stories of
love that follows their story here.*

WHY WE HAVE A SAVIOUR [12]

The littlest scholars retell the story in the very simplest terms
By Sister Eugene, S.C.

Nothing is so empty as a school without children. If you
are in a school building on a holiday, you find yourself almost
tiptoeing down the echoing corridors, as if fearing to disturb
the weekend ghosts.

For a brief hour every Saturday morning, a suburban grade
school in our area comes alive again with catechism classes for
Catholic children who attend public schools. I have been
teaching Christian doctrine to a group of Mexican children
there.

One Saturday, our classroom suddenly became the Garden
of Paradise.

"We'll dramatize today," I announced. "Do you know how
to play act?"

Half-scared but wholly eager, the children prepared to do the
story of the Creation and the Fall. I didn't attempt typecasting.
The Lord was to be a serious lad with a mop of uncut hair.
Adam was a tiny, trim, precocious first-grader with dancing
black eyes, who slanted an appraising look at his fourth-grade
mate, bigger than he. I heard him remark casually, "You're
a pretty fat Eve," as I busily sorted out a volunteer lion, dog,
elephant, and ape.

Everyone wanted to be the devil, (the psychologists can
figure that one out). But since he was a key figure and the
boys were few, I decided on a dainty little *señorita* who could
think fast—just in case she might have a hard time persuading
the First Parents.

The setting was really effective. The regular teacher in that
classroom (whose name I still do not know, though we invade
her domain weekly) could hardly have done better if she had
known what I was to think up that day. On the cupboard was
a collection of plants; on a table at the rear were cans with
sprouts started from seeds; on a stand at the left was some
artificial fruit from which several still-life drawings had been

made.

Best of all, tacked on the front board was a large brown paper tree. Superimposed were colored circles bearing the grammar exercises of the more accomplished. I'm sure that every child before me would have sworn that very real fruit, rosy and appealing, grew there that day.

Then it began. Eve and her half-pint Adam stood up front, not yet saying much. After all, conversation was something new to them, and my First Parents had a critical little audience.

God walked on from the left, "Well," he said, jumping right into the middle of the action, "look what I have done for you. I've given you flowers, and trees, and animals—and trees—and— oh, yes, you can have anything you see." (Bravo, I thought, he's doing it.) "But not those. Don't eat any of those apples," he finished, pointing.

"Why?" demanded Eve.

"Because I said so, that's why," retorted the unshorn one.

"OK," was the meek answer.

Then she and Adam started to look around to see what they owned. They didn't get very far, because the animals without cue went into character. Adam was supposed to name them, but Eve couldn't wait.

"That's a dog," she said as one barked.

Something scurried down my aisle and Eve came after it.

"Get back up in front," I whispered, "and pretend you're going through the woods."

Eve caught on. Looking up, she said, "Adam, I hear birds."

Distracted by what seemed to be a gibbering ape, Adam appeared uninterested. "How do you know they're birds?"

She had no answer, but tried valiantly again. Going over to a larger boy who crouched quietly on his haunches in the corner, she inquired, "What are you?"

He gave her a pitying look. "I'm an elephant," he said disgustedly.

All this time, with the animals all trying to get into the act, I was having a little difficulty hearing. "That's enough of that," I thought. We must get on with the story.

"All right, animals," I interrupted, reluctantly but firmly.

"Lie down and go to sleep. You're tired."

Adam must have decided that he was, too. In the middle of the floor he stretched his two-feet-plus length, and as he rested his head on his hand supported by his elbow, he whispered up at the formidable Eve, "Don't fall over me."

Now from the left slunk the devil. He addressed Eve, pointing: "See that tree?" Eve nodded. "Why don't you eat an apple?"

"I'm not supposed to."

"Eat one anyway. You'll be as great as God."

"OK." Eve toppled fast. Then she walked over to the reclining Adam.

"Why don't you eat an apple?" she asked him.

"Aw, no—" and he put out a restraining hand, never taking his head from the other one. "We're not allowed. You know that."

"Come on," coaxed Eve. "You'll be as great as God."

Adam thought that one over. Eve waited prudently.

"OK," agreed Adam, jumping up all of a sudden. I thought he would just reach for hers, but nothing doing. We were to have a little originality.

Leaning nonchalantly against the doorjamb with one hand on his hip, best Western style, he asked coolly, "Well, do I get yours or do I have to take one off the tree?"

"Get it off the tree," directed Eve, starting to munch again on her imaginary apple.

When Adam reached up, picked his apple, and took a bite, we all looked expectantly to the left. It was God's cue, but he didn't appear.

God was sitting open-mouthed, utterly absorbed in the drama. Everything stopped. Finally, the devil, sitting near him, hissed, *"Get in there, God."* He leaped up and hurried on.

"What's comin' off here?" he demanded. Then he saw.

"All right, you hafta be punished. You hafta get out of the garden. You hafta work hard. You hafta . . . ."

"Suffer," prompted the devil, offside.

"You hafta suffer—and get sick—and then you'll die."

(I was bursting with pride as he pulled all that doctrine out of his tangle of hair.) "But," he continued, his heart taking over, "I'll send you a Saviour."

So Adam and Eve covered their faces and slunk off right; and the animals scrambled up and became their own lovable selves; and lessons went on until the final ritual of every Saturday class—a ritual they never let me forget. Each child dips his finger into a little medicine bottle of holy water and privately but devoutly, while the rest struggle into wraps, looks up into my face and makes that most beautiful sign in the world, the Sign of the Cross.

THE FAMILY IN THE PARKING LOT [13]

Celebrating Christmas turned out to be worth the trouble
By Norman Spray

Have you ever looked at the holidays with a cold and practical eye and then talked yourself into believing that Christmas was not worth all the trouble?

I was making just such a cold and practical appraisal as the Christmas of 1956 approached. On December 11 of that year, another blue-and-purple northern was whistling through our town of Bedford, Texas, and I was in a fittingly icy mood as I drove to work that cold and bleak morning.

I knew that that very morning I faced a deadline on the Christmas issue of the employee news magazine I edited for the Bell Helicopter Co. So far the issue was a mess. Little had been written and, worse, my idea well was dry.

"Why should we bother with a Christmas issue anyway?" I asked myself. "In today's busy world who really cares?" Besides, who was I to write a sermon on peace and good will to interest men and women who built helicopters? After all, we were publishing a line of communication between management and employees—not a Sunday school bulletin.

I drove up to the Bell plant. A car was stopped ahead of me, and the driver was talking to the guard at the gate. Beside the driver sat a dark-haired young woman, and in the back, wedged in among a seatful of battered old suitcases, sat a shaggy-haired little boy holding a puppy. The guard pointed directions, and the car drove off toward the visitors' parking lot. I didn't know it then, but before the day was out, that car and those people would become important to me.

The driver of that car was Frank Gates, and his wife of four years, Eugenia, sat beside him while their three-year-old son, Frank, Jr., sat in the back. Frank was a logger. He had been working in Montana, but logging operations had closed down for the winter a week before and Frank had lost his job—again.

He had heard that in Texas he might be able to get year-round work, so they had loaded their belongings into the old car and headed south. They ate lightly, and at night slept in the car because they had barely enough money just for gasoline.

The family had arrived in Fort Worth on the evening of December 10, penniless, bone-tired and famished. Frank had gone to a construction company which happened to be building a new addition to our Bell plant, and they hired him immediately as a laborer at a dollar an hour. That wasn't much, even in those days—unless you'd just arrived from Montana with nothing at all.

"This is it, honey," Frank had said to Eugenia, elated. "From now on, things are going to be better." On that blustery night they had shared a quart of milk and bedded down in the car in high spirits.

"I'm a new man on the construction job out here," Frank had just said to the guard when I first saw him. "Can I park around here?" The guard had no idea that Frank wanted to park his car and his family there for the entire day.

At midmorning, the guard captain at plant-security head-quarters got a phone call from the gate guard. "A woman and a kid are out here in an old car. They've been here all morning."

The captain and a guard lieutenant went out to speak to the young mother. She looked tired—very tired. "Why," the lieutenant asked, "are you staying in the car?"

Eugenia explained, "We're going to try to find a place when my husband gets off work today."

The two officers both knew that company rules forbade her staying there in the parking lot, so they arranged for Eugenia to park at a service station lot across the street. While the move was being made they overheard the boy plead, "I'm hungry, mommy."

Back at the guard office the two security officers told what had happened. It was then that two other guards suggested that they buy lunch for the mother and son. Instantly, three dollars was on the table.

One guard carried the money to the plant cafeteria. When the cafeteria manager heard the story, he heaped two plates. "It's on the house," he said.

Eugenia was grateful when the guard handed her the plates, but when he insisted she take the three dollars besides, she became emotional. "Thank you very much," she said, her voice breaking, "but we'll pay you back."

The guard returned to the front gate guard station. "These are good people, just down on their luck," he told the other guards. "We ought to help them if we can."

The captain and lieutenant went to talk to Frank Gates. "This young fellow's not about to ask anybody for help," the captain said afterward. "All he wants is a chance."

"Trouble is, he won't get paid for two weeks," the lieutenant added.

The last comment left the guards silent. Two weeks is a long time to camp out in a car.

There was a plant rule against employee solicitation, a rule the guards were responsible for enforcing. But in any plant there is a shadowy information network, the grapevine. And at Bell that day, word of the mother's plight swept through the plant. The guards' first act of kindness was multiplied as secretaries and production workers began building a kitty to help a couple they had only heard about.

And that was when I heard about the Gateses, only ten minutes before I was to meet with my boss to talk about the Christmas issue.

Mildly interested, I took a note pad and ambled out to the security office. By then someone had come up with the idea of offering the family some of the clothing that was being collected at the plant for Hungarian relief.

On Frank's lunch hour, the young logger and his family were escorted to the clothes-collection point. Hesitantly, they picked a few items: a jacket for Frank, a pair of shoes and overalls for the boy. "This is all we'll need until we get started," said Eugenia. She was careful not to take too much from "Those poor people in Hungary."

I went back to my desk and called my wife. I told her about the Gates family. Barby's reaction was instantaneous—and practical.

"Meet me at their car," she said in the definite tone she reserves for times when she doesn't mean to be questioned. "I'm bringing that woman and her boy home with me."

I walked back to the front gate. A riveter from the factory strode up. "The boys around the plant want this to go to that woman and child out front," he told the guards. "Folks just heard about them and reached for their wallets." He laid ninety-six dollars on the desk.

Nobody asked questions—rules or no rules. Another guard, accompanied by the president of the union local, took the gift to Eugenia; I tagged along. There was no fancy speech as the union official said simply. "The folks in the plant want you to have this."

This time the tired, disheveled Eugenia couldn't hold back the tears. She just sat there, stroking her son's puppy, letting the drops fall unashamedly.

Barby drove up. "I want you to come and visit me until your husband gets off work," Barby said.

Eugenia was hesitant, but she accepted. When Barby brought her back to the plant that afternoon at quitting time, she looked like a new woman, years younger, even radiant. She had napped and bathed and fixed her hair, and Frank, Jr., was sparkling clean. She could hardly wait to rush into the arms of her husband.

"You people are wonderful," he said. "I can't say how

wonderful. We'll pay you back. It'll take a little time, but we'll pay you back."

The next morning, Frank appeared on the job thirty minutes before starting time—clean-shaven, rested, the picture of a man with a future. He whistled merrily and strode briskly.

Everyone I met that day wore a cheery smile and had a pleasant greeting. It wasn't imagination—the plant had changed overnight into a friendlier, happier, better place. Suddenly Christmas was everywhere. Suddenly I believed again in its miracle.

In the course of one day I learned that Christmas can never be looked at properly with a cold and practical eye; its value cannot be measured that way. Frank Gates and his family had helped me find a story, and a reason, for the Christmas issue.

OATMEAL FOR CHRISTMAS [14]

Our visitors came at the wrong time but got the right treatment
By John J. Marquardt

Father Marquardt is rector of Glenmary's Major Seminary of Glendale, Ohio. The Glenmary Home Missioners are a society of secular priests and brothers working to establish the Church in rural "no-priest" America. They operate in twenty-two large mission areas in Kentucky, Ohio, Georgia, Virginia, West Virginia, Oklahoma, North Carolina, Texas, Arkansas, and Pennsylvania.

It was the evening of the day before a holiday. Brother Charles and I had not yet eaten supper. We were busy cleaning up the log cabin chapel at Dungannon.

I don't remember now who answered the door, but when it was opened, we saw three of the poorest people in town standing in the doorway. Boo Ludlow, his wife, and their six-year-old son.

They didn't say a word. They weren't asking for anything in particular. They didn't have anything special to say. They just stood there.

While I was fishing for the diplomatic way to tell them we were very busy and that we hoped they'd have a nice holiday tomorrow and "Good-by" and "God bless you" and "Come see us again," Brother Charles said words that went something like this, "Oh, good evening, Boo and Mrs. Ludlow and Johnnie. We're so glad you stopped in. Have you had supper yet? No? Well, come on in and stay awhile. We were just about to eat, and you can join us."

The moment was most inopportune for inviting guests. Our work for the evening would be interrupted. All my plans would go out the window. But Brother Charlie, I knew, would be absolutely deaf to my sighs of protest. Therefore, I really didn't sigh too loudly.

Fifteen minutes later we sat down to our holiday eve supper, oatmeal with milk and brown sugar, and coffee. It didn't seem like much of a meal when we sat down to eat, and I intended to finish in a hurry and get back to my work. But the longer we sat there, the more we talked, the better it tasted. I shall never forget that love feast of oatmeal.

Poor Boo and his little family, so they told us, had been in town all day. They had come into town for no particular purpose. They had no business in town. They just wanted to talk to people, visit with people, any people.

They had had a pretty bad day. I doubt whether they had lunch, and if it had not been for Brother Charles, they probably would have had no supper.

Boo had two nasty red spots on his bald head. Earlier in the day some smart aleck by the general store had exploded a firecracker on top of Boo's hat while he was wearing it. The weatherbeaten hat now had a big hole burned into it and Boo needed a lot of salve for his poor head, burned on the outside, and no doubt aching on the inside,

They didn't say very much, Boo and his wife and his boy. But, oh, how they ate! And how they seemed to enjoy it! Before the meal was half over, they even began to smile.

And Brother Charles began to look so happy and pleased to see them eat his good old oatmeal. And the good old world began to look brighter. The good old people began to look so good and so lovable. It was the intoxication of Christian love foilowing upon one act of charity. I began to feel like Ebenezer Scrooge after his conversion by the friendly ghosts.

A little while later, our visitors said that they must leave. Out the door they went, and down the road, our Joseph, Mary, and Jesus. They had found rest and food in our inn. We shouted to them as they disappeared into the night. "Merry Christmas, Merry Christmas." After they shouted back we closed the door and went back to our preparations for midnight Mass.

SLEEP IN HEAVENLY PEACE [15]

The experience of one Christmas Eve brought home to me the mystery of the cross
By Father John Reedy, C.S.C.

This happened about eight o'clock in the morning on Christmas Eve about a dozen years ago.

Though our offices were closed, I had come over to clear some details from my desk. The phone startled me. No one should have been calling at that time, on that day.

The voice was familiar. It was the high school-aged daughter, the eldest child of a family of friends. A couple years before her parents and I had struggled through religious instructions. They were serious about their search, unwilling to accept easy formulas. When they finally decided to become Catholics, they knew what they were doing. They responded so completely that I could see clearly where my explanations left off and a mysterious religious response took their place.

Over the phone Judy's voice was strained. "Father," she

said, "Dad asked me to call you. We just found Rob. He's dead!"

Perhaps it was the early hour. More likely, it was the complete surprise. I just couldn't function. Instead, I found myself falling back on those routine formulas we use. "Is there anything I can do?" "I'll pray for all of you."

She said, "No, there's nothing. Dad just wanted me to let you know."

The conversation ended and I sat there bewildered. Robbie was their beautiful, wonderfully healthy thirteen-month-old baby. There had been a long gap between the older three children and Robbie's birth, and the entire family idolized him, even though they were now awaiting the birth of another child.

Gradually, a realization began to seep into my understanding. "Good God," I thought. "It must have just happened. They must have just found him."

I grabbed the old jacket I had worn to the office that morning and drove over to their home.

The door opened and I'll never forget that scene. It was as I had thought. All the family were still in their nightclothes. Their home was decorated for Christmas. The tree was lit and surrounded with gifts.

Dick, the father, looked up at me with agony in his eyes. He sat holding the baby's body.

Lois, the mother, came to me. There was nothing either of us could say. I held her, while in the back of my mind I begged God that this shock would not endanger the child she was carrying.

Finally, we began to talk—the kind of halting, strained talk that goes on at the surface when people are unable to say what they are really feeling.

The baby had seemed perfectly healthy the night before when he was put to bed. Although he had signs of what seemed a slight cold, there was nothing that caused concern. (Later, the doctor said it was a fast-acting kind of pneumonia. Even if Rob had been in the hospital, the doctor said, there was little they could have done for him.)

In the early morning someone had routinely checked on him, and their lives fell apart.

We sat there together, but each was isolated in a personal misery: the father, the mother, the two young daughters, and the younger son. And the priest, who felt he should be able to offer some kind of support, only found himself choking on all those familiar formulas which at this moment seemed irrelevant, if not profane.

And the baby, there in his father's arms.

We waited, as mourning people always do. No one wanted to break the moment; no one would have known how.

Finally, after what seemed hours, the undertaker came. And then came another throb of torment. The father was unwilling to hand over his son's body to a stranger.

What then happened grew out of my earlier visits to their home. Tiny children have always intimidated me. I have never been around babies long enough to get used to them. They always seem too fragile to handle, and I fear that in my awkwardness I might somehow injure them. And so, in spite of constant encouragement and teasing, I had never held Robbie. "Wait until he's two," I would say. "Then he can begin to defend himself."

But at this moment, with the undertaker standing awkwardly in their living room, with Dick blindly unwilling to part with his son's body, Lois found the right thing to say to her husband.

"Dick, let Father take Robbie. He'll hold him now."

I caught my breath, I wasn't ready for that. There was a moment of no response. Then Dick slowly held the baby's body out for me to take.

My eyes were so filled that I could hardly see to follow the undertaker to the door. We walked outside the house. He closed the door and I handed the tiny body to him.

He left and I went back to the family.

The next afternoon, Christmas Day, only the parents, their three children, and I went over to the funeral home. Just one member of the staff was present. Because of the day it seemed inappropriate that the establishment should be open at all. And also because of the day, the funeral home atmosphere—the subdued lighting, the muffled sound—seemed horribly inappropriate.

We sat before the coffin, which looked like some grotesque toy. We talked quietly, in fragments, with long silences. The grandparents were as stunned and as helpless as I.

But I began to sense something about this family. The shock and sorrow were, of course, unimaginable. But something else was emerging, a tone which didn't quite fit the utter desolation I expected to find in them.

Along with the grief, there was more composure than I thought would be possible. In words, glances, embraces, there were currents going between Dick and Lois and between them and their children. All of them seemed to draw support from these currents.

We remained at the funeral home for an hour or so and finally left. They knew I was expected at another home for Christmas dinner and they insisted that I go ahead, while they returned to their own home.

The transition from that near empty funeral place to the noisy, jumbled celebration of a happy family was too great. I didn't manage it very well. During the moments when I was not involved in conversation I would find my thoughts drifting off to that other family, their home decorated for joy, filled with grief. I contributed little to the gaiety of the family with whom I shared that Christmas.

It had been decided that Robbie's funeral would be held as soon as possible, the morning after Christmas. I was asked to offer the Mass.

There had been no time for any notice in the newspapers, and I expected the service to be like our visit to the funeral home, just the family and a few close friends.

But the church was almost filled. There had been a lot of telephoning in that parish on Christmas Eve and on Christmas Day.

When the family arrived at the church, I met them. Dick took me aside and said, "Father, we'd like to have the casket open during the Mass."

I was stunned. No family had ever made this request to me

before. I tried to persuade him to change his mind. "Dick, all of you have suffered enough. This will tear you apart."

But there was no uncertainty in him. "No," he said, "we all talked this over. It's what we want."

So I went over and told the undertaker. He said, "Oh, no, Father. We don't do that. It's against the policy of the parishes here."

We argued about it. The pastor happened to be in the hospital and the undertaker wanted to know who was going to take responsibility for the decision.

I said, "I'll take the responsibility. With what this family is going through, the only thing I care about is their feelings."

Reluctantly, he agreed.

When I came out to the altar to begin the Mass, my eyes couldn't avoid the tiny casket. Robbie lay there dressed in a suspendered playsuit, looking as beautiful and healthy as ever.

All through the Mass, whenever I looked up, my gaze returned to the infant who seemed to be sleeping peacefully, unaware of all these people, all this solemnity, all this emotion.

When I pulled my eyes away from the baby, they would always be drawn over to the family. And each time, the tears welled up, producing some long pauses before I could again focus on the words of the missal.

At Mass's end I came down to the communion rail, just a few feet in front of the open casket, and spoke. I cannot remember now what I said, except for one thing.

I said that in searching for some words of support for these friends of mine, I had reviewed all the formulas of faith and hope to which my life was committed. And all of them seemed inappropriate. Not because they were untrue or meaningless—I firmly believed in them—but because all of these truths seemed to speak to the mind. And this family was not hurting in their minds; they were just hurting. With such a hurt, all we could do was be present, grieve with them, try to show our love for them.

When I finished speaking the family arose and came out into the aisle beside the casket. They stood there for a moment. Then the father, the mother, and each of the children bent over, kissed the infant, and turned and walked to the rear of the church.

Through badly blurred vision I somehow followed the servers back into the sacristy.

Later in the day, back at my office, one of my friends who was also a friend of the family came in to see me. He had been at the funeral.

Though he has deep feelings, he likes to project a breezy, hard-nosed image. None of that image appeared in our conversation.

He seemed bewildered by his own emotions. "God," he said, "if anyone had ever told me that the funeral of a baby, at Christmas time, could be beautiful, I would have told him he was out of his mind."

He paused, then added softly, "But it *was* beautiful!"

I have since tried to sort out and understand some of the many perceptions which were churning around inside me during that time.

First, there was the shocking mystery of a cruel suffering I couldn't begin to explain. You can say all you want about God taking Robbie to a happiness ever greater than he could have known in his family. In faith I believe that. But humanly, looking at this child and his family, it sounds like something said in a language I never learned.

Why give this baby to this family for only thirteen months? Why, of all times, on Christmas Eve, a day warm and rich with family love and joy and anticipation?

Through the years, of course, I've seen other tragedies come into lives I have known, tearing at good, sensitive people in a way which seems almost whimsically cruel. But in all the years of my priesthood, no other tragedy hit me quite as hard as Robbie's death in those circumstances.

And none of those formulas from theology or spiritual reading provided an explanation which makes sense to me.

Only the phrase, "the mystery of the Cross," suggests that those who profess to follow Christ do, in fact, accept a vulnerability beyond our expectations.

It is an openness to God's will, a fierce commitment to

belief in his love, no matter how difficult it might be to feel that love in our lives. And it is truly mysterious. Why does such a thing happen to these lives when other Christians, the same kind of people, never encounter anything like it?

While I was completely incapable of understanding the mystery of the suffering my friends endured, I was able to perceive signs that beyond the cloud of pain—beyond the cross—the loving Father was present.

How else could anyone understand the strength, the faith of this family? It was an acceptance not of their baby's sudden death, but of the fact that somehow even such a horrible loss has meaning and purpose in the providence of a loving God.

This experience also brought some humbling thoughts about my own faith, and my priesthood.

I couldn't walk away from my participation in this family's suffering without wondering how my own faith, so easily professed, would have survived if this had been my child. The things in my life which I call hardships seem trivial when compared to such naked suffering.

Also humbling was the recognition of just how incidental, how instrumental, my ministry to them had been.

Most of the time we had spent together during their course of instructions was spent on all those details common to such presentations—everything from indulgences to Lenten fast and abstinence, to the whole catalogue of mortal and venial sins.

In one of our first discussions, Lois said frankly, "Father, I guess I just don't want to be a Catholic. There are a lot of things about Catholic life and belief that I just don't like."

I felt rather smug about my answer. I told her, "There are a lot of things about Catholic life and belief that I just don't like either. If I felt I had a choice, I'm sure I could find a religious belief that would be more attractive."

They pushed me hard, challenging and questioning, sending me back to my books. Then suddenly, without any reference to what we were discussing, it all changed. It became, "You don't have to prove all that. Just tell us what the Church teaches. We accept the Church and its teachings."

It was obvious that the significant change which had occurred was between God and these people. As far as the reality of that change was concerned, I could have been juggling apples instead of explaining indulgences.

Though the realization shook any vanity I had in my effectiveness as a catechist, it also was reassuring during a time when a lot of priests were having second thoughts about the effectiveness of what they were doing.

To me, the basic question came to be not whether I was achieving the maximum effectiveness with my ability and training. Instead, it was a matter of being available, with all my limitations, to serve as God's instrument in his mysterious dealings with the people I encounter.

And that awareness was immeasurably deepened as I watched the faith of this family in their suffering. There was no doubt in my mind, nor in the minds of their friends, I believe, that their extraordinary ability to endure and grow through this loss was rooted in their faith in God and in each other.

Such recognition puts the success or failure of human projects in a different perspective. For me it has been a reassuring perspective.

Finally, seeing this family's humanity infused with a religious response to God, I can see the wonder of the Incarnation in a new reality.

Scripture doesn't say much about the family life of Jesus, but the fact that God chose to redeem humanity through this universal human experience has to be important. It requires people to use their understanding of family life as a way of looking at God's plan.

Certainly the family and friends of Jesus knew the ordinary joys of warmth and rejoicing in the joys of those they loved. They also know the reality of loss, the human bewilderment at what must have been seen as unjustified suffering.

In all of this human experience of Jesus, shared in varying degrees by most families, God's immediate design was being worked out.

Surely this says that for most people a loving response to the Father is to be expressed not in deep theological speculation or in extraordinary commitment, but in the ordinary patterns of family relationships: in service to others through work, in openness and response to friends and others in need.

At a time when many people seem distressed because they can't find meaning or achievement in their lives, this memory of Christmas seems to say: The meaning is in the living itself. Don't be blinded by regret over accomplishments unattained. Open your eyes and your lives to the God revealed in a newborn infant, in a family called Holy, in a teacher's modest accomplishment, in a man's suffering and death accepted as God's mysterious will.

None of these reflections is very profound, but they are much more real to me for having emerged from the reality of that Christmas loss suffered by my friends.

In the intervening years, their lives have gone on. All three of the children who shared that Christmas are grown and married. Two younger children are at home with Dick and Lois.

Curiously, though I'm sure our lives are intimately linked through the sharing of that tragedy, I don't see them very frequently. When we do get together I have the feeling that all of us are conscious of that moment which was too painful and too rich to be the subject of reminiscence.

This is the first time I've tried to express to them and to others what it meant to me. I hope they will understand what I've said, and what I've left unsaid.

JOE'S CHRISTMAS GIFTS[16]

A bag of coal once meant Santa's disapproval, but Joe changed all that

By Vincent Argondezzi

Our family was fortunate in living so close to the freight yards, for in those days, when every penny counted, we got a lot of help from the railroad.

The old ties were discarded along the side and all the people in our town had permission to take them. On Saturday mornings you would hear the sound of many saws cutting the ties into small blocks, which were then split into fours. They fitted perfectly into the castiron stoves, and were fuel during the fall, and made a good base for the coal fires in the long winter.

We were also allowed to go along the railroad tracks and pick up the coal that fell when the freight trains were being made up. The shifting and bumping of the cars caused big lumps to fall off. This black gold went to anyone who wished to pick it up. You could look out our back window almost any day and see people walking along, bent over, and picking at the ground. I took many a turn, as did my neighbors, in filling 100-pound burlap bags.

The champion coal picker was Joe, one of our buddies, the son of Zio Giovanni, who lived near Ferry Alley. We always referred to him as Zio Giovanni Near the Alley to distinguish him from Zio Giovanni the Tavern Keeper.

Joe was a hard worker, and he moved fast at coal picking. He would come down to the railroad with an empty bag on a coaster wagon and work until it was full. Then he would pull it home. Joe's mother, Zia Marianne, died when he was young, and he was like a son to the women in our neighborhood. My mother in particular loved him very much, and he was at our table often. Mom knew he liked homemade bread, and she baked it especially for him. If his clothes got torn she mended them, and she gave him spending money now and then. The other women did just about the same. We boys often said that we had one mother, but Joe had many, and he was very grateful.

One night after a hearty meal Joe said, "You are so good to me, Zia Louisa, but I cannot give you anything to show you how much I appreciate it."

"Now, never you mind, dear, just be a good boy and always say a prayer for me, and that will be more than enough," Mom replied.

But Joe was preoccupied the rest of the evening. Just before he left, my stepfather asked him to go into the cellar with me to get a quart of wine to take home to Joe's father. While my stepfather was filling the bottle we talked about the coming Christmas holiday.

"My father is going to buy me a new suit for Christmas," said Joe.

"I'm going to get a new pair of shoes and a Buck Rogers gun," I said.

"I wish that I had a lot of money. I would buy everyone here in this neighborhood a gift! I would be a regular Santa Claus."

"It's all right, Joe," I said. "Your friendship is enough of a gift."

Suddenly I noticed his face light up as he gazed in the direction of the stove.

"I have it, I have it!" he exclaimed. "I can give everyone a gift, I can."

"But what?" I asked.

"I'm going to keep it a surprise," he said.

After that we didn't see much of Joe at our house or any other house for he was out along the railroad track right after school every day. We had never had much luck getting him to play in our games; now it was impossible, for Joe was always at the tracks. His wagon would hold only one bag at a time, so after he got it full he would pull it home and in no time be back.

"Joe does not come to see us anymore, Antonio," said my mother. "He is always on the railroad picking coal. Now, what is he going to do with all that coal?"

"I don't know," said my stepfather. "Maybe he wants to get the bin full so he can stop for a while, instead of picking a little every day."

One day I stopped Joe as he was pulling home his wagon of

coal.

"Joe," I said, "Mom misses seeing you, and she wonders why you don't come over to our house anymore."

"I'm very busy," said Joe. "I don't have time, but I love your mother and everyone else in the neighborhood, and like I said, I don't have time to stop. I have to get as much coal as I can."

"But why?" I asked.

"I can't tell you," he replied.

As Christmas drew near we saw even less of Joe. Christmas Eve arrived and we sat down to our traditional dinner and afterward went into the living room to trim the tree. Usually about this time, Birch, Sal, Bill, Mike, Joe, and the others, together with their parents, began arriving. But thus far none had come. Joe always had been the first, and Mom looked disappointed.

"Perhaps I said or did something to hurt the boy's feelings," she said.

"Mom, you could never hurt anyone's feelings!" I told her. I knew how she felt though, for she and Zia Marianne had been very close, and after Zia Marianne's death Mom felt that it was her duty to keep Joe as happy and well as possible.

Finally Zio Vincenzo arrived with Zia Lucia, Billy, Mike and Jim. *Buono festa's!* filled the air, and there were kisses and warm embraces.

"What is wrong, Louisa?" Zia Lucia asked. "You are so sad tonight, and it is so unlike you, especially this night of festival."

"Wait, wait, let me tell you what happened tonight at our house," interrupted Zio Vincenzo. "We heard a noise at our back door, and you know me, brave and fearless."

"Tell the story," said his wife, "and never mind the brave-and-fearless talk."

"But please, let me build up the suspense of the moment!" replied Zio Vincenzo. "As I was saying, we heard a noise at the back door and I—well, courageous and daring as usual—went to investigate. Do you know what I found?"

"Santa Claus," chipped in Chris, Vicki, and Tess, my three little sisters, in chorus.

"Ah, something almost as great, if not as great. We found a bag of coal!" said Zio Vincenzo.

"Who was bad?" asked Tess.

"Yes, who was bad?" asked my sister Sue. (Mom had often told us that if we were bad Santa would bring us only a lump of coal.)

"But my little dears," said Zio Vincenzo, "no one was bad! This was a gift of love, bought with sacrifice and hard work. The bag of coal was marked, 'To Zia Lucia and Zio Vincenzo with all my love. Joe.' "

"Mother, I, too, heard a noise at our back door," Tess said.

"Why didn't you tell me?" asked Mom.

"I was afraid it might be Santa Claus, and they told me that if someone sees him he goes away without leaving any gifts, is it not so?" asked Tess.

"It is true," said Mom. "But let us look, for we know that Santa Claus does not come at the back door but down the chimney when children are fast asleep."

Mom opened the back door and there on the porch was a bag of coal, Joe's Christmas gift with a note attached. "To Zia Louisa and Zio Antonio and family. Love. Joe."

There were tears in Mom's eyes, tears of happiness, mixed with sadness that her friend and ours, Joe's mother, Zia Marianne, couldn't be there to see the beautiful spirit of her son in this gift.

Soon Joe arrived with his father, and Mom hugged Joe until the redness lit up his ears. But you could tell how happy he was, for truly he had brought the living spirit of Christ into our home. Or rather, it had always been here, but he added new meaning to it. Joe had filled ten bags of coal, one for each of our families.

That night Joe was the center of attention. After eating and drinking and exchanging gifts we gathered around our beloved Christmas fire, now our torch of love.

THE DAY AFTER CHRISTMAS [17]

The joy delayed was mine, not the little girl's
By Paul C. O'Connor, S.J.

I am a missionary. A quarter century ago I was serving at
Hooper Bay on Alaska's Bering Sea coast. I had been on the
trail for nearly two weeks and I wanted to get back to the
mission. But as we dropped down to the beaten trail of the
Black River, my guide asked me about visiting a little village
three hours off in the tundra. I thought of Honnoe, an Eskimo
lass of ten, who lived in the almost-deserted village. I was the
only white man she had ever seen and she would be expecting
me.

I turned my dogs off the river, up through some tortuous
willows and into a blanket of fog smothering the trailless tundra.

On we traveled at a good clip for three hours, and I knew if
the fog did not lift we would be spending the night on the
tundra. Then we heard the barking of dogs that led us to our
village.

As my assistant removed our food box, I walked up and was
greeted with a shy, little smile from Honnoe. She told me that
she had been waiting for me for a long time. I slipped some
English walnuts into her hand, which I called "big peanuts" in
Eskimo.

Little Honnoe and her aged mother were the only ones in the
village. She had arrived late in her mother's life, and here in this
tiny village I doubt if she met more than ten strange faces a year.
Soon she was showing me her crude toys, including a doll she
had made for herself.

I remarked that if she came to the mission I would give her
a doll that would make her eyes pop. It was an oft-made offer,
for I dearly loved to give dolls to these little tykes.

The year slipped by and soon the Christmas season arrived.
It was a busy time for me, with confessions for the hundreds
of people who arrived by dog team. With three Masses, sermons,
decorations, a Christmas play and other holiday affairs, I was
one distracted missionary.

I did notice little Honnoe, but hers was only one face in hundreds. I had completely forgotten about my promise of a doll.

The day after Christmas shone beautifully and clearly. I was congratulating myself on the happy departure of all the visitors when a timid knock came to my door.

There was Honnoe and her aged mother. I indulged in small talk, gave them my blessing and wished them a safe journey home. They seemed reluctant to go, and I thought of the long journey ahead of them. They had probably never traveled so far from home.

Then it came to me in a flash—the doll that would make her eyes pop! This tiny girl had come a good two-day journey just to make me keep my promise.

Anguish struck me. I had given away a hundred or more presents and, of course, the dolls were the first to go. I was in trouble, and as I rushed upstairs I asked the angels to help me out of my predicament.

My heart was in my mouth as I looked over a bunch of toys, all broken discards. It was then I spied a carton back against the wall completely forgotten in the frenzied confusion of Christmas. I reached for it, ripped off the wrapping to behold a beautifully-made rag doll. She was at least three feet tall with flaxen curls, a prize for any girl.

I hid the doll in the back of my cassock and slowly descended the stairs with hands empty and faced my little maiden.

I said in a slow and measured voice that I had no small dolls, but would this do? As I produced her gift, Honnoe's eyes bulged and her thin arms hugged the doll with all her might.

Making children happy is the supreme joy in life but this was something special. The look of gratitude in that little girl's eyes will live with me forever. She put the doll on her back, Eskimo style, and then solemnly walked up and down the room, patting it as real mothers do.

Her mother could hardly believe I would part with such a grand doll, but Honnoe knew it was hers completely. As she left she beamed with joy. In limpid Eskimo, she said, "Father, you make me so happy."

But I was the happy one that day.

A CONTEMPORARY CHRISTMAS CAROL [18]

In the light of the stars
By Marvin R. O'Connell

Wendell Jackson's tiny grocery store stood there, or rather
crouched, in the basement corner of a drab apartment house
not far from the city's industrial center. The stock was not
impressive when compared to the wonderland of the nearby
supermarket; it was made up mostly of things people tended
to run out of unexpectedly or to want on the spur of the
moment: milk, bread, beer, potato chips, cold meats. Wendell
charged more for his wares than the supermarket did, but that
was the price people paid for having him and his store available
at odd hours, and Wendell thus scraped out a living.

It was not much of a living. As Wendell looked out from
the empty store at the snow drifting down through the arc light
onto the sooty street, he reflected on how very little he had
gotten out of life. This was a thought that oppressed him often,
left him feeling bleak and hollow inside, turned his mind's eye
backward, where he saw disappointment and shattered dreams,
and then forward, where he saw nothing at all. He looked at
his watch. Quarter of six, December 24. "Merry Christmas,"
he said aloud, though there was nobody to hear the harsh note
in his voice.

Christmas was one of the rare days that Wendell did not
open the store, and on Christmas Eve he closed it early. This
was not because he had any celebrating to do himself but
because he knew from experience that nobody came to buy.
He would spend the time the usual way, by himself, in an
empty apartment; he would idly watch the phony jollity on
television and would realize with a stab at the heart that he
was almost an old man.

And what to show, he now asked himself. All that he cared
about was gone, for all he had ever cared about was Sarah, and
Sarah, beautiful and good, was dead and gone and would never
come again. He even had trouble now, after all these years,
remembering what his wife's face had looked like or how her

hand had felt.

Might as well close now, he thought, and as he walked toward the back room for his coat the shrapnel splinters he had brought back from the South Pacific caused the familiar dull ache in his leg. It always happened in damp weather. He had his coat on when he heard the front door open. The customer, Wendell saw, was a slight young man, with long hair and a thin, unkempt mustache, dressed in boots, worn jeans, and a windbreaker zipped to the throat.

"May I help you?" Wendell asked. The young man ducked back toward the cooler and then reappeared with two half-gallon cartons of milk. He put them down on the counter next to the cash register, where Wendell had already set his hat. As he reached for the cartons to put them in a bag, Wendell saw the gun. The hand that held it shook visibly.

"Gimme the money," the young man said.

"Now listen, son," Wendell began.

"Don't gimme any crap, mister, just gimme the money." He waved the revolver in what he must have thought was a threatening gesture, though the motion reminded Wendell of an awkward little boy writing on a blackboard. "Put it in there," the young man said, pointing to the brown bag.

Wendell opened the register and scooped out the silver and few bills and dumped them in the bag. "Mister," said the young man, as he took the bag, almost gently, "I'm no thief, but I got a sick wife and a sick kid and I got no job and it's Christmas." He paused and breathed a deep, choking breath, and Wendell thought he was going to cry. Then he was gone.

Wendell leaned against the counter for a long time staring at the spot where the young man had stood and seeing nothing. He roused himself then, picked up the phone, and began to dial the police number. Suddenly, as his finger moved across the dial, he saw everything. He saw the Christmas tree in the front room of his father's house, and he saw the crude Christmas decorations they had rigged up in 1942 amid the smoking ruins of Guadalcanal, and he saw how the apartment had looked the first and only Christmas he had spent with Sarah.

Most clearly, he saw Sarah's face, lovely and serene, as though it had been there all the time, as though the bitterness and despair he had cultivated like a garden for these long years had never happened. And when he felt Sarah's hand on his he hung up the phone without waiting for anybody to answer.

By the time he got out to the sidewalk the snow had stopped, and he looked up past the dark blur of the surrounding buildings at the bright but moonless sky. He turned up the collar of his coat against the wind, and he said, "Merry Christmas." He smiled as he said it this time.

This time, though as before there was no one in sight, it was heard ringing like a bell as it pealed through a billion trillion stars.

CHRISTMAS STOCKING [19]

Of considerations elating and depressing
By Bob Considine

The greatest news story ever written was committed to papyrus by a man called Luke, some thirty years after the crucifixion of Jesus of Nazareth.

Luke, who was primarily a physician, not a writer, told the story in a few hundred words. But he wrote it in such a way that each succeeding age of reasoning man has regarded it as the very essence of all that is wondrous in the printed and spoken word.

It was in the form of a letter to a convert to Christianity, one Theophilus, and was part of his instruction in the faith for which he had renounced his paganism. Luke, bolstering his own authority, said that he had talked with Peter before putting the story down.

"... In those days," the letter continued, "there went forth an edict from Caesar Augustus for the registration of the whole world."

81

Luke, which was a nickname for either Lucius or Lucanus, wrote his fabulous words in Greek, though he was then an honorary citizen of Rome, as were all physicians who made their homes in the realm of Caesar.

". . . And Joseph likewise went up from Galilee into Judea, from the town of Nazareth to the town of David which is called Bethlehem—for he was of the house and family of David—to enregister himself together with Mary, his betrothed, who was with child."

"And it came to pass that whilst they were there she completed the days of her delivery and brought forth her first born Son."

No one can tell us what Luke looked like, how he dressed, or anything about his exact background. We do know that he was from Antioch, in what is now Syria, and that he was the best phrasemaker of the Gospel writers.

Luke traveled a great deal among the rich and poor, as doctor, friend, and aide to Paul. They had met either in Antioch or Paul's home, Tarsus, and were inseparable during the difficult early years of Christianity. "I am all alone, save for Luke," Paul wrote shortly before he was put to death in Rome in the summer of 62 A.D.

Luke may well have been with Paul when the latter visited the aged Peter and James to hear from their lips the stories of Christ they knew so well, and of the Blessed Virgin who bore Him.

She "brought forth her first born Son; and she swathed Him round and laid Him in a manger, because there was no place for them in the inn."

Luke was more than a physician to Paul. Often he preached or wrote report of what he had learned, and he shared with Paul the ecstatic vision of a Saviour glorified on earth.

"And in the same district were shepherds living out in the fields and keeping night-watches over their flock. And an angel of the Lord stood by them, and the glory of the Lord shone about them, and they feared with a great fear."

"And the angel said to them, 'Fear not, for behold, I bring you glad tidings of great joy which shall be to all the people; for there has been born to you this day a Saviour, who is Christ the Lord, in the town of David.' "

Luke died in Bithynia, in Asia Minor, at the age of seventy-four. There is some evidence that he may have been murdered. But nothing could kill the simple golden words that had rolled from him in his letter to Theophilus—words since framed into more than 1,000 languages and spread through every country the earth has known.

"And this shall be to you a sign thereof: ye shall find a Babe enswathed and lying in a manger."

"And suddenly there appeared with the angel a multitude of the heavenly host praising God and saying, 'Glory to God in the highest, and peace upon earth among men of his good pleasure!' "

The Burning Babe

Once upon a time in Baltimore there was a guy named Mike who faced Christmas Eve with pockets that were cleaner than his neck. Mike had had a bad year. He wasn't a bum, but he was so closely related to the species that the Christmas shoppers edged away from him. Mike felt bad, but looked worse.

He was a sentimental soul, Mike. He didn't mind when the shoppers took a quick gander at him, and looked away. He hardly noticed them, except to feel sorry for them, and to wonder what had become of the spirit of Christmas. Mike was a little funny that way. He could see no sense in one rich person's giving another rich person something he didn't need. There was no generosity in that, Mike thought.

Mike felt it was all right to give a present for Christmas, if it hurt you a little to give it, and if it went to someone who could use it, and who would be surprised and pleased by it. Mike had a couple of friends—down around the Baltimore water front—bums.

So Mike walked along the cold street, vaguely warmed by the yellow lights that spilled from the store windows. He liked the sounds of horses' hooves, the murmur of the smart carriages that went past him.

Mike walked faster now. He had caught a whiff of the wharves. It gave him an idea. He had a dollar in his pocket—no, it was crumpled in his hand. He had found it that day and said a little prayer of thanks for it. It was the first break he had had in days. Now he knew what he'd do with it! He'd go down to the flop

83

house and find his friends. And he'd say to them, "I found a buck today. Let's go down to the corner and drink it."

That was a good idea, he thought, as he automatically stopped to look into a sports goods store. Himself, he'd take rye. It gave a man a warm and rugged feeling. It would make him forget that in a little while he would stop trying to find a job, and begin to bum like his friends. It would be hard for him, for the thing that was still fine in him was taking a long time to die. "Rye for you, Michael, m'lad," he said to himself. "It'll be a Merry Christmas you'll have."

But even as he mused he knew, somewhere inside him, that there would be no rye. He knew there would be nothing at all, except the bread-line beans and a flop in a wintry room. He squeezed his dollar into a tighter little ball. He looked again at a baseball bat in the window. It cost one dollar.

It was a beautiful thing, that bat. It glistened in its coat of varnish. Mike's bleared eyes roamed up and down its slim grip and the great solid batting surface. He wondered what sacrifice he would have made as a kid for that bat, and he could think of none too great.

In a little while he was walking again, the bat under his arm, his palm damp where the crumpled dollar had been. For a moment he felt a little sorrow for his friends at the flop house. There would be no drinks for them. For a split instant he even felt sorry for himself. But in a little while he thought only of the kid who would get that bat, never knowing where it came from. That to Mike was joy enough. That, to Mike, who would never see the kid, was Christmas.

He knew where he'd leave it, because often he walked by the old place and saw the boys in the yard. He walked to the door of St. Mary's Industrial School, and leaned the bat against the door. Then he rang the bell, and walked down the dark street. The Christian Brother who came to the door did not even see him. But he took the bat in. He said to himself that he'd give it to the boy who had the least of all the boys.

The Brothers gave out the presents after Mass on Christmas morning: presents that the police had mended, or charitable organizations had sent to the home. The kid who got the bat

84

was a chubby boy who had no real home, who had no chance. He was a homely kid, with a broad nose, a great humorous gash of a mouth and lively dark eyes. There was a strange look in those eyes when he held the bat, the first bat he ever owned. He set his thinnish legs in a stance and swung his round body.

That was the day a Babe was born. It could have been the day another Babe was born.

Mistletoe and Water Cooler

The Christmas Eve party has become as much a part of the American office building as the typewriter. The writer has certainly joined in his share, but, as the years pass, with growing misgivings. Maybe I'm getting old. But what logical connection can there be between the birth of Christ and a hangover?

Is there a greater obscenity than the typical office Christmas party? I've been to some in recent years that had about as much to do with the meaning of Christmas as a night in a Bombay opium den.

They seem to consist of bad, cold food remnants on soggy paper dishes, half-consumed drinks in paper cups which also have been used as ashtrays, and sedate working people who—with a snootful—are sure it's time either to tell the boss what a louse he is, take a punch at him (which, in prescribed cases is, of course, to be urged), or ask him for a raise.

All the pretty stenogs get bussed and pinched under the questionable truce of the mistletoe. The boss smiles until his jaws ache and then begins to look around for an exit. Some pest with hardly enough brains to eat a banana has him by the lapel, blowing bad whisky in his face and telling him, the boss, what a lucky stiff he is to have him, the pest, working in the outfit.

It all seems to have precious little to do with the birth of Jesus Christ.

Silent Nightmare

"Silent Night, Holy Night" has long since been drowned out by the scuffle of feet and the elbowing of cracked ribs, as millions spend billions in a grim—and often losing—battle to give as much as they receive.

The din and fury of the modern Christmas doesn't subside in a hurry. In the week that follows Christmas there is always the rush to exchange the handsome statue of Venus for something useful, like a blurry print of *The Laughing Cavalier.*

The last known citizen to feel wholly rewarded by the gift of gratitude, instead of merchandise, seems to have been Scrooge. That miserable old crock underwent not only an emotional U-turn but got a great spiritual lift out of doing something nice for a change, and doing it at a time of year when he—a hard man— was least likely to experience a change of heart.

We had a guy around New York a couple of Christmases ago who emptied his cash-register of bills and loose change and just gave the stuff away to the poor bums along the Bowery. The cops wanted to arrest him for acting as people once acted at Christmas time.

"What are you getting out of this?" asked one stern custodian of law and modern mores.

"I don't want *anything* from these poor guys," the man protested.

The flabbergasted police wanted to put him away in a local snake pit. Matter of fact, not long after the incident he was ticketed by the police for having on his premises two chance-books put out by a deserving charity.

And the reason they nabbed him with the chance-books is that he naturally had been under suspicion ever since he exhibited the rudimentary generosity that was the origin of Christmas giving. What made him a sinister figure, in this day and age, is that he asked for nothing in return.

O, Tannenbaum!

Christmases seemed so much simpler twenty or thirty years ago. And more real.

Even the trees were real. Nowadays I'll bet that a vast majority of all the trees placed in U.S. homes are either made of nylon or have been dipped and sprayed with enough white stuff to repaint Brooklyn bridge.

Come December 28 or 29, they are ripped up, folded or put to the torch in the ignominy of the gutter.

I remember when one of our kids reached a sobering milestone.

86

He had reached the advanced age of thirteen, going on fourteen, the period in a child's life when he misses the happy expectation of toys and bikes and punching bags and faces the prospect of getting something as unromantic as shoes, socks, and shirts.

In my own youth the transition was especially abrupt, and I always felt it marked the dividing line between the wonderful world of childhood and the drab responsibilities of adult life. On the last memorable "toy" Christmas of my life I received a new sled—a Junior Racer, it was called—and a pair of skates.

But by the following Christmas I had moved, like a small planetoid, into another orbit. I got an umbrella and a pair of rubber overshoes. It was a pretty bleak Christmas morning. I wondered whether it was worth growing older. And sometimes I still do.

If I were king (and I may be one of these days, for I am in the direct line of descent from King Gillette) and I had the power to give gifts of any magnitude, these would be my choices for Christmas:

To the world I would give peace.

And health.

And the gift of understanding the purpose of Christmas, and the chance it offers people for a re-birth of the spirit, the character, the courage, the faith, the dignity.

And, to signify this re-birth of the spirit, I'd order a silence of at least one minute—each Christmas Eve—when not one cash register in the world would clang, when not one bottle would crash, when not one human would cry out in anguish, "Look at the cheesy tin earrings the bum give me, and I give him a smoking jacket!"

From Our House to Your House

Christmas card manufacturers, those wholesale purveyors of a sentiment which neither they nor the rest of us seem to understand, are studiously eliminating the Christ from Christmas.

We received some pretty cards one recent Christmas and appreciated same very much. Had a card with a tenderly tinted view of a battleship belching a broadside, a lot of wistful dogs, horses, cats; views of the Manhattan skyline from Brooklyn, a bewildering variety of front doors, a pretty painting of a

Swedish bridge, a superbly embossed card giving the first breath-taking sentence of the Constitution, and even one with a shot of the Kremlin. As I said at the start, the remembrance was warming.

About one out of twenty has anything to do with the birth of Christ. Perhaps the card companies, or the people who this season are exchanging the dizzy number of one and a half billion cards, have decided that since everything else in life seems to be moving along, they might as well view Christmas with a progressive eye and eliminate its traditional aspects.

Whatever the reason, there aren't many mangers floating through the mails these days, nor Infants, nor Marys, nor Josephs, nor Magi, nor oxen, nor Bethlehem stars, nor shepherds, nor heavenly hosts.

For me there's something less than goose pimples in the picture of a chubby kitten who, while playing with a ball of yarn, has spelled out: "To my cheery chummy pal, mighty square and true. Kind we don't so often meet, but lucky when we do! Merry Xmas!!!" Worries me. How did she cross that "X" so well, at her age? Things like that. Anyway, I can't squeeze from it the old feeling I had as a child, when after midnight Mass the bundled parishioners would troop down into what we called the "lower church," darkened and spooky, and marvel at the unveiling of the creche.

The average family sends seventy-five Christmas cards; eleven percent of the cards you'll receive come from persons you omitted from your list; sixteen percent of the cards arrive after Christmas; more than three percent wind up in the dead-letter office. The last item is interesting. And appropriate, when one considers the new trend in Christmas cards. Their designers appear to have given up the symbol of life.

MY CHRISTMAS STORY [20]

I'll never forget how these people remembered
By Leon Williams

I was for a while one of the lads in the Franklin County Children's home in Columbus, Ohio. At Christmas, it was the custom of the home to put all the boys' names on slips of paper, and place them in a bowl. They were then drawn by kindly people who had each volunteered to take a child into his home as a guest for Christmas Day. We children were not allowed to be present at the drawing. The event took place long after our bedtime.

This Christmas in 1930 was my first Christmas away from my mother. She was ill and unable to care for me, and I was a thoroughly lonely little boy. I looked forward to an empty Christmas, and on Christmas Eve I cried myself to sleep.

Next morning, after breakfast, I stood at a window overlooking the main driveway to watch the children and their hosts for the day enter automobiles and drive away. Suddenly my name was called. I turned to find the matron waiting for me. She told me to go to the superintendent's office.

The superintendent introduced me to a charming middle-aged Irish couple. They were, I learned, to be my hosts for the day. I was awed, and a little afraid. Could this be true? I was colored, my parents were from the South; I was born in Kentucky, and my mother had taught me a great deal of respect for the "white folks," as well as a certain amount of fear. Could these two people possibly want me to go home with them? Hurrying to my locker, I got my best coat and cap, and scurried back to the office. A few of my playmates still waiting for their hosts to show up made dire predictions concerning my probable fate.

I was trembling with fear and happiness as my hosts led me to a modest sedan. Wonder of wonders, I was permitted to sit in the front seat between my hosts. They soon put me at ease by pointing out places of interest we passed.

As we pulled abreast of St. Anthony's church, we stopped. We went into the beautifully decorated main chapel. It was quiet and almost empty except for a few people scattered along the altar rail at prayer. We went to the shrine of the Holy Mother, and knelt down together. After a few minutes we arose, left the church, and continued on our way.

I don't suppose I shall ever forget the wonderful kindness and hospitality shown me by these people and the members of their family. I played games with the children, devoured a huge Christmas dinner, and had my picture taken. The climax came when, loaded with gifts and radiantly happy, I was told it was time to take me back to the home.

As children are so likely to do when occupied with pleasurable things, I had almost forgotten my mother. Now, after all my fun, I thought of her in her lonely bed at the county infirmary. I did not even know where or what it was, except that aged and sick poor people were sent there. Imagine my surprise when the car eased to a stop before a grim red-brick building with a widespread lawn.

Although it was quite late in the evening, a few tactful words from my host got us the permission to go in. We went up the stairs to the third floor, where we stopped before the door leading into a small six-bed ward. I shall never forget how tears of happiness sprang into my mother's eyes when I was ushered into the room. There in her arms I eagerly told her of the day's thrilling events. I presented her with a bouquet of flowers given to me by my thoughtful benefactors. After introducing my friends to her, we started back to the children's home.

It was a perfect ending for a truly wonderful day. Two kindly people had shared their Christmas with a little colored lad, and showed his mother that life is good and worth living.

WHEN CHRISTMAS CAME AGAIN [21]

It wasn't only for children
By Dina Donohue

Many people knew that Frank Hinnant had no use for
Christmas, but few understood why. As the head of his own
multi-million dollar contracting business, he discouraged yuletide
office parties. He gave no Christmas bonuses, though his
employees received generous fringe benefits.

His wife, Adele, loved Christmas and she longed to celebrate
it with all the fuss she could stir up. It was the one chronic
disagreement the Hinnants had every December. Adele wanted
decorations, a tree, gifts, parties for employees—and Frank said,
emphatically, "No." He would go along to other people's parties,
and Christmas services, and for Adele there would always be a
costly gift. But beyond that, "Nonsense," Frank would say,
"Christmas is for children!"

And that is precisely the reason Frank Hinnant had locked
Christmas out of his heart: children.

One brisk December morning Frank decided to walk to work.
He did this occasionally, varying his route each time. He was
a man with a giant curiosity, fascinated by people. This morning,
reaching midtown, he noticed a cluster of people standing in
front of Leeson's department store. They were looking at the
Christmas displays.

One window had a manger scene. Frank looked at the créche:
at Mary, Joseph, and the shepherd in colorful costumes; the
donkey, cow, and sheep. All were life-size. And there was the
Child.

Frank turned away.

He started to move on. As he did, a sign across the street
caught his fleeting attention.

HOLY INNOCENTS HOME in huge golden letters framed the
arched doorway of an old brownstone building surrounded by
a forbidding iron fence. Frank had only half noticed this
building before.

"Holy Innocents. Holy Innocents." Frank repeated the

name in his mind. He stood there staring at the orphanage across the street, seeing something else, a long-ago morning in Sunday school. There was Miss Raymond, a skinny woman with black hair pulled back into a knot, and Miss Raymond was telling the class about King Herod and all the male children under two, "and the wicked king had had these little children slaughtered because he feared the Baby Jesus."

"The Holy Innocents," Frank said to himself. "That's odd, you don't hear about them much. Christmas is just this sentimental mush, like Adele's joy-on-earth stuff. There's more to Christmas than syrup. There's misery, too."

Frank turned back to the windows of Leeson's. He looked at the smiles on the faces of Mary and Joseph. But what about the parents of the infants who had died? What about their faces?

And for the millionth time Frank remembered the desolation of the day that his son David had died. David had been eighteen months old. In the twenty-two years since then, Frank had not been able to bring himself to mention his name.

Frank walked on towards his office. At the corner he turned and looked back. "The Holy Innocents," he said, almost out loud.

Impulsively he struck out on a new course. An idea had come to him. Quickly he covered the four blocks to the public library. A librarian gave him assistance.

"Holy Innocents," she reported, book in hand, finger pointing, "Their feast day is celebrated on December 28 by the Anglican and Roman Catholic Churches, on December 29 by the Greek Orthodox Church. They are among the early martyrs."

The information she gave him mounted, some of it conflicting. Some sources stated that thousands of infants had been slaughtered by Herod, others reported only a few. Frank was most impressed by the historian who very carefully deduced that since only about 2,000 people were living then in Bethlehem, no more than 20 children had been killed.

"Imagine that," he shouted to Miss Summerwell, "only 20 children!"

Very politely Miss Summerwell asked this extraordinary man

to try to keep his voice a little lower.

When Frank left the public library he went back to Holy Innocents Home.

That evening, Frank and Adele dined alone. It was a leisurely dinner, yet Frank was ill at ease. He was searching for the right moment, the right phrases to use when he told Adele what, sooner or later, he had to tell her.

"I had an odd kind of day," he said finally. "I went to visit an orphanage."

Adele was surprised, but registered only the mildest curiosity.

"It's that bastille of an orphanage across from Leeson's," Frank ambled on. "Really a dungeon, dear, cramped and dismal."

Adele was fascinated. Frank was building up to something. Now he told about the walk downtown, about the creche at Leeson's. At last he told her about his visit to the orphanage itself. "It made me realize how little I really know about kids. What strange little ugly creatures they are! When I went in they stood around looking at me like I was a movie star, not one of them saying anything. Later one of them came up to me—I'll never forget it—this little boy came up and he stood there and he stroked the sleeve of my coat."

Adele was quiet, but her eyes urged him to continue. Frank was embarrassed now. "You know full well what I've always said about Christmas," he blustered. "Christmas is for children!"

"Yes, you've always said that."

"Well, it's about time people started doing something for them. Today I gave that place some money. They're going to build a wing with it."

Adele had loved him so long she thought she knew him completely, but she was unprepared for his next announcement, "They're going to name the wing for David."

It was the first time in twenty-two years that Adele had heard Frank mention their only son's name. It made her do something she never did when Frank was around. She wept.

Frank never told her how, as he held her in his arms, he saw again the vision he had that afternoon. He saw a room full of children. There were twenty of them playing in a bright new wing at Holy Innocents. But now, suddenly, instead of twenty, there were twenty-one.

GRANDFATHER'S CHRISTMAS STORY[22]

How the neighbors helped a family too proud to receive gifts
By Nova M. Lee

Grandfather was a good story teller and his grandchildren loved to listen. We liked the stories about sleigh rides over the icy snow. He made them so real that we could almost feel ourselves cozy and warm under the heavy robe as the horses' hoofs clopped against the snow.

One story none of us ever forgot was about a family in the valley who had experienced misfortune.

"There never was a better family than the Bates," Grandfather told us. But it had been one hardship after another for them. "They lost old Bessie," Grandfather remembered. "There never was a finer sleigh horse."

A little daughter "took the measles." It was a cold dark night with lots of snow and ice. The roads were not good. "Old Doc Clemens had many sick folk to take care of that night," Grandfather said. "And by the time he reached the Bates' farm, it was too late."

Spring brought a tornado that seemed to pick out the Bates' house. It demolished it completely (the family were saved because they had fled to the cellar) and even blew the chickens and turkeys away.

The people of the valley had gone in and rebuilt the house and given the Bates' enough furnishings so they could again start housekeeping. But the family refused any other help. They struggled through the summer and fall on their own. The older children dropped out of school.

It must have seemed a forlorn future as Christmas approached. Then three days before Christmas, things began to happen at their farm.

Tom, the oldest boy, came in from the woodshed with a large box. "I don't know where it came from, Ma. I found it on a stack of wood."

Mrs. Bates went through the contents for any clue that might tell them how it got there, but who can identify gingerbread, a glass of jelly, jars of fruit, and a gallon of molasses?

When Lucy, the eldest daughter, went to draw a bucket of water, she found another box at the well. Again a search was made. It held two long sacks of sausage, a bag of dried peaches, and a chunk of salt pork.

For the next two mornings, things such as this kept turning up around the barn, woodshed, and smokehouse, but it was not until Christmas morning they discovered the big find.

When Mr. Bates went out to feed the horses, there stood a sleigh, bright red and trimmed in green, under the shed. As he opened the barn door, a big tom turkey stared right back at him. And other members of the family were coming upon surprises of their own around the farmhouse.

Mrs. Bates found that the pantry shelves, which had been sparsely stocked, held rows and rows of home-canned fruits and vegetables. There was also a five-gallon stand of lard, a sack of cornmeal, two sacks of flour, and twenty-five pounds of sugar.

Too stunned to move, Mrs. Bates stood looking, until Lucy came dashing in calling, "Ma—."

It seemed when she had opened the front door to let the cat in, there was a box filled with packages, all wrapped neatly in red and green paper and tied with striped string. They were obviously toys so they were quickly put out of sight.

Carrie, the second daughter, opened a cupboard to get a skillet and called out that she, too, had found something. It was a bucket of cream, a basket of eggs, and a jar of honey.

Before poor Mrs. Bates could collect her wits, Tom came in with a ham he had found in the woodshed. He announced he was going back for a side of bacon.

When the family sat down to breakfast, Mr. Bates announced that he was going to pay a call on some of the neighbors.

"Something is going on," he said, "and I aim to find out what it is."

Since Grandfather was the closest neighbor, it was only natural he would go to his house first. "Now, William," he began, "I know the people mean well. But we don't aim to take charity."

"All right, Thomas," Grandfather said. "What are you going to do about it?"

"Take it back," Mr. Bates said.

"Well, if you have got to be so stubborn," Grandfather said, "go ahead and take it back. But you are going to look pretty silly toting everything all over the valley trying to find the right place for it."

Mr. Bates had not thought of this. "But—." He stopped.

Mr. Bates returned home and did not seem the least surprised when his children told him that a bag of turnips, a sack of potatoes, and two large pumpkins had turned up in the harness shed.

He took Tom and went into the woods to cut the Christmas tree. And what a tree! For in the box of gifts there had been strings of popcorn, cookies, candies, fruits, nuts, and a chain made from colored paper (contribution of the children of the valley).

After a dinner of roast turkey and all the fixings, Mr. Bates hitched old Nellie to the new sleigh and he and Mrs. Bates spent the afternoon driving over the valley to say, "Merry Christmas," and to thank their neighbors.

But the part of the story that amused the grandchildren was the part the Bates family never knew. Grandfather had organized the affair and all the people of the valley had agreed to go along with him. They brought their gifts to Grandfather's house. No doubt many people wondered how things got into the Bates' house without the Bates' knowing, but no one ever asked.

It seemed there was one man in the valley who in his younger days had gotten off on the wrong track, as Grandfather put it.

Fortunately, the Bates' were the only people in the valley who did not own a dog and, of course, in those days, no one ever locked up at night.

Many years later we learned it had been Grandfather who had helped the one-time thief to go straight and become a respectable citizen, so it was little wonder he was willing to help carry out Grandfather's scheme.

"And you know," Grandfather chuckled, "I believe that fellow actually got a big kick out of being able to slip in and out of a house again without being caught."

THE CHRISTMAS AFTER ALICE DIED [23]

Never had I felt more alone, or been more mistaken
By Harold Melowski

Until last year, the greatest sorrow of my life was that my
wife Alice and I could not have any children. To make up for
this in a small way, we always invited all the children on our
street to our house each Christmas morning for breakfast.

We would decorate the house with snowflakes and angels in
the windows, a nativity scene, and a Christmas tree in the living
room, and other ornaments that we hoped would appeal to the
children. When our young guests arrived—there were usually
ten or fifteen of them—we said grace and served them such
delicacies as orange juice garnished with a candy cane (which
could be used as a straw once it began to dissolve). After the
meal we gave each of the youngsters a wrapped toy or game.
We used to look forward to these breakfasts with the joyful
impatience of children.

But last year, about six weeks before Christmas, Alice died.
I could not concentrate at work. I could not force myself to
cook anything but the simplest dishes. Sometimes I would sit
for hours without moving, and then suddenly find myself crying
for no apparent reason.

I decided not to invite the children over for the traditional
Christmas breakfast. But I did not have to be alone for the
holidays. Kathy and Peter Zack, my next door neighbors, asked
me to join them and their three children for dinner on Christmas
Eve. As soon as I arrived and had my coat off, Kathy asked me,
"Do you have any milk at your house?"

"Yes," I replied. "If you need some, I'll get it right away."

"Oh, that's all right. Come in and sit down. The kids have
been waiting for you. Just give Peter your keys and he can get
it in a few minutes."

So I sat down, prepared for a nice chat with eight-year-old
Beth and six-year-old Jimmy. (Their little sister was upstairs
sleeping.) But my words wouldn't come. What if Beth and
Jimmy should ask me about my Christmas breakfast? How

could I explain to them? Would they think I was just selfish or self-pitying? I began to think they would. Worse, I began to think they would be right.

But neither of them mentioned the breakfast. At first I felt relieved, but then I started to wonder if they remembered it or cared about it. As they prattled on about their toys, their friends and Christmas, I thought they would be reminded of our breakfast tradition, and yet they said nothing. This was strange, I thought, but the more we talked, the more I became convinced that they remembered the breakfast but didn't want to embarrass Grandpa Melowski (as they called me) by bringing it up.

I didn't have long to ponder this. Dinner was soon ready and afterwards we all went to late Mass. After Mass, the Zacks let me out of their car in front of my house. I thanked them and wished them all Merry Christmas as I walked toward my front door. Only then did I notice that Peter had left a light on when he borrowed the milk—and that someone had decorated my windows with snowflakes and angels!

When I opened the door, I saw that the whole house had been transformed with a Christmas tree, a nativity scene, candles, and all the other decorations of the season. On the dining room table was Alice's green Christmas table cloth and her pine cone centerpiece. What a kind gesture! At that moment, I wished that I could still put on the breakfast, but I had made no preparations.

The next morning at about eight, a five-year-old with a package of sweet rolls rang my bell. Before I could ask him what was going on, he was joined by two of his friends, one with a pound of bacon, the other with a pitcher of orange juice. Within fifteen minutes, my house was alive with all the children on our street, and I had all the food I needed for the usual festive breakfast. I was tremendously pleased, although in the back of my mind I still feared that I would disappoint my guests. I knew my spur-of-the moment party was missing one important ingredient.

At about 9:30, though, I had another surprise. Kathy Zack came to my back door.

"How's the breakfast?" she asked.

"I'm having the time of my life," I answered.

"I brought something for you," she said, setting a shopping bag on the counter.

"More food?"

"No," she said. "Take a look."

Inside the bag were individually wrapped packages, each bearing the name of one of the children in the dining room and signed, "Merry Christmas from Grandpa Melowski."

My happiness was complete. It was more than just knowing that the children would receive their customary gifts and wouldn't be disappointed; it was the feeling that everyone cared.

I like to think it's significant that I received a gift of love on the same day that the world received a sign of God's love 2,000 years ago in Bethlehem. I never found out who to thank for my Christmas present. I said my "Thank you" in my prayers that night—and that spoke of my gratitude more than anything I could ever say to my neighbors.

NO ROOM AT THE MOTEL [24]

But people's hearts were open,
and provided all the warmth of a shelter indoors
By C. W. Chambers

As a TV technician who's low on seniority, I often work on holidays. The station's cafeteria is usually closed then, and the guy who supplies the canteen in the snack room is probably off. So for supper I can either haul in my own brown bag or go over to Howard Johnsons.

Eddie and I found a table there about 10 P.M. last Christmas Eve. We were making up our minds over the menu when we sensed something going on. Somebody from the motel part of the establishment came hurrying over to the restaurant manager, and they both went into the kitchen. There we could see them talking to the cook.

It was the expressions on their faces that did it. Half smiling, half unbelieving. Snatches of their conversation drifted out to us.

The motel manager was saying, "The place is full. We've no room for them."

The restaurant man said, "They're snowed in out there on the parking lot and they want to stay until it's over."

The cook: "In all that cold and snow? Have they got anything to eat?"

"No. They ran out of food yesterday."

"No money, either, I suppose?"

"Not a dime."

One of the waitresses said, "Fix up something, I'll take it out."

Another said, "Be sure it's good and hot."

The hostess put in: "OK, girls, let's take care of the customers, too." They fanned out to their stations, but kept whispering to each other in passing.

"What's happening?" I asked the waitress who finally appeared at our table.

"Oh, a girl is going to have a baby in an old bus out there on the lot," she answered.

"No rooms available?"

100

"No. People are even doubling up."

"Isn't it cold out there in that thing?"

"I guess so, but they won't leave it. They just want to stay on the lot. They say they don't want to be a bother and they'll manage. They've been driving all day and have no place to go."

"But," I said, "they'll need a doctor, won't they?"

"Hah!" she snorted. "Where are you going to get one at this time of year who'll make a house call on a parking lot?"

"Listen. Forget the order. C'mon Eddie."

He came along with me to the car, willing enough. We could see the beat-up VW bus out there, all painted with those wild patterns and psychedelic colors the kids like. It had been a camper once. The now raggedy curtains were still at the windows. I supposed a bed and some furnishings were inside. There was a luggage rack filled with colorful, lumpy parcels. A few people were standing around blowing on their fingers and trying to get a look inside.

Eddie said, "Listen, Chuck. Maybe we can get the company doctor, or maybe somebody in the news room has a connection."

"Good idea. Also we can scare up a few blankets in the guest house."

"And grab some brandy from the old man's stock, huh?"

"Now *that's* a practical idea!" We grinned impishly at each other.

It was a short drive. We wheeled up to the station's door like we were on fire and narrowly missed skidding into the pillars of the long promenade. We fell out the doors at once, leaving the motor running. Eddie headed down the promenade to the guest house for blankets. I went into the station itself to see if the man in the news room could rustle up a doctor. While he started phoning, I cracked open the old man's booze-bin for a bottle of something to warm the gizzard. I took a first-aid cabinet from one of the studios, too, just in case.

Eddie met me back at the car and we loaded the things in. We left the night man still trying for a doctor, but one idle reporter and a cameraman came along for the possible story.

The crowd had grown by the time we reached the parking lot again. A car with a medic's tag closely followed us in. The newsman had succeeded. We were all approaching the van together when we heard the baby already crying.

A cheer went up from the people outside the vehicle. Then the double doors in its side were thrown open by a young man in faded blue jeans and blue denim jacket. He had long, faintly wavy hair and an uncut beard. But the faint illumination of the bus's dome light we could see an excited, long-haired girl in a nest of tattered quilts. She was holding her red-faced infant with undisguised care and love.

I handed the brandy to the couple, Eddie passed in the extra blankets, and the reporter dug down into his pockets and came up with a ten dollar bill. Some other people put up money, too, and waitresses with jackets or coats flung over shoulders came out of the restaurant carrying food and hot things to drink. Many of the onlookers had left their meals cooling at the tables to come out and see what was going on.

The doctor had managed to get to the van, so the doors were briefly closed. A maintenance man had found an electric heater and was running an extension cord to the nearest outlet.

We backed off a bit to survey the scene before we left to go supperless back to work.

"I'm still hungry," I grouched to Eddie.

"We can get something to take back. I guess the guys will understand when we tell them."

Doc, the two newsmen, Eddie, and I were waiting inside the restaurant for fish and chips to go, listening to the hum of conversation as the remaining diners discussed the event outside.

"Will they be all right, Doc?" I asked him.

"Oh, sure. She's a healthy girl. The baby's fine, too. Ought to be in a hospital, formally speaking, but they won't go. They feel it's the most natural thing in the world, and I tend to go along with that. I'll make my services their Christmas gift."

Eddie was all wrapped up in his thoughts and hadn't spoken for some time, so I nudged him with my elbow. "What new wisdom are you mulling over in your tiny mind, Old One?"

"Oh, something I found out listening to the people talk. The kids' names are Mary and Joe."

It's a small world, I guess, and sometimes the centuries can go like minutes.

Chapter III
Joyful Complaints

*Most people are much too enthusiastic to
celebrate Christmas as perhaps it would be best
celebrated—in thoughtful lonely meditation.
As a result our culture has built up an enormous
amount of fuss over the season, shopping, gift
giving, eating, tree decorating and visiting.
Certainly and surely these activities bring on
annoyances and anxieties but nearly all
persons who write about such aspects see the
humorous angles and, in view of the happy
time, are not at all as bitter as they pretend
to be.*

THE TWELVE DAYS OF CHRISTMAS[25]

A carol is updated
By Ralph Reppert

On the first day of Christmas, my true love said to me, "Hey!
The needles are dropping off the pine tree."

On the second day of Christmas she spoke again to me, "You
really ought to be more careful around the big candles. Every
time you bump them they drop melted wax on the rug." So I
get a brush and the can of carbon tet, clean up the rug, and sweep
up the needles 'neath the pine tree.

On the third day of Christmas, she still won't leave me be.
"For three days now we've been up to our hips in this litter.
Get it out of here." So I gather up wastepaper, empty boxes,
scraps of ribbon, haul them out to burn, then do my bit again
with candles adripping and needles adropping 'neath the pine tree.

On the fourth day of Christmas, I have to referee. With too
little sleep, too many sweets, too much excitement, the kids turn
bratty. I break up a fight, lay down the law, then take care of
the Christmas trash apiling, candles adripping, and more needles
'neath the pine tree.

On the fifth day of Christmas, the mailman brings to me a-l-l
s-o-r-t-s o-f t-h-i-n-g-s. Messages from department stores. Now
they don't begin with "Dear Preferred Customer," as they did a
few weeks back. Now they get down to the nitty-gritty right
away with just plain "Sir." Also a note from the bank about our
being overdrawn.

So I hustle downtown, cash a bond, make an emergency
deposit, and deal as best I can with department stores adunning
and bad checks abouncing. There's barely enough energy left to
lead with the two kids afussing, trash can abrimming, candles
adripping, and the needles 'neath the pine tree.

On the sixth day of Christmas, we get the fa-mi-ly—sisters,
cousins, uncles, nieces, the works. Also several neighbors. I hop
into an apron, turn bartender, and somehow manage with the
in-laws ayakking, neighbors asipping, stores all adunning, bathtub
over-running, the kids all afighting, ashtrays aspilling, candles

adripping, Uncle Phil anipping, the toy train achugging, my true love still abugging me about all those needles 'neath the pine tree.

On the seventh day of Christmas, it catches up with me—head aspinning, radio adinning, neighbors still asipping (three quarts are missing), credit people acalling, needles still afalling.

By the eighth day of Christmas, we are running short on glee. The kids' brattiness has begun to rub off on the adults. I don't think I can stand to listen through "The Little Drummer Boy" one more time, and I say so. Having eaten leftover turkey, turkey hash and turkey salad, I would sell my car for a big, fat hamburger.

Fat chance! On the ninth day of Christmas, my true love says to me: "You look like you've put on ten pounds. Cottage cheese and grapefruit for you, Buster."

On the tenth day of Christmas, traffic is acreeping, office work aheaping, stomach arumbling, bosses all agrumbling.

The eleventh day of Christmas is rough as it can be. Calories acounting, mistletoe amissing (nobody kissing), in-laws afighting, fretful kids abratting, the drummer boy adrumming, the vacuum cleaner humming, fruit cake acrumbing, more company acoming, my wife and me astalling, and needles still apiling up 'neath the pine tree.

On the twelfth day of Christmas, our tree's a sight to see. It hasn't got a needle left, its branches droop, and the poor thing is so worn out that it has to lean against the wall to twinkle.

My true love and I know precisely how it feels.

CHRISTMAS GROWS ON MANY TREES [26]
Memorable mistakes can be better than the right answers
By Harold Dunn

During the fourteen years that I have taught elementary school youngsters, I have been saving the "wrong" statements found in Christmas essays that are twice as delightful as the right ones.

Every Christmas season I read urgent news about Round John Virgin and partridgenipur trees. One little fellow spoke out on the subject of mistletoe, "Mistletoe means watch out for slobry girls." It must have been one of his best friends who declared, "The most dangerous thing about Christmas is standing under the kisseltoe."

In this world of uncertainty, when a child learns a fact for certain he hangs on to it. Here is what I mean: "Another name for Christmas is Xmas but I think I will just stick with the first name and learn it good."

Everyone has heard the story of Dickens' *A Christmas Carol,* but here are some "facts" about that masterpiece that I never suspected: "There is no such thing as a humbug but it is old and grouchy when there is." "Everybody was taught how to act Christmasey by Tidy Tim." "Tim taught them about the spirit that was started when the little Baby Jesus was born in Creche, a suburb of Bethlehem."

There are times when the truth sounds unbelievable to a child. When a lad reads something he does not believe, he has to be especially adamant when he writes about it in a report to his teacher: "At one time there was not even any Christmas at all. No there wasn't! I can show where it says!"

Then I do not suppose I will ever forget this remark by a brown-eyed lass: "When I learned we were going to see a movie about Christmas customs in England, I told my feet to quiet down but they felt too Saturday to listen."

Four very young poets had these charming observations about Christmas trees: "A star is for living in heaven when it is not for wearing in a Christmas tree's hair." "Needles are found in both pin cushions and Christmas trees." "Pine trees give us Christmas and turpentine." "Pine trees are not the only Christmas trees." "Christmas grows on many kinds of trees."

Here is a remark as captivating as childhood itself: "I was thinking all pine trees were small enough to take into the house and put Christmas decorations on. When I learned different, all the thoughts I was going to say went in a swallow down my throat."

You are probably familiar with the way very young children can inadvertently twist the words of songs into entirely different sentiments. Christmas carols are no exception.

Being responsible for the preparation of a Christmas program, I tried to teach "Silent Night" to a group of first graders. The first time through, it sounded as though the entire class had changed "Round yon Virgin Mother and Child" to "Onion version, Mother and Child."

They concluded their "onion version" of "Silent Night" with these lyrics: "Sleep in half and in peace . . . Sleep in half and in peace."

A demure little moppet told me her favorite carol was "Old Cumalye, Faithful." Who was Old Cumalye? Jesus' dog, of course.

An obviously more knowledgeable second-grade tyke sang these lyrics to me: "We three kings safari ain't are, bearing gifts we trap us a fire." When I mentioned that those words didn't make much sense, he said: "I know, But it rhymes, and things that rhyme don't have to make sense."

Here are some other lyrical lapses that I would not have noticed if I had not tape-recorded them: "Peace on earth, good wilted men." "Dark the hair, old angels sing, Glo, return the newborn King."

Santa has certainly come in for his share of comments through the years. Here are four of my favorites: "Santa Claus was born in the family branch of the Christmas tree." "Santa lives just north of the imagination." "He always has fatness and not just skinny bones." "Clauses are found in both sentences and Santas."

Samuel Butler, the seventeenth century author, once remarked that "Great resolutions do not always lead to great actions." Still, to many grade school youngsters, New Year's Day would be

110

quite hollow without some resolutions. One boy wrote: "I only made one New Year's resolution. I resolved to always finish everything I start because"

(By way of explanation, he told me the bell rang at that awkward moment.)

Sometimes a child is caught in the cross fire between the high ideals of yearly resolutions and the realities of everyday behavior. One young seeker of truth proclaimed: "It is more important to be honest than rich and famous and happy." Then the idea began melting away on him like a popsicle, as he added: "Or at least any one of these. By itself. In most cases."

The problem of which comes first, Christmas or New Year's Day, seems to be more perplexing to some children than the chicken-or-egg puzzle. Here is a logical explanation: "New Year's Day comes first in the life of a calendar, but Christmas comes first in the life of a person."

Additional thoughts on the subject: "Christmas comes some time before New Year's Day. Maybe it comes one week before. Maybe it comes two weeks before. I do not know. It takes all my knowing to know Christmas comes some time before New Year's Day."

"Christmas just barely sneaks in the nick of time before every new year. We try to hurry it up along about Halloween."

"I observed New Year's Day last year. What I observed was that New Year's Day comes quite late in the night."

Another little moppet wrote: "Now that I know that Christmas and New Year's Day are just seven days apart, the next time I notice them coming on the same day of the week I will just twinkle an eye and know why."

Perhaps that is an important part of education, anyway—to be able to "twinkle an eye" occasionally.

THE CHRISTMAS WE HUNTED HENRY JAMES [27]

**An old man needed the ultimate in last-minute shopping as proof
that somebody cared**
By Richard W. O'Donnell

Charles Flinn was probably the crankiest old soul ever to enter
the Catholic rest home in South Boston. He arrived there one
year in the early fifties, a week before Christmas. The Sisters of
Charity who ran the place were dismayed by his grumpiness.
During his first week at the home, Charles hardly spoke, and
when he did open his mouth, his explosive language made the
nuns blush.

Nevertheless, Sister Matilda, who supervised the home, was
determined to win Charles's friendship. She believed that
despite his gruffness, there might still be some human warmth
inside the man.

On Christmas morning, after Mass and breakfast, all the
residents at the home would customarily assemble in front of
the giant tree in the main hall. Carols would be sung. The many
gifts that had arrived during the week would be distributed.
It was a happy time that Sister Matilda relished.

This year one thing troubled her. There would be no Christmas
gifts for Old Charles. He had no family left to send him presents.
He certainly had not acquired any friends at the rest home.

Sister decided to buy Charles Flinn a Christmas gift. If he
received a present, she reasoned, the holiday mood might over-
whelm him. He might even start smiling.

A few days before the great holiday, the silver-haired nun,
herself almost as old as Charles, asked the sullen senior citizen
if he desired any special Christmas gift. The stony one just
grunted.

She tried again after breakfast on Christmas Eve. Charles
growled this time. But as the day progressed, he mellowed.
That evening, some carolers visited the rest home, and their
beautiful Christmas songs finally melted the ice that had coated
Charles's heart. After the concert, he approached Sister Matilda.

"Know what I'd like for Christmas?" he asked.

112

"What, Charles?" responded the surprised nun.

"I'd love to sit down in a comfortable chair and read a book by Henry James," Charles revealed. "He's my favorite author, you know. Haven't read anything by him in years."

Then Charles stomped off. He had issued his challenge. It was up to Sister Matilda to prove her sincerity.

Locating a book by Henry James proved to be a problem. The nun checked the small library on the first floor. There was no Henry James available there. She then dispatched the night custodian to a local drug store to find a paperback. But the drug store was closed for the night, as were all the pharmacies in the area. The weary janitor returned empty-handed an hour later.

"Everybody's gone home to their families," he told Sister Matilda.

There were seven Catholic churches close by. The nun phoned all of them, hoping to locate a pastor or curate who had a Henry James handy. All the priests in South Boston were reading other authors that year.

For a few frantic moments, Sister contemplated phoning the other denominations in the district to check their libraries. But it was close to midnight, and she abandoned the idea.

Nevertheless, Sister Matilda was determined to find a Henry James, even if she had to stay up all night. She also planned to do quite a bit of praying during the small hours of the morning.

"We've got to come up with that book," she confided to Sister Mary Margaret, her second-in-command. "If we don't, we may lose Charles Flinn forever."

It is here that John Landers and I enter the story. I was a young reporter for the Boston *Globe*. Landers was my photographer. We worked what newspapermen called the "lobster shift," roaming the city from midnight to eight in a *Globe* radio car, checking out police calls.

Landers loved his family, and hated to be away from them on Christmas Eve. I was a bachelor, and also knew a few places I would rather spend Christmas Eve than a *Globe* radio car. To add to our gloom, snow started falling as we rolled on to the main drag; the driving would be hazardous. It did not look like a very merry Christmas.

We were in Park Square in downtown Boston, just leaving the car to get some coffee, when Phil Deniver, the night city editor, came on our two-way radio.

Deniver was a city editor of the old school. When he snapped his fingers, his staff leaped to attention, and obeyed all commands immediately. When he called us, Landers and I forgot about our coffee. We were poised for action!

"Get me a book by Henry James," ordered Deniver.

"What was that again?" Landers called into the car microphone.

"I said I want a book by Henry James," barked the city editor. "And I want it in a hurry." Then Deniver told us all about Flinn, Sister Matilda, and the book. Sister had called the *Globe* city desk and asked for help.

"It's Christmas Eve, boys," Deniver added. "When you're not busy chasing two-alarm fires and automobile crashes, I want you to show a little bit of the Christmas spirit. I want you to get that book and rush it over to the rest home."

First Landers and I looked for a drug store, smoke shop, or delicatessen. An all-night drug store near the Massachusetts General Hospital was open, but they didn't have the book. Everything else was locked up tight.

We tried the newspaper stands at the railroad stations and bus terminals, but they were featuring Mickey Spillane that year. We even made a trip out to the Logan Airport newsstand, but once again it was Spillane and no James.

Next, we checked all the "after hours" joints in town. We did not expect to find a Henry James in one of them, but we hoped one of the bartenders or customers might be able to give us a lead. For a change, though, they were obeying the law. They had all closed.

"Let's try the press room at police headquarters," I suggested. Some reporters had actually been known to read a book once in a while.

Jack Ferris of the old *Herald-Traveler* was the lone man in the press room that Christmas Eve. Ferris was a Mickey Spillane reader.

"How do I know where you can get a book by Henry James at this hour?" he said, slightly annoyed. "I haven't read one of his books in years."

Then, as an afterthought, he added: "Why don't you try Station Four? There's always something doing in the South End. Maybe somebody down there can tell you where to get your book."

So we motored down to the South End station, only a couple blocks away.

"You guys are crazy," the desk sergeant informed us. "Nobody in this part of town reads Henry James. You ought to try Station 16. The heavy readers all live in the Back Bay."

Needless to say, we tried 16. Needless to say, the desk sergeant sent us scurrying to another station house. In all, we tried six police stations that night, without success.

Fortunately, there were no serious fires, crashes, or crimes that Christmas Eve. Landers and I had plenty of time to search for the book. We tried Boston Fire headquarters, City Hospital, State Police headquarters, several old friends, and a fraternity house at Harvard University.

We struck out every time. Harvard was a stab in the dark. The college lads usually had plenty of books on hand, but all of them had apparently headed home for the holidays.

At dawn, Landers finally admitted defeat. "It looks like we're going to need a miracle," he conceded.

At that moment, there was a call on the police radio. A burglar alarm had gone off at a store in the Back Bay. Burglar alarms are always going off in the middle of the night in big cities. Mostly, they are triggered by heavy winds, electrical freaks, or mice nibbling on wires. They seldom go off when there are burglars around.

Landers, who was driving, took off as soon as the call came over the radio.

"Why are you chasing that one," I asked.

"It's a book store," he said.

"But there will only be a couple of cops there when we arrive," I pointed out.

John asked, "Why will the cops be there?"

I thought that one over. "They'll be waiting for the owner to arrive and unlock the front door of the store. Then the two officers will accompany the owner inside, check the place and shut off the alarm. It's strictly routine."

"Absolutely correct," declared John, beaming. "And when that owner arrives to open his store, we're going to talk him into selling us a book by Henry James."

At first the owner did not want to sell us the book. Two police officers were close by. It was illegal for him to sell anything on Christmas Day. But after hearing the story of Flinn, Sister Matilda, and the Christmas gift, he finally and quietly surrendered.

While the officers were at the rear of the store checking windows, he sold us a book of short stories by James. His price was two dollars more than the figure printed on the book, but Jack and I were not about to argue. The collection included such favorites as "Four Meetings," "The Turn of the Screw," and "Paste." Even at two dollars above market price, it was great reading.

Landers and I were not present when all the senior citizens gathered around the Christmas tree in the main hall of the rest home. Still, I have often wondered how Charles Flinn reacted that morning when he received his Christmas gift.

I would like to think that he smiled, and called out, "Merry Christmas, everyone! And the merriest Christmas of all to you, Sister Matilda."

CHRISTMAS KIDNAPING [28]

**The generosity of the people of Jacksonville was overwhelming,
but that made it tough for the Navy chaplain
By Maurice S. Sheehy (U.S.N.R.)**

Sometimes I wish Congress would set up a Committee to
Find Out What's Right About Us Americans. That's one
committee before which I would like to testify. Since there
isn't any such committee I should address myself, perhaps, to
the Special Senate Committee on Investigating Organized Crime.

I should like to inform it about one of the greatest mass
kidnapings in history. It happened at Christmas time during
the war while I was serving as chaplain at the Naval Air station
at Jacksonville, Fla.

I had been asked to look after a little matter of 1,100
invitations which came from the people of that hospitable Florida
community who wished sailors to go with their turkey dinner.
The first 500 invitations went like ice-cream sundaes in the
Indian Ocean. After that, I had to check cadets and sailors to
be sure that no one was overlooked on Christmas Day. For
their first time, most of the men would not enjoy Christmas
in their own homes.

At midnight Mass, sung by eight fliers (four weren't around
for the next Christmas), I managed to dispose of my few
remaining invitations. I told the boys they might replace some
missing son by accepting one.

All seemed to be going well. About noon, I settled down to
a little rest. I did not suspect that the army, by calling an alert
at Camp Blanding, would destroy whatever naval peace I prayed
for on Christmas Day.

The radio carried the news that none of the 60,000 soldiers
at Blanding would be free to come to Jacksonville.

That is when the kidnaping started. An innocent little
sailor would stroll through the front gate of our station.
Instantly, he was waylaid, set upon, abducted, and thrown
into the nearest car. At one time more than fifty kidnapers
were lined up in front of the station. The names and addresses

which I had laboriously prepared were completely ignored.

About one P.M. my telephone began ringing. "Where are my sailor guests?" "Our turkey is done!" "We've still got six extra places." These were the wails which reached my ear.

To say I was mystified is to understate. Green though I was in the ways of navy men, I know they didn't ordinarily act like that. Yet, as far as I could discover, about 1,100 had vanished into thin air. Sailors don't run away when there is turkey in the offing.

One of the cadets called me early in the afternoon. "I got here, Father," he said, "But what a struggle! You can't get through the people trying to grab you off."

Typical of the experiences of others was that of a seaman in our service school. "As soon as I got to the front gate, a guy in a Cadillac grabbed me. He asked me if I had relatives in Jacksonville. I told him, 'No.' 'Okay, kid,' he says, 'you're eating at my house.' Boy, what a dinner! Then I thought you'd be sore because I didn't go where you sent me, so I went over there. They were still waiting for me. I ate all I could and ducked out to a movie. About eight P.M. I came out, and I heard a woman say to a man, 'There's one.' Before I knew it, I was on my way to another Christmas dinner. Really, Father, I'm afraid I can't take much more of life in Jacksonville. I've only one stomach to give to my country."

One of the cadets got through the lines by pretending he had a wife to see (which shouldn't have fooled anyone, because cadets weren't allowed to marry). His name was Smith, and I had given him an invitation to a family by the same name. There he met a charming young Miss Smith. She liked his name and he liked hers. Shortly afterward, he told her he thought it would be a shame if she should ever change her name, and she thought so, too. The last time I saw them there were four new little Smiths in Jacksonville.

Then about six o'clock, after a worrisome and futile Christmas Day, I just remembered that Percy Zacharias was expecting me to send some guests for his Christmas dinner. Percy was a brother of a most distinguished naval officer, an admiral—but admirals don't bother me much. I was concerned because when I went to Percy for 1,600 toys for children from ages two to twelve, he got them for me. They were all wrapped up and ready for delivery at our Christmas party. This was the man I was letting down, a Jewish merchant who had helped to bring Christmas to the navy children.

One last chance, I dashed to the hospital. There I found a couple of convalescing aviators who would accompany me if I would go with them to the Zacharias home. I did. I had to escape from my telephone for an hour, anyhow.

I was driving back to the station when I saw some sailors in trouble. Three Negro boys! They were loaded down with packages.

"What happened to you?" I asked them.

"Chaplain," said one, "we were just born lucky, I guess. These are our presents." Then he grinned, "Believe me, if anyone asks where Santa Claus lives, I'll tell 'em, 'Jacksonville, Fla.'"

Not to prolong this story, my charge is that the people of Jacksonville kidnaped, some with threats of duress and others with turkey, a whole mob of sailors, in bright daylight. Something should be done about it, especially since it ruined one day of my life. We, the people, expect the Committee on Investigating Organized Crime to keep this country of ours law-abiding.

P.S. On further thought, so many of these sailors married Jacksonville girls that it may be hard to distinguish at this late date between abductor and abductee, so maybe the committee ought to lay off the whole business.

CHRISTMAS CARDS ARE CLUES TO CHARACTER [29]

Think twice before you choose a Scotty dog or a "sick" cartoon to convey your greeting
By Diana Serra Cary

One brisk fall day it suddenly dawns on us that we have only a few weeks left in which to choose, buy, address, stamp, and mail anywhere from 50 to 500 Christmas cards.

Cards are among the earliest harbingers of the holidays. They are also the last glittering remnants of it to be swept or filed away. To most of us comes that January morning in the silent living room, when the tree has just been hauled out and our carpet is crunchy with mica and parched pine needles. Seated purposefully at a desk heaped with cards cleared from the mantle or the pegboard, we finally look thoughtfully at pictures we only half noticed before: a colorful gallery of subjects, from ice-skating penguins to Da Vinci's *Nativity*.

Have you ever wondered as I have sometimes done, if the Christmas cards you sent to your friends revealed your temperament as closely as those they sent revealed theirs?

Is it just coincidence that my gourmet friend, an expert cook, invariably sends a card featuring steaming plum puddings or mince pies? It seems more than accidental that another friend, who was orphaned as a child and enduring a youth of grinding poverty, now always selects a card with a cozy fireside scene.

Look at the formal charcoal silhouette of a coach-and-four on heavy gold foil; it came in the gold-lined envelope. The couple who sent it used to live next door, but every year since, they have gone steadily up in the world. Their cards have mirrored their climb. This year they moved into a home in an exclusive suburb. Their card is an elegant understatement of their new status. The names are engraved.

It might be an appropriate card to send to a special customer or to a fellow executive—but to an old friend? Years ago a note was always scrawled inside, but one doesn't write on gold foil. That card is an austere reminder of the ever-widening gulf between us. It gives me a feeling that next year, or the year after, we are to be dropped from their list.

Of course, there are plenty of rather dreadful examples of artistic overstatement in my stack, too: the garish, gaudy Santa Clauses and the religious prints which almost cancel out with their ugliness the sincerity of the message. And there is usually a handful of sad, tasteless "joke" cards.

Apparently a card design can be found for just about every shade of nature lover. I always find the lone deer in the deep woods, the furry rabbit in the snow, the stately arch of trees that forms what we are told is "nature's own cathedral."

One friend waits every year until the gift shop she patronizes gets in the scheduled album of Scotty dogs. It wouldn't be Christmas for her without them. And don't we all know someone who connects Christmas with cats? Before the card is out of the envelope, when just the ears are visible, you know who it is from.

There is also a postgraduate nature-lover school of cards with a way-out-West theme. In these a cowboy drags a fir tree home behind his horse, decorates sagebrush with Christmas ornaments, or shares his saddle with a load of exquisitely gift-wrapped packages. (Who ever wrapped them for him, I'd like to know?) And have you ever received that Old Gray Mare of all Western cards, in which the cowboy holds a skillet over his campfire and the rising smoke spells out "Merry Christmas"?

Perhaps it is because we are still a very young nation that things have a way of becoming "traditional" with Americans in a short time. We have come to regard the custom of exchanging annual greetings (which is actually little more than a century old) as an ancient practice—almost as though the early Christians had mailed cards to each other, or had scrawled on catacomb walls a cherry "Merry Christmas to All!"

Therefore, it sometimes comes as a shock to Americans who go abroad or who have friends in foreign lands to find that Europeans have never observed the custom at all. Italians, Spaniards, and Latin Americans regard it as a Yankee custom. If they do send cards it is only as concession to our quaint folkways. (The French have the practice of sending a simple calling card, timed to reach their friends just before New Year's

Day. In longhand the sender laconically wishes the recipient *bonheur,* or good fortune in the new year.)

The custom of sending printed greetings at Christmas is as strictly Victorian English as Mr. Dickens, the bonneted heroines of the Brontë sisters' novels, and the romance between Robert Browning and the fragile Miss Barrett of Wimpole St. Victorians were forever dashing off notes in violet ink and sending a servant round with them to the neighbor's house (or the beloved's). It was all in the plush-and-damask tradition of paying calls on stated days, of saving every trivial note, and pressing each wood violet and rose between the leaves of the massive parlor edition of *Pilgrim's Progress.* (In well-to-do American homes it might be a volume of the *Memoirs of General Grant.)*

The hero (or the villain, if you prefer) who put the imposing machinery of Christmas cards into motion, was a sixteen-year-old printer's apprentice, William Maw Egley, Jr., who worked in a London shop. Just before Christmas in 1842, the youthful line engraver hit upon the idea of sending engraved cards to his friends.

He designed and printed a series of panels, depicting a children's party, a Punch and Judy show, a poor family receiving baskets of food, a yuletide banquet, skaters gliding around a glassy pond, and a band of muffled street musicians serenading in the snow.

As though it were not enough to have created practically every "traditional" card design in a single stroke, young Egley inscribed over the whole the legend which has since become the most hackneyed phrase in the long history of man's communication with man: "Merry Christmas and a Happy New Year to You!"

The novel idea caught on, and was developed in artistic forms that for a time were as unyielding as a pudding mold. By a happy accident, Dickens' *A Christmas Carol* appeared on London bookstands in 1843, just a year after Egley turned out his first cards. Now were crystallized forever in the public mind such yuletide archetypes of piety and parsimoniousness as Tiny Tim and Ebenezer Scrooge.

In Victorian society it would have been unthinkable to send

a comic Christmas card. Religion was acknowledged with an artistic nod toward a church with hoop-skirted and top-hatted worshipers streaming in. The charitable spirit of the season was captured in cards portraying young misses bearing gifts to the "deserving" poor. (Remember *Little Women?)*

America imbibed all the traditional English ideas, most of which were first set down by the remarkable Mr. Egley. We also evolved our own distinctly American symbols: the farmhouse, the skaters in Central Park, and Santa Claus. Although most of us are two or three generations removed from the land, Grandma Moses' bright glimpses of a bygone age still lead the field with many American card buyers.

Religious cards have enjoyed a great upsurge over the last few years. Among cards I receive, they now outnumber all the other kinds two to one. Classics among the religious cards are mainly reproductions of the Renaissance masters' portrayals of the Nativity, the journey of the Magi, the shepherds hurrying to the stable, or the angels filling the starry sky with Alleluias. Increasingly, fine original religious card designs are being turned out by modern artists.

Since Christmas is Christ's birthday, it should be more "traditional" to send a religious card than one of other types, especially since so many forces in the modern world tend to obliterate all Christian meaning from the holy season. Some of the cards I receive indicate that many of my acquaintances still think Christmas is a sort of winter carnival in which Santa is king.

During that January session at my desk, I always am tempted to save all the cards I received, the ugly as well as the beautiful. Think what a historical treasure they would be for someone a hundred years from now!

Chapter IV
In Brotherhood

A large part of man's history here on earth is the story of his wars. Saddest of all to say, religious conflict has been as bitter as any other. It was once recommended to the Jews and Arabs in the council of the United Nations, that they settle their differences in a Christian spirit. The speaker was not trying to make a joke, he spoke naively. Cynics laughed because they thought Christians as war-like as Jews and Moslems and more war-like than Buddhists or Hindus. But the speaker had forgotten that failing, he was thinking only that both sides should act with more charity, which is the deepest meaning of Christianity to those who truly believe and practice it. In most of the world now, former religious conflict has left a legacy of prejudice if not of hatred. About the only time this dark cloud lifts away seems to be during the Christmas season as the stories in this chapter testify.

MY CHRISTMAS TREE ANGEL [30]

**A family's bad luck on the Saviour's birthday melts all the
hardness of bitter hearts**

By Miriam Lynch

Everytime Christmas rolls around, I think back to a certain
Christmas when I was sixteen. That year was special for two
reasons. One was that Herbie Hillier had lately come into my
life. Our "romance" meant only walking home from school
together, dates at the movie house, a sly exchange of greetings
and scribbled notes, but it was mighty important to me. The
other reason was a particular Christmas tree angel I wished to
buy at the Methodist church bazaar.

I had seen the angel the year before, hung on the crossbar
of a booth. It was a lovely, storybook little figure in a pink
gauze gown, with a tiny halo above its pale gold hair, and a
cherubic smile on its face. I hadn't been able to buy it then.
Its price was two dollars, and the little store of pennies in my
pocket didn't come to nearly that much.

I watched all day, in an agony of dread, for someone else
to buy the angel. When the lights in the hall began to dim,
I went back to the booth for one last glimpse.

"What do you do with things that aren't sold?" I asked the
woman in charge.

"They're put away until the following year," she told me.
"So save your pennies, maybe you can buy it then."

I did exactly that. During twelve months of baby tending
and running errands, I hoarded my money like a miser.
I longed for the lovely little figure, imagining it on the top of
our Christmas tree in place of our tarnished old silver star.

The day of the next bazaar finally arrived. It was a Saturday,
but I was up at daylight to be at the church when the doors
opened.

I still remember the breath-taking cold of that morning.
My toes and fingers ached with it and my sharp panting made
little plumes in the air. There was a new fall of snow softening
the ugly outlines of the houses and hiding the scrawny bushes.

The world was white and shining and still, and my overshoes whispered as I walked.

My made-over coat was not warm enough, but the cold and my shabby clothing could not chill the excited happiness that was warm and sweet in my veins. There were two crumpled dollar bills in my pocket and I was going to buy my Christmas tree angel.

I reached the church, and went straight to the Christmas ornament booth. The angel was not in sight, but the woman I had spoken to the time before was there, busy arranging her display.

I couldn't wait for her to turn in my direction. "Where is it?" I demanded. "I've come for the angel."

She looked at me with an unseeing glance. I cried, "You told me I could have it if I came back this year."

She took a tack from her mouth and spoke unconcernedly. "You mean that pink angel we had last year? I remember now. It's been sold."

"Sold!" I swung around. There were only a few boys near the food booth and a few coatless women wandering from table to table. "Who?" I shouted. "Nobody's come in yet."

She explained patiently, "Before we officially open, we allow the workers to buy whatever they want. That's only fair, my dear. After all, we've been at this all year, making things, putting up the preserves—"

"Who?" I croaked, "who bought it?"

She gestured toward another table. "Mrs. Hillier. But I mean, after all—"

I darted across the hall, my breath choked in my throat. Herbie's mother stood behind an array of old gas lamps, chipped vases, old pieces of crockery. I had known her by sight for a long time, but I think I would have recognized her anyway. Her pale eyes and bony wrists were like Herbie's. She was not attractive. Her hair was drawn back so severely that her features appeared to be pulled into a taut mask.

"You took my angel!" My voice cracked. "I wanted it! I want it! I've waited all year to buy it. I'll pay you. Look—." I thrust out my hand with the wrinkled bills in it. "Oh, you've got to give it to me."

She seemed shocked at my rudeness. "Got to, young lady?"

"Please," I amended, "I came to get the angel."

"I'm sorry." Her hands became busy re-arranging the articles on her table. "I bought it, and I intend to keep it."

Several of the women had turned to stare. Now there was a little pool of silence around us with Herbie's mother and me in the center of it.

"It's mine!" I kept repeating. "She promised. A year ago she said I could have it!"

Herbie's mother kept shaking her head, staring at me with her pale expressionless eyes, her lips drawn into a disapproving knot.

I finally gave up. I turned and ran home, swallowing hard sobs all the way.

There seemed to be more people on the streets then. I heard sleighs creak past me, and the tinkling of their bells and the shouts of coasting children. But I paid no heed to them.

I burst into the kitchen. My mother was dyeing something in an old pot on the stove. The rank smell filled the house, and I choked on it.

"Mama!" I wailed, my sixteen years shrunken in my heart-break. "They wouldn't let me have my angel!"

Mama usually had all she could do in her endless household chores, but now she put down her stirring stick, ready to listen. I told her the whole story. The words were sometimes drowned in my blubbering and sniffling. But she understood, and when she spoke, her voice was loud and angry.

"I told you it wouldn't come to any good, you going where you don't belong. Not that it excuses them! Not a bit it doesn't! It's a wrong thing, to break a promise to a child."

She wiped my eyes and nose, her rough hands tender, as though I were a baby. She was still muttering over me when my father came in. He was wearing hip boots, as he always did during the day, for most of his small income came from odd jobs, cleaning drains and pumping cellars. He was a big man, and when mother told him what had happened, his bellow shook the house.

"A meaner trick I've never heard of!" He tore off his boots and heaved them across the room as though he was aiming at the women of the Methodist church. "So that's the way they treat a child, is it? Sure, if it's the angel you want, my girl, I'll see you get it." He started for the church, but my mother restrained him.

That evening he went out to play cards with his cronies, still boiling with rage. He told the other men the story, and there was heated discussion.

The story spread. It passed among churchgoers, over Sunday dinner tables, in the saloons, along factory row. Within three days, the whole town knew it, and people were taking sides.

The Mahoneys, close friends of my parents, refused to go into McDonald's pharmacy. Instead, they crossed the street to trade in the chain drugstore because Irving McDonald was a cousin by marriage of the Hilliers.

Mrs. Pearl Peterson, a sister of the woman who had promised me the angel, called Addie Cullinane, the dressmaker, and cancelled a dress she had ordered because Addie had been heard to say she believed the Mahoneys had done exactly right.

Addie then made her daughter Theresa take back the Christmas present she had bought for her chum, Doris Mellen, because the Mellens and the Petersons were members of the same whist club.

And so it went. The town split into two factions, those who believed I was the victim of a scurvy trick, and those who sided with the Methodist ladies. Old friends refused to speak when they met. New friendships and alliances were formed, solely on the great issue of a Christmas tree angel.

On the Sunday before Christmas, Father Gallagher of St. Peter's discarded his prepared sermon, and preached on the theme, "Love Thy Neighbor." His old voice rang with pleading and reproach, but many of our faces remained sullen.

The Reverend Mr. Belkins, the Methodist minister, preached practically the same message as Father Gallagher. But when he stood at the door to shake hands with his parishioners, faces turned away from him and his greetings were returned through thin, tightened mouths.

It rained that evening. A slashing New England northeaster

beat the snow into floods of swirling slush. "There'll be many a wet cellar," my father said with grim satisfaction. And he was right. Late that night and all through Monday morning, people who lived at the bottom of the hill came to ask him to pump their cellars.

But he always refused with great, chortling glee. "For they're all the other ones," he would say as he came stomping back into the kitchen. "They can all sail away in the water for all of me. I'll not raise a hand to help them."

Mother remonstrated with him. "We need the money, Dan," she pointed out. "And in some of those houses there are small children. They might catch colds, or something. Do you think it's right not to go?"

"I have a child of my own," he countered. "Did they think of right or wrong when they treated her that way? It was sickness they brought to the heart of her. Let them find someone else to clean their dirty cellars."

Herbie no longer waited for me after classes. No more notes passed from desk to desk across the room. I was lonely and uncomfortable. Open quarrels flared up. It was the unhappiest time our town had ever known.

On Wednesday evening, the tree-lighting ceremony was to be held on the Common. Electric Christmas lights were still new and exciting. Other occasions had been festive, with carol singing by the crowd, speeches by the selectmen, small gifts and string stockings filled with candy for the children.

This year it was different. The bad feeling was something you could almost see, hanging black and ugly above us in the cold winter night. People gathered in groups, their backs stiff and set. Men peered into the faces of those standing near them before speaking. Women turned away from next-door neighbors with no sign of recognition. Children huddled close to their parents, uneasy and frightened.

When the switch was pulled and the lights of the tree threw their colored brilliance across the crowd, there was no sharp intake of breath, no quick babble of admiration, as there had been in other years.

I saw Herbie a few feet away, shivering in his short mackinaw.

He and his sister stood on the fringe of a little knot of people. He kept his eyes away from mine, and pretended not to see me, although I knew he did.

On Christmas Eve, my brothers and sister and I were shocked to see mother finishing her last-minute cleaning with tears on her cheeks. Not illness nor any other crisis of family life had ever made her cry. Now, she would not tell us the cause of her sobbing, although we begged her to, almost in tears ourselves. Not until father came home did we know, and then only because we listened at the kitchen door.

It came out in a rush of shrill words, "So there I went, straight into the market and asked for a turkey like I always do. And Roy Mitchell—him that I've traded with for twenty years—looked me right in the eye and said, 'I haven't a bird in the store.' I could see there were a-plenty in the showcase right in front of me."

"I said, 'What about those?' But he wouldn't answer me. You see what it is, don't you, Dan? He's one of them others, the ones which side with the Hillier people. That's why he wouldn't sell me a turkey, and he wouldn't sell one to Bridie Mahoney nor the Cannons nor Francie McGinn, either."

Father let out a roar. "Then he may keep his scrawny birds if he's a mind to!"

"But there's no other butcher shop in town," mother sniffled. "We'll have no Christmas dinner. Oh, Dan, what will we do?"

We huddled closer to the door and to each other, scarcely breathing. Never on Christmas, in good times or bad, had our table been without a turkey.

"I'll go into Westville or Boston even," father vowed. "We'll show that spalpeen, Roy Mitchell, that we don't need his old poultry."

"Too late," she moaned. "By now, there will be nothing decent left."

"Then we'll eat potatoes, as we did many a time in the old country. But don't worry—we'll eat something."

We turned away, not looking at each other. That's the way it went all day, all of us avoiding each other's eyes, as though we were ashamed.

Father came home late that evening. His face was grim, and he was, for once short of words. He had a small brown bag under his arm and our hearts sank when we saw it. He opened the bag and tossed on the table a skinny, pale chicken of not more than five pounds.

"That will have to do us," he said sourly. "I near walked my feet off and it was all I could get."

We went to bed, still heavy-hearted and silent. Our Christmas tree stood in a corner, bare of ornaments. It was to be trimmed later, after we were asleep, as was our family custom. The gifts would be brought out from hiding places and put around the tree and in the stockings that hung under the mantel. But there was no joy in the prospect that night. I only wished that Christmas was over, and I was anxious to go to sleep.

I was awakened in the middle of the night by the fire whistle, so loud that it seemed to be right there in the bedroom.

From my parents' room, I heard the flurry of footsteps, and the sound of a window shade being pulled up. Then came my father's muttered exclamation as he searched for a boot.

Mother put her head in the doorway. "Now watch the little ones," she cautioned me. "We'll be back soon."

We dressed hurriedly as though she had not spoken, snatching mittens and scarves, and rushed out after mother and father. Fires were something big in our uneventful lives. We scurried along the streets. Oblongs of orange light were beginning to spring up in the dark houses.

Dennie Mahoney's Overland went lurching by us, and someone leaned out from the back seat, pointing and shouting, "Hilliers'!" I knew a short cut to Herbie's house, and we hurried through a vacant lot, stumbling over the ruts in the frozen ground.

The fire had a good start by the time we reached the Hilliers' corner. We could see its dull red reflection against the black sky and could smell the stench of burning wood. Jake Bancroft, the fire captain, was shouting orders, and we could hear the ringing of the firemen's axes.

Mother saw us, and warned us sternly that we were not to

try to get near the front lines, nor go looking for our friends in the crowd. And then, slowly, with her little procession of children behind her, she edged closer. She sighed over each ruined piece of the Hilliers' furniture as it was tossed or dragged out into the street.

Father, in his boots and long, flapping coat, had pressed close to the fire lines to volunteer his help. We could see him towering above the crowd, his voice louder than Jake Bancroft's.

We stood silent, awed by the sight of the burning house, stretching and craning to see over the shoulders of the crowd. I could not see Herbie nor any member of his family. Finally, father came shoving his way back to us, followed by all the Hilliers.

I felt mother stiffen beside me, but as the little group stopped near us, she burst out. "I want you to know, I'm sorry!"

Mrs. Hillier looked unfamiliar, her hair disarranged and the tight mask of her face cracked into lines of distress. In the weird light, she seemed more than ever to have no eyebrows nor eyelashes, but tears glistened in her eyes, and her mouth was shaking.

"You sorry?" she whimpered, "How do you think I feel? I've been punished. You see that, don't you? I took the angel away from your little girl and it was like a curse on me. I lit the candles on the Christmas tree, to see how the angel would look. And its gauzy dress caught fire from the candles. That's how all this started."

Her voice rose. "The angel was angry at my selfishness, and this is the way I was punished. I deserved it, I deserved it!"

Mother caught at Mrs. Hillier's hand, and patted it. "Hush, now," she soothed, as though she were speaking to one of us children. "It was an accident only as might happen to anyone. And don't be talking about curses, for there's no such thing. If we were to get punished for all our selfish thoughts and actions, I'm sure we'd have all burned up long ago. An angry angel, indeed! 'Twas just a Christmas tree ornament and nothin' else, and could have no feelin's at all."

She went on patting the other woman's hand. "You're all unharmed, so think of it that way. God spared the whole family. And nothing's lost at all except what can be replaced."

Herbie's sister was sniffling into her mother's skirts, and the faces of the man and boy looked stricken. When she turned to them, Mrs. Hillier burst into fresh tears.

"Christmas!" she wailed. "And us without even a roof over our heads!"

"You have," denied mother stoutly. "Ours! You'll come along with us now. Though there may be some that will have to sleep on the floor, it will not be our guests. It would be a real favor of friendship if you would come to our house."

Mrs. Hillier mopped at her eyes. "Then we will."

"Tonight and tomorrow you will spend with us."

Mother broke off suddenly, remembering, no doubt, the small chicken in the icebox. And at that moment, a man tapped her on the shoulder. It was Roy Mitchell.

"I'm sorry about the turkey," he said with a shamefaced grin. "I'll open up now, and you can take your pick. I got plenty of birds left. If you can find your friends, the Mahoneys and Cannons and them, get them to come along, too. There's enough for everybody."

Not to be outdone, my father cried, "And if there's anyone of you with a wet cellar still, I'll be there to pump it out if you just raise your voice and say so. Christmas or no, I'll work tomorrow for them that asks me."

I've seen many Christmas Eves since that one, but it's the one that remains most vivid. These things I remember: the smoking ruins of the Hilliers' house; eating Mother's holiday pies that night in the kitchen with Herbie beside me; father coming in to join us, puffing and wheezing under the weight of a huge bundle containing not one turkey, but two; the lumpy daybed in the dining room.

On Christmas morning, the bells of all the churches in town rang out, not drowning each other but making a lovely harmony. Our dining room table held all its extra leaves, but we still sat shoulder to shoulder. Father and Mr. Hillier took turns carving, and mother and Mrs. Hillier did the serving.

Whenever I hear the phrases, "peace on earth," and "men of good will," I think of my hometown. And I remember that we learned their meaning only after a flood, a famine, and a fire.

MY FIRST AMERICAN CHRISTMAS [31]

A small girl's gift of love moved a mountain
By Louise Sottosanti

It is Christmas Eve. All my children and grandchildren have gone home. I sit by the fireplace and watch the dying embers glow. The snow falls softly, and in the distance I hear carolers. The hands of the clock point to the midnight hour.

As I glance about the room my eyes fall on a white popcorn ball wrapped in red cellophane. It is my grandson's gift, made by his tiny hands in kindergarten. Suddenly, I remember another popcorn ball that once changed my life.

The years fall away as if by magic and I am a little girl again. I see myself on a cold winter day long ago, standing alone, my lips pressed together to keep from crying, my hands clenched tightly at my side, waiting. Waiting for the blow to fall.

My tormentor was a schoolmate. Butch, freckle-faced, red-haired, was the toughest kid in the Franklin Elementary School. Suddenly, his viciously hurled snowball struck me squarely in the eye. With gleeful shouts and choruses of name-calling, Butch and his gang raced around the corner. Their taunts echoed in the winter twilight.

I rubbed the spot where the snowball had struck. It hurt. But I didn't care so much about that. It was the other thing that really hurt: what they said. It was not the first time this had happened. I should have been used to it by now.

Why couldn't I just laugh it off or throw stones and snowballs back at them, or call them names, too? Why was I so afraid? And of what?

But I knew, even if I could not put it into words. I couldn't fight back because there was a mountain between us, and I was the stranger on the other side.

Holding back my tears, I picked up my scattered books and turned toward home. The icy November wind cut through my coat and high boots. I shivered, and something in my throat choked me.

I climbed the steps of our house and thought about Butch

and his sister Maggie. They were my enemies, the ones who always started the name-calling. They were a part, safe and secure, of a world I never could hope to enter. They were Americans. I thought about that word.

Miss Bennett, my fourth grade teacher, had told us that all who lived in America were Americans. So it seemed in the classroom. But once we left the room, things changed. We fell into different classifications. There were Americans and there were others.

The unfortunates who did not belong to that elite group were not welcomed in the games and play. They were chased, laughed at, and scorned.

As I pushed open the front door a wonderful smell of cooking hit me. The odor was familiar and comforting. This was my home and my world, warm, safe, and secure.

My mother stood at the highly polished coal stove. She stirred the food and greeted me in her hesitant English. "How was school today?"

My answer was always the same. "All right, Momma."

I made my voice happy and enthusiastic, keeping from my mother the secret of my private troubles. She must never know about the unkind world that existed just outside this house.

A few minutes later my father came home from work. He also asked about my school day. Then we sat down to eat. I was glad that my parents did not include me in their conversation. I could think while I ate.

The following week the fourth grade began preparing for Christmas. We were told to make window decorations. I produced a decorated tree that pleased my teacher. She smiled and honored me by pasting the tree on the window where it could be seen from the street.

It was a wonderful triumph for me. I felt happy all morning. But as I was hanging my coat in the cloakroom after lunch Butch and Maggie started pushing me around. I tried to squeeze past them and Butch tripped me.

I guess that was the last straw. I kicked and punched until we all landed in a heap on the floor. Miss Bennett rushed in, untangled us, and stood us in a row like a police lineup. She demanded an explanation. Since I was the one who hit first, I had to stay after school and write a 500-word task.

On my way home after school I busily invented excuses to explain my lateness. As I opened the door I was enveloped by the Friday cleaning smell, that wonderful mixture of lemon-oil polish, ammonia, and brown soap that I loved. I walked through the parlor, admiring its spotless perfection. The Victrola and piano were mahogany mirrors, the white lace curtains stiffly starched, and anti-macassars placed with geometric precision.

In the kitchen, my mother was at her post by the stove. Questions, explanations, lies. I was determined that she would never know what I endured on the outside. Then I received a pleasant surprise.

"If your report card is good this month, I will make you a velvet dress for Christmas, maybe," my mother said as casually as if such dresses happened every day.

"Oh, Momma!" I screamed happily. "Would you?"

I was beside myself with joy. A velvet dress! Wait till Maggie saw it! So the day ended on a happy note, my school troubles forgotten at the thought of owning such a marvel.

On Monday morning Miss Bennett announced that the fourth grade would take part in the P.T.A. Christmas program. We were to do the Nativity scene. Everyone was excited, wondering who would be selected to take part. All eyes were on Miss Bennett as she began to choose the participants.

"First, let's see . . . is Joseph." She ran an expert eye over the boys. "Someone tall and stocky. How about Peter Jones? Now . . . for Mary," she continued her gaze sweeping over the hopeful, eager girls.

My heart pounding, I prayed hard that Miss Bennett would pick me. How wonderful it would be to appear before the P.T.A. Perhaps my father and mother would see. The teacher's glance had stopped at me!

Please, God, I prayed. For a second she hesitated. Then she went on to the next girl. I looked down at my desk to hide the tears. It was the fight in the cloakroom. A little girl who picked fights certainly wasn't suited to take the part of Mary. Or maybe it was the mountain again, separating us.

138

"Maggie," the teacher was saying. "I think we'll let Maggie be Mary. She'll look nice in blue with her blonde hair."

I was stunned. Maggie to be Mary! With her round face and short yellow hair!

After school I lingered in the cloakroom watching Miss Bennett try costumes on the children who were to take part in the program. When the teacher saw me, she told me to run along home.

I walked out into the dark afternoon. It was snowing, a fine powdery snow driven by a sharp wind. I didn't feel like going home yet. I walked in the opposite direction, wandering aimlessly up and down streets and through alleys.

I reached the public library and sat down on one of the benches. When I heard the five o'clock whistle I began hurrying toward home. The street lights were on and the snow fell thicker and faster. Near the school I saw my father looking for me. I ran up to him and explained, "I was just coming home, Poppa. We had to stay and practice for a play."

All that night I shivered with cold and by morning I was burning with fever. My mother called the doctor. He announced I had pneumonia, an alarming verdict in the days before antibiotics.

For the next four or five days I existed in a half-world of shadows and hazy impressions. At times, I forgot who I was, where I was. I thought I was on fire, twisting, turning, choking, crying for water. Tight bands of steel crushed my chest.

One night, very late, the doctor came again. I felt hot, stinging cloth on my chest and a needle stabbing my arm. Then the room faded away and I floated in darkness for a long, long time . . . .

The sun streaming in the window awakened me. I recalled being away for some time in a sort of dream world. Now everything was bright and clear again. The school bell ringing brought remembrance. The fourth grade, the P.T.A. program, Christmas, Maggie. What day was it? Was Christmas gone?

I cried out for my mother and she tried to answer my questions one at a time. "Yes, yes. You were very sick. But thank the good Lord you are well again. Yes. No, Christmas is not gone. It comes still. In one week. What is today? Friday,

139

the eighteenth day of December. Yes, many children come and ask. So. You miss party. Don't worry, many more. No, we have not tree yet. Poppa will buy tonight when he gets money. Now you rest. Sleep a little. Momma have much work to do. Much sewing."

Pulling down the shades a little, she hurried into the next room where I soon heard the whirring of the sewing machine. The sound was soothing and I fell asleep.

When I opened my eyes again the shades were raised to let in the remaining afternoon light. Hanging on the wall facing my bed was the most beautiful dress I had ever seen in my life. The red velvet dress my mother had promised me for Christmas!

I heard the school bell again and the children passing on their way home. I thought of all I had missed. Most of all I missed the joyous feeling I always had when all the children sang carols together. Then the doorbell rang and I heard a familiar voice ask for me.

It sounded like . . . but no, it couldn't be. What could *she* possibly want with me? Someone was clumping noisily up the stairs. I sat up, clutching the covers to my chin, my eyes wide in surprise and fear.

Maggie walked shyly into my room. She hesitated a moment, then walked slowly to the bedside. In her outstretched hand she held something red and sparkling. It was a popcorn ball, wrapped in gleaming red cellophane and tied with a ribbon.

I stared at Maggie as she said, "I made this for you. Here. Take it."

But I couldn't move or speak or lift my hand. Maggie, smiling at me? No snicker, no leer, no name-calling? What was Maggie saying?

"We missed you. Miss Bennett and the kids and everybody. We're sorry you were sick and missed everything. Merry Christmas, and come over to my house when you feel good again."

Too surprised to talk, I made no reply. Maggie repeated, "Come over to see my tree and we'll play with my dolls and stuff." She stopped, waiting for me to say something. But I remained silent. Maggie continued, "Butchie's sorry he hit you

140

with that snowball and I made him promise he would never be mean to you again."

And then she began to stammer, her face reddening, "And I won't ever be mean to you again. I promise. Here, take this. Don't you want it? I made it for you." She began to look hurt at my refusal to take the gift.

Then, very slowly, I began to realize that Maggie meant what she said. She was offering me her friendship.

Very far away, it seemed that someone was singing "Hark the Herald Angels Sing," my favorite carol. And Maggie was the most beautiful angel of them all, her yellow hair a golden halo, the age-old spirit of Christmas shining from her eyes.

As I lifted my hand to accept the gift, I knew with soulfilling happiness that I had entered Maggie's wonderful world. I was an American at last.

IN A LITTLE METHODIST CHURCH ON CHRISTMAS[32]

Sincere "Amens"
By Joseph O'Donnell

The message of Christmas struck me last year at 6 A.M. in a little Negro Methodist church. I had been invited to be with them for their sunrise service and to join them for breakfast afterward. It seemed right for me to go, to bring the gift of my good will and to honor this occasion with my priestly presence.

I came to show my love, but they outdid me with their own.

The little church had been freshly cleaned for this welcome to the newborn King. The roaring flame in the potbelly stove kept us fairly warm as we hovered near. Below the simple pulpit a small tree had been decked with a single string of lights.

There seemed to be so little to start with here. The depth of their poverty hit me when a deacon announced that their woman preacher had been called away to the deathbed of her daughter. Now they had no one to lead the service, no one even to read them the Scripture about the birth of Jesus.

Almost as a group, they turned to me. I was a preacher! Would I read to them the words of life? Would I lead them in some prayers? Would I join with them in singing carols? I had not come for this, but I had no choice! Picking up their worn Bible, I slowly read to them the story of the birth of Christ. They listened and responded, as they saw fit, with nods of the head or shouts of "Amen."

Then in honor of Jesus' birth, one by one they stood to tell what they were thankful for this Christmas Day. "I thank the Lord for bringing up my children right," said one. And all answered, "Amen." "God, I thank you for leading me back from my sinful ways," said another. Then an elderly lady arose to utter a prayer I shall never forget. "Lord, I am going blind, but I do thank you for the seventy-five years of sight you gave me to see the beautiful things you made."

It was my turn to give thanks now. They all bowed their heads to listen and to save me from my embarrassment, I rose and looked toward heaven, praying, "Lord, I thank you for this morning. I thank you for the message that rings so clear today, that poverty can make us rich and that riches can make us poor. Lord, I thank you that we are all learning to love each other more."

"Amen, Amen," they chanted as I sat down.

I REMEMBER HANDEL'S *MESSIAH* [33]

And all the members of the choir, too
By Joseph Sittler

St. Peter's Lutheran Church endures in my memory. It is in the small southern Ohio town where I lived from my tenth year until I entered college.

The annual rendition of Handel's *Messiah* on the Sunday evening preceding Christmas Day was the event of the year. The choir was directed by a cranky old physician. I think his practice of medicine was only a way of making a living until Christmas and the *Messiah* came around.

The bass in the choir was Jake, who ran the grocery store, which had a bakery where real bread was baked daily.

Jake was a big man. At nine o'clock, after the bread had been taken from the ovens, he could usually be seen walking down Main St. in his great white apron, his huge arms floured to the elbows, on his way to Happy Mock's saloon for a mug of beer. Happy, by the way, was also a communicant of St. Peter's; he showed up regularly on Ash Wednesday and on Easter. When my father, the pastor, was leaving the parish to assume another task, Happy made it a point to tell him that he would miss his sermons. Father reminded Happy that he had been missing them for many years!

Anyhow, Jake was the bass. What he lacked in finesse and precision he made up in power and enthusiasm. I have heard "Why do the nations so furiously rage together?" sung better, but I have never heard the question put more forcibly. Jake sang it as if he really wanted to know! When he dropped off to that spine-tingling note at the end of the aria we small boys, amazed at the performance, poked each other with delight.

The organist's name was Ethel. She was the perpetually jolly wife of the local undertaker. She was an indifferent organist but imperturbable. A few dropped notes here and there were silly details, not to be remembered in the total impression.

On that old tracker-action organ was a four-foot flute stop
of such liquid quality that I can hear it still. The flute stop
was commonly used on the great annual occasion to accompany
the aria "Comfort ye, comfort ye, my people." The line of
that phrase in Handel's notation was utterly melting; when
our George sang it, accompanied by that four-foot flute, strong
men paled. George was an incompetent, lackluster, weak,
indecisive, harmless young man who clerked in the post office.
He moved like a wraith through the town, never uttering a word.
It was old Doc, I suppose, who found out that George had a
tenor voice that was pellucid, sweet, and of angelic purity.
And once a year George sang in the *Messiah.*

The week before the performance the members of the choir
became quiet, almost morose. Only with difficulty were their
minds kept on their work. During these lapses, families and
fellow workers would be indulgent: "She's singing in the
Messiah on Sunday you know." The participants would look
at themselves in the mirror to detect any evidence of illness,
open wide their mouths to catch signs of a bad throat. They
would wear heavy mufflers to protect their voices and lie down
every afternoon to ensure full power on Sunday. I assure you
I don't exaggerate. They would nod to one another on the
street with enigmatic smiles. They shared a secret: whoever
was not in the choir was for that week a lesser being.

How can one account for the popularity of this music?
I think the answer is quite simple. Text, score, the magic of
the season all converge in a single event with absolute good
fortune.

First, the libretto. It is not of Handel's day; it was
assembled from Biblical texts by Charles Jennens and handed
over to Handel all complete. He confidently strung a few
Biblical texts together to suggest the entire Biblical drama.

What is surprising is the sheer success of it! For the texts
are representative, the episodes *are* crucial. The texts have a
rhetorical quality that pleads for singing. From prophecy to
eschatology to the epilogue in heaven where ranks of angels
sing "Blessing and honor and glory and power," it is impeccable.
The few texts chosen for the ministry, life, work, and sayings

of Jesus astound us by their felicity and propriety. The King, the Servant, the Healer, the Consoler of human misery, the Shepherd, the Lamb of God, the Man of Sorrows—they are all there, and there in the most memorable text for each.

Second, the music has simplicity and harmonic purity. It is rich without cloying, sweet without superfluity, moving without loss of majesty, heavy with legitimate sentiment but always stopping a safe distance this side of sentimentality.

This achievement is the more amazing when one recalls that Handel was German, that English was not his mother tongue, and that the lineage of his melodies is Italian. The English oratorio is a development of the Italian opera; its forebears are secular, whereas the German oratorio is a development of the religious chorale. The English work does not in the same way spring out of folk sources. The *Messiah* keeps right on rocking through the decades because it represents a happy marriage of four elements: the power of music, a simple and solid theological structure, Italian grace and style, and English religious sentiments.

After all this one might suppose that I am a true believer, a *Messiah* patriot. I am not. I never go to hear it any more. Except for the memories clustered about my early experience it would not have great significance for me. I like Bach better.

The *Messiah* music does not, like the *Passion,* the cantatas, and the *Mass* of J. S. Bach, really assault my mind. It does not, as Bach continues to do, bring under a fierce, relentless gaze my actual performance in life. For instance, I can know a great deal about the Christian faith in historical and theological terms, but Bach's *O Man They Sin Bewail* stands over against me as a deep accusation, putting under moral question my entire career. Bach musically set forth the Word. Handel wrote to please men.

145

THE CHOIR FROM LITTLE HELL [34]

The great Boy Soprano Battle set the Paulist Choir on the high road
By Robert Hardy Andrews

I didn't know what kind of story I was looking for when I
walked the Levee's dark side streets. In 1930 only fools roved
alone in Chicago's Little Hell. Rotting buildings stood vacant.
Dark doorways held dregs of down-and-done humanity.

Then I heard angels singing. I looked up, and saw Old
St. Mary's Church, on its South Wabash corner. My plans for
that night had definitely not included going to church. But
the doors stood open, candles burned inside, and the angelic
voices were clear.

I went up the stone steps into an oasis of peace. Hours
later, I was still trying to convince Father Eugene O'Malley
that he and his Paulist choirboys belonged in *Midweek,* the
supplement I edited for the Chicago *Daily News.* Without
knowing what I sought in Little Hell, I had found it in Angels'
Half Acre.

Father O'Malley was slender, stooped, spectacled, mild, but
with steel behind the mildness. He had a dedication to Young
Men Going Somewhere. His men were eight and ten and twelve
years old. Hard-eyed, underfed, suspicious, insolent, ragged,
they were mirthless copies of elder brothers who ranged the
Levee district mugging pedestrians, stealing cars, robbing filling
stations, ganging up on cops. They were growing up to be the
two-bit punks used by the syndicate to drive beer trucks and
bomb dry cleaners and do minor gun jobs, and die young, or
a day at a time for twenty years in an iron cage.

Father O'Malley would not talk about this work, however,
but only about Father William Finn, founder of the choir.
He had been taller, tougher, with large hands almost always
balled in fists and a self-sharpening tongue. "Me, train boys
to sing?" Father Finn objected when his superiors gave him
his assignment. "I'd sooner be sentenced to a cannibal's
stewpot in Senegambia!"

But in the black-robed army without banners, soldiers go

146

where they are needed. During the black hard-times winter of 1903, traveling on a pass, lacking money for a meal on the train or for streetcar fare when he reached Chicago, Father Finn had arrived at Old St. Mary's.

He walked up and down the Levee hunting volunteers for his choir. He got just two. One sang like a nightingale. He attended two rehearsals, then was never seen again. His father had just killed his mother.

The other choirboy was a big eight-year-old, Johnny Keely. He couldn't sing for sour apples, but he had all the rest of the kids on his block buffaloed, so Father Finn made him peace enforcer.

Desperate for more singers, Father Finn appealed to the Christian Brothers. They helped him enlist his recruits. The Paulist Choristers sang publicly for the first time in September, 1904. But it was the great Boy Soprano Battle that set them on the high road.

Episcopal choirboys from prospering Grace Church, bound for a picnic, collided with the Paulist boys, who thought a street brawl was picnic enough for anybody. The ensuing war with fists and stones and barrel staves stopped streetcars, tied up traffic, and hit page one in every paper.

Father Finn was apologizing to Grace Episcopal's choirmaster when both heard simultaneously that boys were besieging their churches, demanding a chance to join their choirs, now that the papers said boy sopranos need not be sissies.

Thereafter Father Finn had all he could handle, in the rehearsal hall next door to McNally's undertaking parlors, which was also the polling place to which Hinky Dink and Bathhouse John brought their voters (50¢ a vote, $1 for repeaters) on election day. Nearby was the biggest gambling dive between New York and California.

Eight years after their first concert, the Paulist Choristers sailed for Europe. They were to have been aboard the *Titanic*, but just missed the boat. They won medals in Paris, and sang for the Pope in Rome.

The President, Teddy Roosevelt, summoned them to sing in

the White House, specifying that they must appear before his Cabinet in executive session, "because I hope you can soften the hearts of some of the members and especially of William Howard Taft." But when the Rough Rider asked the boys to sing his favorite, "Drink to Me Only with Thine Eyes," a twelve-year-old Jimmy Kearn (later a priest in Cedar Rapids) declined to sing the solo part because he thought the lyrics were too frivolous. Father Finn always had a stand-in ready. Ralph Summers sang the solo. T.R. shook hands with him, and with Jimmy, too. "I like a man," the Rough Rider said, "who sticks by his principles."

In the great days, the Paulist Choristers made 241 public appearances. Then war and other distractions halted the meteor in its course. Father Finn was needed at the Paulist mother house in New York. Al Capone took over at the nearby Hotel Metropole. Youngsters stopped coming to Angels' Half Acre. But in Rome, there was a young priest who had been one of Father Finn's boy sopranos.

Father O'Malley was recalled to New York and told, "See what you can do." So he returned to the Levee, as poor as Father Finn was in his generation, as much a stranger, and facing a greater challenge. In Father Finn's days, boys who went wrong turned thief. In 1930, they turned murderer.

I said this. Father O'Malley didn't. I promised, "We'll give you two full pages in the magazine, and a color picture on our cover. That should sell a lot of tickets for your annual concert." The concert paid for shoes and underwear and hot meals for the boys, and supported their summer camp in an abandoned icehouse on Crystal Lake.

"Well," Father O'Malley granted dubiously, "you may come around if you wish. But go easy in writing about the boys. They've known shame enough already. Don't brand them. Don't let people think they have to be what their fathers and elder brothers have become."

Some of my story was sure-fire. The voice of a boy soloist changed without warning in the middle of an aria. Flawlessly, his stand-in took up the note on which he had begun to fail. None in the audience suspected they heard a solo turned into

148

a duet.

"The change can be heart-stopping," Father O'Malley said. The boy pours out a pure note, and hears a faltering croak. He thinks he is disgraced, and done. This finishes the first happy years he has had. If he can no longer sing, he is back where we found him. Or so he fears. But God be thanked, it isn't so."

It wasn't so because of the Old Paulist Boys. They were lawyers, storekeepers, dentists, plumbers, judges, truck drivers, doctors, salesmen, priests, postmen, streetcar conductors, college students now. Few were rich, and many were out of work.

But each one did the best he could for a younger Paulist boy as foster brother. A thousand had made good, and a hundred more were climbing the straight road.

Strangely, hoodlums wanted to help. Some sent anonymous donations, or bought blocks of tickets for the annual concert. Some even dropped in at St. Mary's. A gorilla with a record for brutishness came to Angels' Half Acre dragging his small son, "Put the fear of God in him. Don't let him turn out damned like his old man."

A boy whose dead mother had been a Protestant, whose father had asked for a priest before he walked the last mile in Stateville prison, chose his mother's faith though he sang with the Paulist Choristers. When Cardinal Mundelein heard him and praised the devotion in his voice, the boy said politely that he didn't propose to be converted to Catholicism. The cardinal placed both hands on his head. "It was a very special blessing," Father O'Malley told me, "and it was deserved."

I wrote this and more for *Midweek*. But I left out the story of Solly Levine. He appeared one day in the rehearsal room. "I decided to join your gang."

Father O'Malley asked, "Are you sure you understand about the choir? Are you sure you can sing well enough?"

Solly asked, "Am I maybe an amateur? Since I'm knee-high to a lamppost I'm singing for throw money in saloons."

He considered the discussion closed. But Father O'Malley asked, "If you're earning your living as a professional, why do

149

you want to be in a choir for twenty-five cents a rehearsal and fifty cents on Sundays?"

Solly said, "They ain't throwing much these days." Then it came out in a rush. His father, unable to find work, had disappeared. His mother scrubbed floors when her strength permitted. "I gotta get some school," Solly said. "If I have a square meal here, my mom don't starve herself at home to feed me. If I get free shoes, she don't have to scrub a week to buy me some. Please, Father, let me in!"

Father O'Malley let him in, and held a conference with the other choirboys. Rules they agreed on were never broken. Nobody argued the New Testament against the Old with Solly. Saturdays, when Catholic boys were fined a quarter out of their Sunday half dollar if they missed rehearsal, Solly was excused for synagogue.

But when I said Solly belonged in the *Midweek* piece, Father O'Malley said No. I was not to make Solly feel he was separated from the rest by anything. So I didn't. I was glad I hadn't when on Christmas morning the choristers filed into the choir loft at Old St. Mary's caroling the "Adeste Fideles." Leading them, singing his soul out, was that day's soloist, Solly Levine.

Chapter V
All Nations Know Him

Christmas has spread around the world. Even in Japan where the percentage of Christians in the general population is very small, Santa Claus, complete with red suit and long white beard, has become a familiar figure in the shopping centers at Christmas time, which the Japanese do not otherwise observe.

As Christians believe, Christ came to save all men and to teach all mankind. Consequently, He founded a missionary church, which has sent messengers to all available parts of the world to gain Him followers. Most of the Asian religions are utterly indifferent to making converts. The average Buddhist or Hindu cannot understand why you should want to convert him, since he has no desire to convert you. In the days of their expansion, the Moslems were interested in gaining more adherents only in connection with making territorial conquests. But Christianity has always felt a duty to go forth into the whole world, and that is why there are so many Christmas stories with backgrounds not only in Christian lands but in the far corners of the earth.

THE ANGEL SONG [35]

My little cross on a chain was the most valid of my passports
By Janos Varkonyi

In December, 1956, I, like the other Budapest University
students, was on the job clearing the streets of the rubble left
by the October revolution.

Many of the students I had led in the fight on the rooftops
already had escaped across the border. But some of us ignored
the danger and stayed. We still expected UN intervention.
Why else would the communists want the district to look
orderly? If Dag Hammerskjold should come, he would need
witnesses for the Hungarians.

We worked so slowly that two days before Christmas ample
evidence of the paving-block barricades remained. The buildings
still spilled their ruins through gutted walls onto the sidewalks.

Around 3:00 P.M. a tough-looking student came by motorcycle to the area where I worked. "Varkonyi, they've been to
the college looking for you. You're on the list."

So here it was: my final choice—death or Siberia. I'd get
my submachine gun—Russky guitar, we called it—and mow
down as many as I could when they came to get me. My friend
must have read my thoughts.

"Take my motorcycle and get to the border before the list
does. The holiday will slow things." he said.

I stood there debating.

"Under the seat is a gun." He handed me a Red Cross arm
band, a stamped identification paper, and a gas ration card.
"Fill in your name. Head for the border, and don't go back
to the college."

He hesitated a moment, then he pushed back the neck of
his sweater and unfastened a gold chain and cross. I looked
away, embarrassed for him and astonished that a person who
looked so tough could still be religious. I had discarded my
cross shortly after my mother died and the communists took
charge of me.

"Take this memento." He thrust it into my hand. "I know

155

you are not religious."

"I was once," I muttered. I shoved the cross deep into my pocket, and started the motorcycle.

Just outside Budapest on the road to Gyor a Russian tank, its gun turned toward the traffic, blocked my way. I stopped. The guard, bundled in a dirty gray coat, slung his submachine gun over his shoulder and asked for my papers. He pretended to read the identification although I doubted he knew Hungarian. He studied my arm band, then returned all my papers, and waved me on.

Getting past the Russian tank gave me little assurance that I could escape across the border. The tight squeeze would be slipping through the twenty-five mile border zone.

By sundown the fallen snow began to freeze, and the cold wind whipped through my jacket. To keep my hands from freezing I rode with one in my pocket. Even then, my fingers were almost too cold to hold the handlebars.

I concentrated on the houses along the road. The windows poured beacons of light into the darkness. I thought of that last Christmas with my family before the communists came. I could almost hear the fire crackle warmly while I waited for the angel to come.

In Hungary, it was not Santa but the angel who came. Children lighted candles in the window and waited for the bells to chime out. Then they sang:

From heaven the angel descended
To bring you the news.

I used to rush out into the snow, barefoot and in my bed clothes, I was so excited. But the angel no longer came to Hungary. Few people still dared to light candles in the windows on what was now Pine Celebration day. I hummed the song and felt strangely warmer.

When I stopped for gas in Gyor, the man wiped his greasy hand on his overalls and reached toward me. "Your gas ticket," he demanded gruffly.

I pulled the ticket from my pocket, horrified to find the chain tangled around it. The man watched me intently while I freed the card.

"Keep your ticket. How many liters do you want?" The unexpected kindness in his voice encouraged me to ask for more help.

"Five, please. How far to the border zone?"

"Twelve kilometers past Gyor. But only people who live there or have special permits can enter," he warned.

I had no future in going back, nothing further to risk by going on. I shrugged and started the motor.

"Isten vele," he said. His soft "God be with you" took some of the chill from the night.

At the border zone I saw the flashlight but did not stop until it waved violently and moved in front of me. "Trying to run the border zone!" the burly guard shouted while the other one pointed his Russky guitar at me.

The sight of the green Hungarian uniform fired my imagination. "I didn't know this was the border zone."

"State your business."

"The Soviet commander of Buda, Tovarish Umersky, is ill and wants his old friend Dr. Forr from Sopron to operate. I am to bring the doctor." I handed him my Red Cross identification, amazed my hand was so steady.

"No border-zone permit?"

"There was no time." I stuffed my hand into my pocket.

"You speak Russian?"

I answered in Russian.

They conferred for an eternity. I could easily have shot them, but the fingers which should have reached for my gun was holding the cross. Finally one spoke. "We do not believe your story, but the police at the border will stop you if you try to escape."

I needed no urging, and left, oddly exhilarated. The border police, I knew, had orders to capture or kill anyone trying to escape. Yet I felt no fear of death. I had seen too many die. But as I came closer to the Austrian border, the desire to live became more compelling. Beyond the border was freedom, and life might take on meaning.

In Sopron, the deserted streets warned me that it was past curfew and dangerous to ride through the city. Then I heard a vehicle behind me. I turned into a side street, expecting to hear shots any moment. I left the motorcycle on the sidewalk and raced up some wide steps toward the nearest building. Not until I saw the dim light glowing and then the altar did I realize I was in a church.

Although I had not been in a church for years, I instinctively blessed myself. I knelt and tried to say the Rosary on my fingers. My mind would not furnish the words. Embarrassed, I gave up.

My eyes, now accustomed to the dim light, made out the crèche. The Christmas my father went to war, my mother and I lighted our candles at the Nativity scene in church, then knelt and prayed that he would return to us alive. My father never came back, and my mother died, too. Prayers seemed to me wasted efforts. I closed my eyes and fell into an exhausted sleep.

I awoke at dawn. Again, I knelt and tried to pray. The words would not come. I escaped into the foggy morning.

I found my motorcycle where I had deserted it and rode to the nearest gas station.

The man's mustache stood out straight. "You need gas?"

"No, information," I said, "in exchange for my motorcycle."

"You trying to get across?"

I nodded, taking the gun from under the seat and stuffing it in my belt.

"The fog will help," he assured me. "Go through the fields instead of the woods. If you hear many dogs, that is an Austrian village. If you hear one dog, that's the patrol. There is some barbed wire and maybe some mines." He handed me pliers. "Avoid the watch towers. The walk takes two to two and a half hours."

I hurried toward the border. Only once did I stop and look back at Hungary, wrapped in fog and communism. My throat tightened. I could hardly swallow the tears. I took one final look at my country and walked on. Very soon I would know if I would escape or die.

For the next two hours, I moved steadily westward, where I heard shooting and dogs. Then suddenly the dogs seemed

to bark behind me. I was moving in the wrong direction!
I altered my course and kept changing it, trying to put the barks
ahead of me. Eventually, I lost all sense of direction in the
thickening fog.

The dog leaped on me and knocked me down in the snow.
He held me there until two figures emerged from the fog. They
ordered the dog back and pointed two machine guns at my
stomach. "Stand up."

I stood up. One held the gun while the other took my
possessions and stuffed them in the big pockets of his coat.
The cross seemed to cling to his rough hand.

"Take him to the guard station," the one with the gun
ordered. "I'll go back to the watch tower."

Through patches of clearing fog, I could see the border I
would never cross. Freedom was only a few feet away.

My guard nudged me in the back with his gun. "Move!"
We walked along until we reached a spot where the fog was
very heavy. "Stop!" He dangled the cross close to my face.
"Take it!"

He wanted to taunt me with the cross. I took it.

"Remember the song the little ones sing to the angel when
the bells chime?" He chanted the song in an off-key fashion.
"Sing it."

When we finished he seemed to be listening for something.
"Each Christmas Eve, I think I hear the bells chime and the
laughter of children. I tell nobody, but you can understand."

"In a minute, I shoot in the air. You run fast," he directed.
"Help little ones to sing the 'Angel Song.' "

The gun exploded behind me. I ran as I had never run in
my life. The cold air knifed through my lungs, and the cross
cut into my hand. I did not stop until I was safely in Austria,
alive and free. I fastened the chain around my neck and fell
on my knees. Prayers I had not used in years found my lips.
It was as if I had been born again.

The years stretch out since that eventful Christmas Eve, but
I will not forget or cease to hope. Each Christmas I pray that
my friend in the border police may again hear children sing
the "Angel Song."

ON CHRISTMAS EVE [36]

**A true story found among the effects of an American soldier
killed in action twenty-five years ago
By James Wolfgram**

It began as a trickle: an occasional *papasan* with tall hat
and crooked cane leading wailing women and children down
the slippery mountain trails that led to the beach at Wonsan,
North Korea.

Behind them sounded the dull thunder of artillery. With
each muffled burst came a bitter memory of their ruined
villages, whose younger men had been systematically
slaughtered by the Chinese communist army advancing south
from Chosin Reservoir. Before them lay a vast fleet waiting
to pick up retreating U.S. Marine and Army units.

Soon the trickle became a flood, a stream of humanity that
poured from the mountains six days and nights, intermingled
at times with gaunt, bearded Americans, heads down and faces
immobile.

Little by little the boats were loaded. The 100,000 weak
refugees begged to be put aboard. They had been subsisting
on C-rations and whatever else they could forage.

Amid the embarkation came four American soldiers of the
Tenth Engineer Battalion of the Third Infantry Division.
They had been fighting a rear-guard action for a Marine
regiment that had arrived on the beach the previous day.
One, a corporal named King, told the beach commander that
the rest of his unit had been captured or killed. The four men
boarded a ship already filled with civilians.

His men secured, King set out to find a medic to treat his
frostbitten fingers. He stumbled through the crowd of huddled
refugees, and suddenly tripped. To a cacophony of Korean
chatter, he screamed an obscenity. The past month of combat,
carnage, and misery swiftly combined with the pain in his
fingers, and his feeling of futility was finally unleashed. He fell.

A wrinkled hand touched his face and he looked up to see
a yellow-toothed grin. An old man was saying something to

him, but King's gaze was fixed on the beard, about ten long strands that flowed from his chin, the mark of a village elder. The old man took King's good hand in his and in sign language asked if he could borrow the mitten to cover the feet of a shivering child nearby. Why not? King thought.

A South Korean soldier came up to them and, in his best pidjin English, told King that the old man was grateful and would like to offer something in return for the mitten. The elder, he said, had heard King yell the word *God* before he fell to the floor and that was why he felt bold enough to ask for the mitten, for the old man was a Christian, too. He had not understood the rest of King's curse.

The old man removed his back sack, and King wondered how anyone so skinny could be so agile. He used only one flowing motion of his left hand; the right remained tucked in his shirt. He rummaged for a while and gently removed a small plaster statue of the Christ Child, Joseph, and Mary.

"He wants you to have it," the Korean soldier said. "A missionary gave it to him many years ago. He says that now he is like Joseph and he welcomes the pain."

King studied the man as he slowly pulled his right arm from his shirt. There was only a bloody cloth-covered stump. "The communists cut the hand off when they came to his village," the soldier said.

King looked at the statue. The right hand of Joseph had been chipped off, too.

"He wishes you a most joyous Christmas," the Korean soldier continued. "He wants to know whether it is today or tomorrow that is the traditional eve of Christ's birth."

"Today," King told the interpreter, just realizing that it was December 24, 1950.

AN OLD-TIME CHRISTMAS[37]

In my childhood we didn't need to be reminded of whose birthday it was
By Doran Hurley

I was startled last September to hear "Hark the Herald Angels Sing" coming over the radio, and shocked to find it being used as a commercial gimmick to exploit something or other. A celebrity prattles about how she purchases her Christmas gifts away back in June, seemingly to get as far away from the true spirit of Christmas as possible. As Scrooge said, "Bah! Humbug!"

When I was a boy, not too long ago, it was very different. The Christmas season did not begin until long after Thanksgiving.

"Do it yourself" hobbies of today were routine practice yesterday. In our school we painfully pasted little boxes together out of heavy paper and crayoned them with holly leaves. Hopefully we put together circles of chamois for that now-forgotten article, the penwiper.

We were proud of our handicraft, for these were to be gifts for our parents. If we had elder sisters or young aunts, they were always around the dining room table, busy in the spreading glow of the Welsbach mantles, crocheting or knitting or tatting or doing "drawn work," making their own gifts.

We believed in Santa Claus even if we sensed that he really had his physical being in our parents. But we were never taken "downtown," in our New England phrase, to see him in a shabby department store replica. We did write letters to Santa that our mothers posted. They reached him, of course—there was proof on Christmas morning of that.

Then finally came the Eve of Christmas, and somehow that Eve is still capitalized in my mind as it was in my childhood. In the early morning began the final scrubbing that the house should be in order, just as we cleaned every Saturday in preparation of the Lord's day. From the oven of the coal range in the kitchen came the glorious smell of pies baking, apple and mince and pumpkin if the season had lasted. As New England Catholics, true to the same American tradition as their Congregational or Methodist or Baptist neighbors, our mothers would have scorned setting a festive table with only one kind of pie. The Christmas fruitcake, of course, had been mixed and baked near Thanksgiving time; is now merely wanting icing.

In the afternoon, everyone went to Confession. It was not quite the thing to wait until evening, because Christmas Eve was to be spent at home. If our elders walked back from church sedately, we younger ones certainly did not. We skipped like lambs of the flock in that inexplicable lightness of being that the sacrament gave us.

The evening meal (since the day was what the older people called a black fast) was meatless, of course. My New England city was near the sea, so we were not reduced to eggs or cheese. Although it was a fast-day meal, the feeling was that it still should be something special. At our house the tradition was clams fried in egg batter and cracker crumbs, with oyster stew.

My mother had a "clam man," a tall, gaunt Yankee named Jesse Shaw. Jesse, a rugged individualist and a man with kinship to Thoreau, came to town when the spirit moved him, with heavy baskets of clams or mussels, and maybe a few lobsters. He consented to sell his stock—almost grudgingly it seemed—to a few privileged customers. But no matter what the weather, old Jesse always showed up at our house on the morning of Christmas Eve with a "mess of clams" for my mother, for which he would take no payment. It was his way of saying "Merry Christmas," although no such sentimental non-Puritan words would ever cross his lips.

Once the pies were set to cool, my mother would go to our neighborhood grocery for the holiday turkey or chicken, picked out well in advance after much pressing of the breast bones. And of course the Christmas candle!

At Abe Yokum's, the grocer's, the ritual was always the same. Elderly Mr. Egan, the butcher, with his straw hat and paper cuffs, would say, "Gotta candle put aside for you, in case Yokum is waitin' on and don't see you." Mother would smile, make her other few selections, and move on to the cashier's cage. There little Miss Estes, of a Yankee Congregationalist family that had "come down in the world," would whisper, "I put aside a candle for you, in case he —?" And then Abe Yokum would come thundering over, his Jewish face smiling with true affection.

At this point each year we would interrupt mother. "All right, which candle did you take?" And she would say, "That poor little thing's: Miss Estes. You know she said to me, 'I'd love to light one myself. Say a prayer for me on yours, won't you do that? And I can think of it shining for me with light in the night.' "

The Christmas Eve supper; and then the lighting of the candle, placed on the table in the kitchen as the real heart of the house. The table was now spread with a fair cloth. And not only the lighted taper of welcome but beside it a bowl of fruit and a goblet of milk for the Holy Travelers if they should come by in the night. The tradition was that the candle should be lighted by the father or the oldest male.

Earlier, just after the candle lighting, mother would always point out the Christmas star to us. It was always there, I remember, brilliantly in the heavens. That Christmas star that guided the Magi shone alone and resplendent in my boyhood. It made you feel one with the shepherds, and all holy and warm inside.

In the old parish in those days everyone, children and adults, would go early to bed. Midnight Mass was not observed in our diocese. The single (and an exquisitely lovely) exception to the early-to-bed rule came in my youth. In the parish lived the Sullivan "girls," four sisters of great graciousness and Catholic dignity, to whom our Lord had given exceptional talents and the understanding to use them in his service.

Marian was our organist, and Sarah and Elizabeth soprano and alto soloists, at the old parish church and later at the cathedral. Julia was the housekeeper, adoring her more resplendent sisters. The custom they inaugurated, for themselves at first, then for a few friends, was this: shortly before midnight all the lights in their pleasant house would be lighted. A moment before the stroke of the hour Julia would rush about, opening the front door and all the windows in the parlor and in the living room across the hall. Then, with Marian at the piano, Sarah and Elizabeth standing beside her would welcome the Child in their glorious voices with a fervent "Adeste Fidelis."

As the years passed, silent groups of men and women used to assemble across the street to hear this lovely welcome to the Christ Child. Priests no less than their people would come and listen to the five minutes of beautiful song. The old bishop was believed to have come unobtrusively one year; and there were always non-Catholics in the throngs.

In the old parish of my New England our great and most important Mass was not at midnight, as I have said, but at five o'clock in the morning. The reason was part of our hard-won American acceptance. When our grandfathers and great-grandfathers came to this country as workmen in our factory city, they went into the cotton mills. The mill hours then were from six o'clock in the morning until six o'clock at night. Under Puritanism, Christmas was a working day. It was not until the 1850's that in Boston it became a day of ease.

So old Father Murphy, first resident priest of a parish and a church that are now the cathedral parish and church of a great diocese, set the single Christmas Mass at an hour the parishioners could attend—at five o'clock, before they hustled on to a dreary, unhallowed long day's work.

The tradition held fast among the descendants of those early Catholic settlers—doctors, lawyers, judges, priests, bishops, and an archbishop of my knowledge—so that somewhat in tribute to those who had gone before, the five o'clock Christmas Mass in the old parish was one of dignity and circumstance.

It was a solemn Mass with the massed parish choirs singing; and a long double train of altar boys, of which I was one, to add to the dignity of the three priests as they went in processional about the church before Mass. The church was crowded, but there was no nonsense about standing up in back because you could not find a seat. At the five o'clock Christmas Mass you came to pray. You stood prayerfully in your pew through all the verses of "Adeste Fidelis" at the close of Mass. And never did "Merry Christmas" ring out with more meaning through the crisp shining morning air than from the little knots of neighbors on the way home over the crisp snow.

It was a common thing then to seek to share in the privilege accorded the priests of saying three Masses. It was not only the old people who went to Five and the Nine and the Eleven. The teen-age Children of Mary were on hand to sing in their junior choir at the Nine and to supplement the senior choir at the last Mass at eleven, as they had at the solemn Mass at five.

Since every house was wakened by the cheerful return from the Five, it was then that the children leaped from bed to inspect their stockings. Christmas trees were held more or less in suspicion by both ourselves and our Yankee neighbors. The Boston Tea Party and Lexington and Concord were still too much in mind to favor a custom introduced in England by Victoria's Albert.

Our Christmas dinner was, of course, as American as our neighbors', a differing only perhaps in the form of the grace that was said to invoke God's blessing on it.

The day was a restful one of little movement save for those of us fortunate enough to have grandmothers. There were sometimes early afternoon visits to those mothers of our mothers and fathers, who were always especially precious at Christmas time. But the usual old parish visiting was done after Grand Vespers. Just before four o'clock, the same family groups that had hailed each other at Mass in the morning would set out for Grand Vespers and Benediction. For Vespers the children would always be taken along, to visit the crib.

For us children, those visits would continue until Epiphany, Little Christmas. But we did not simply continue to visit our own. Our mothers or aunts would take us in turn to the cathedral, to the French church, and the Portuguese and the Polish churches, where the crib was always a little different but always the same.

It was on those visits that our Catholicism embraced a truer Americanism than was possible to our Yankee friends, who stood apart from the newer aliens among them. For the Christ Child in the crib of the poor little Polish church held out his arms in the same embrace as in our own, and with the same message: *Glory to God in the highest; and on earth peace to men of good will.*

HELPING OUT—MY TWO WEEKS OF CHRISTMAS MASSES [38]

One morning I saw eighty-eight brides with their grooms lined up to be married—not surprising in India
By Alcantara Gracias, S.F.X.

December 23, 1975. The sun was not yet hot when I left the house. My destination: a mission station sixty miles away. It was my first missionary experience in this part of India, Ranchi. I was going there by bus to help the parish priest out at Christmas.

When I reached the bus stop, I was disappointed. The bus was packed to capacity, and there was still a line of about 50 people.

I learned that the next bus would not come until ten, which meant four hours of waiting. "Don't worry," the conductor said, "you can get into this bus." And I did, and so did another 30 passengers who lined up after me. When the conductor finally blew the whistle, 137 of us were packed in a bus meant for 46!

Once we started moving, I tried to settle myself. I was completely sandwiched, precariously standing on one leg, when the driver suddenly pressed the brakes hard.

The stop was to make place for more passengers! By the end of my journey five and a half hours later, the number was nearing 200, and I was on the roof of the bus, along with some 30 other passengers.

Outside the church, children were playing. As they saw me walking in, they greeted me in unison: "Praised be Jesus!" One of them, Munu, came out to greet me from the group and extended an emaciated hand, repeating the same greetings. I lifted her up in my arms.

Right after I had finished lunch, the parish priest, a devoted missionary for nearly fifty years, asked, "Will you join us, Father, in hearing confessions? Today our Christmas Mass starts at 2:00 P.M."

Christmas Mass on December 23? The priest explained that Noatoli parish is forty-two villages with a total population of 45,000 people. Of these 14,500 are Catholics, spread in a radius of fifteen miles. The missionary can tour all the villages only once or twice in a year, which means the people can attend Mass only once or twice a year, unless they walk the considerable distance to the church. So everyone could attend the Christmas Mass, he had the Christmas celebrations start a week before. Every day at 2:00 P.M. for seven days there was a Christmas Mass preceded by confessions and followed by dances to the rhythm of drums.

From the distant villages people came in groups, walking sometimes four hours or more. Like the shepherds of Bethlehem, they came to pay homage to their Savior. They came to offer Him not silver or gold, of which they had none, but something more: their hearts.

It was a moving scene: hundreds of them lining up for the Sacrament of Penance and the Eucharist, and though illiterate, singing beautifully in unison the praises of Someone who was born like them in utter destitution.

December 24, 1975. I visited several families in the morning, all of them poor. But however poor they were, their houses were immaculately clean.

As you enter the house, the host welcomes you by offering water and a towel to wash your hands. This must have been a very ancient custom dutifully preserved here. Didn't Christ himself once complain to his host: "I came to your house and

168

you didn't even bother to give me water to wash my feet."

In the evening, confessions. For six hours, until 11:30 P.M., four priests continually imparting God's pardon. Was it said that religion is the business of women? The thousands of devout men, beating their breasts, invoking God's mercy, and asking absolution from the priest, seemed to prove the contrary.

And then at last came the Christmas midnight Mass. By that time the crowd had exceeded the estimate of 6,000 people, men and women, young and old, mothers with their young, some tied to their backs. It was a magnificent manifestation of their love and faith in Jesus. Nothing could prevent them from coming for this festive occasion: neither fear of their houses being robbed (not unusual), nor the dangerous swim across the river. The chill was penetrating and the wind biting, and the people had just rags around their shoulders. It required tremendous sacrifice.

The church was too small to accommodate such a crowd, so the ceremony was held in the open air. There were no benches to sit on. The only light came from the stars, the moon, and a few lanterns. It was truly in the spirit of the first Christmas.

The way people participated in the Mass was especially edifying. And when the time came to kiss the Babe, every one of them threw a coin or two, a symbolic gesture of their love of Jesus. There came an old lady, stick in hand, bent by the weight of age. She could hardly walk and I went to help her to the crib.

As she bowed to kiss the infant Jesus, I felt drops of water falling on my hands—tears, her tears. I asked her why she was crying. "I had saved a few coins to give to Jesus, but have lost them on the way. I have nothing now left to give to Him except these grains of rice which I have kept aside before I prepared my meal here this evening." It was too much for me. Soon, I, too, felt tears on my cheeks.

December 29, 1975. Traditionally the people of this area consider Monday an auspicious day, and it is generally marked for weddings. Weddings here are not an individual but a collective affair. This morning at 6:30 when I saw eighty-eight brides lined up before me with their grooms I was not surprised.

One incident, however, made the occasion memorable. When I called out the name of the boy before me and asked him whether he would marry the girl standing next to him, the answer was No. I repeated the question, and quick came the same answer. Then I turned to the girl and she nervously shook her head. When confronted with the same question again, she burst into tears. The confusion was soon cleared up: the bride had been misplaced in the line.

These mass marriages are preceeded by an intensive three-week instruction. Boys and girls about to be married stay in two houses belonging to the parish. They are given religious instructions, and talks on the beauty of love and the problems of married life. The course closes with a three-day retreat ending on Christmas Day.

During my stay in Noatoli, I had made friends among the children. Munu, the first I met when I came to Noatoli, was my best friend. At a tender age, she had already tasted the bitterness of life. Her deep-sunken eyes and rickety body were the sure signs of undernourishment. Nevertheless, Munu was a child full of life: intelligent, playful.

I had a small gift for her: some chocolates, which she was very fond of, some pencils (she liked to draw), and a piece of cloth for a dress. But for the last two days I had seen no sign of her. In the evening I went to visit the sick people around the village, and as I was passing by Munu's house I called to her. I had brought the little gift packet with me. I imagined how she would come running out to me the moment she heard my voice. But no answer.

"Munu!" I called again. Then I saw Munu's mother coming out of her little hut, sobbing. I entered. Munu was there, motionless, cold. She had died a few hours before, a victim of dysentery.

Her parents, poor and illiterate, had not sensed the danger to Munu's life when the first symptoms had appeared three days earlier. Besides, there was no doctor in the neighborhood, and no medicine available.

Back in my room, I was haunted by Munu's picture now lying on the bare floor, covered with flowers. She was to me the symbol of the thousands of children dying every day all over the world—unwanted, uncared for, in utter destitution. We bury them with flowers, but in their lives they have known only thorns. Like Mary and Joseph, they have found no room to stay.

FIRST CHRISTMAS IN THE NEW WORLD [39]

It brought both disaster and joy to Christopher Columbus
By June A. Grimble

It was a languorous night of stars and setting moon, and it was Christmas Eve. Off the northern coast of the recently discovered island of Hispaniola, now Haiti, two vessels, the *Santa Maria* and *Nina,* made their way eastward.

Moonlight and shadow mingled in rippling mystery on the sea. The wind was barely strong enough to billow the canvas into a proud display of a green cross on a white field, flanked by the crowned initials *F* and *Y.* These were the initials of King Ferdinand and Queen Ysabella of Spain and the insignia of the first voyage of discovery to the New World, headed by history's most famous explorer, Christopher Columbus.

On the deck of the *Santa Maria,* fourteen-year-old Pedro blinked hard to keep his eyes open and to concentrate on the grains trickling through the sandglass. He was a "gromet," or cabin boy, and his job was to watch the sandglass and turn it every half hour. When he turned it, he took a deep breath which he let go in sound, if not song, that could be heard from end to end of the ship. By the words of his ditty the sailors could tell the time.

Now, it was eleven o'clock on the night of December 24, 1492, just one hour before Christmas. As the last grains settled in the base of the sandglass, Pedro turned it and rent the air with:

Seven has just fallen,
Eight is in the mill.
More time in sand will grind
If the Lord so will.
To our God above we pray
For a safe and good journey.

"Amen say I to that, boy!" said a voice behind him. "And may I not hear the clamor of your tongue again till dawn. I'll wager you could founder the walls of a dozen Jerichos!"

Pedro turned to the tall figure pacing the quarter deck. Penetrating blue eyes were scrutinizing him with something that suggested amusement. But Pedro was discomforted. He did not enjoy a very good conscience and could never make up his mind as to whether Christopher Columbus was teasing him or not.

The mass of white hair framing a long, lean face, the high cheek bones and aquiline nose, gave his admiral an air of great authority. He prayed so much that Pedro was convinced he must usually be engaged in lofty thought. Pedro fervently hoped that all that prayer did not give one the power of knowing what he had not seen. How he, Pedro, for example, would sometimes break the ship's strictest rule and snatch a turn at the great tiller. His burning ambition was to be a helmsman, but Columbus had expressly forbidden even the touching of the tiller by any boy, "in calm or storm."

"Don't look so frightened, boy," said Columbus, laughing. "I'm joking. That's what gromets are for: to make a rousing noise and pray vociferously over the sands of time. You, for one, could not be said to have missed your vocation."

"Yes—I mean No, Sir Captain," said Pedro dubiously, eyeing the tiller.

At that moment Juan de la Cosa, part owner of the *Santa Maria* and second in command to Columbus, arrived on the quarter deck to take over the night watch.

"Ah, there you are, Juan," said the admiral. "Good. I can go and bunk down now. Two days and a night without sleep leave a man weary. I can hardly keep my eyes open. At least, there should be no trouble tonight. The sea is as

172

motionless as a cup of water."

"That's right, sir," said Juan. "What's more, it is the first time during the entire voyage that we are covering charted waters. It was a good thought to send the ship's boat ahead to map our course along the coast. Bunk down while you may, Sir Captain. You're not likely to get a more propitious night for it. And for what better Christmas gift could a man ask than a good night's sleep?"

"Just one," murmured Columbus almost to himself, but with an intensity that was surprising. "Just one, Juan."

"And what is that, Sir Captain?" asked the ship's master.

"Gold, man, gold, so that our sovereigns may regain the Holy Sepulcher!"

"Well, there is still hope, Sir Captain," said Juan. "We are not done with discovering yet, and there is already evidence that this land we have found that looks like a terrestrial paradise will yield up gold."

"The Indians wear gold ornaments, Sir Captain," cried Pedro hopefully. "They must have got them somewhere."

"True enough, boy, but where? I tell you. I need a whole mine to yield enough to furnish an expedition to the Holy Land. I would willingly circle this world to find it for such a cause. May our Lord in his goodness guide me."

"But," he added, with a smile, "Christmas or no, that is a prayer that is hardly likely to be answered tonight. To your duties now, lads, and may God give you good eyes."

"And good rest to you, Sir Captain" called Juan after the retreating figure, "and may you dream of mines enough to furnish a thousand holy expeditions."

But the admiral did not hear him. He had reached his cabin and was already lost in meditation.

Gold was not the subject of his thoughts. He was remembering that it was Christmas. In his mind's ear he could hear the bells of Europe tolling, as was the custom of the time, a sonorous warning to the powers of darkness that the Prince of Light and Peace was about to make his entry into the world. He was remembering that at midnight they would burst into peals of jubilant chimes to welcome God incarnate as the Babe

173

of Bethlehem. Comforted by his brief meditation, Columbus gave thanks and fell asleep.

On the quarter deck, Juan de la Cosa was giving instructions to the helmsman to steer by a star and, surprisingly enough, ordering the man to wake him at the slightest change in wind or weather. Surprising, because Juan de la Cosa was responsible for the night watch and his duty was to keep sleepless vigil until 3:00 A.M.

It was only a very short time after the ship's master had retired that the grizzled helmsman kicked Pedro, who was nodding over the sandglass, and startled the boy into wakefulness. "Wake up, boy! Wake up, I say! If it's a helmsman you would be, come; I give you the tiller for a Christmas present. Steer by that star now, and if there is change in wind or weather, rouse me." And without more ado, the old seaman curled up on the floor and promptly went to sleep.

The first exhilaration of an independent turn at the great tiller was indeed like a Christmas treat to Pedro. His heart soared and he was happy.

But presently, straining his ears, and hearing nothing but the jarring of the rudder on its gudgeons, and all the creaking, slapping, rattling discord that wood and rope and canvas combine to produce in a calm, Pedro became apprehensive. He listened with all his might, but no murmur of human voices came to his ears, nor the familiar padding sound of bare feet on board. Nothing, in fact, that he could trace to human sources but the heavy snoring of the sleeping helmsman.

Apprehension turned into fear. Pedro's heart froze as the realization dawned that out of the forty men and boys aboard the ship, he alone was awake.

Desperately the boy looked seaward for assurance, and found none. Even the ghostly silhouette of the *Nina* had disappeared. Pedro tightened his grip on the tiller, and looked frantically towards the sandglass. There, at least, was some comfort. Only a little while now and the sands would be run out. Then he would launch into his midnight ditty. That surely would wake someone.

"I must stick it out," thought Pedro, "I must. If they think

I'm scared they'll laugh at me and never give me another chance at the tiller, maybe. There's not long to go now. God help me, what's *that?"*

Out of the night, a distant booming came to his ears, muffled but persistent, and seeming to draw nearer.

"It must be the wind," thought Pedro. "I can wake the helmsman. But no—the billowing of the sails has not changed. What can it be? If only that sand would run a little faster!"

The booming increased in volume, and Pedro began to feel a rising panic. As he clung to the great tiller, fear streamed in icy rivulets down his face, and his eyes became glued to the sandglass like those of a bird hypnotized by a snake.

At last, the grains settled in the base of the glass. Pedro snatched it up and took a deep breath for his song—the song announcing the first Christmas in the New World.

Even as he did so there was a crash, so resounding "that it might be heard a league off." The tiller shuddered and trembled under his grip as if caught in the strain of a mighty current, and the booming turned into the thunderous roaring of waves hurling themselves against the hull of a grounded ship.

It was no pious ditty then, that heralded the first Christmas in the New World, but a protracted, earsplitting yell, because as Columbus later recorded in his logbook, "the boy gave tongue." And he did mightily, fit to scare the wits out of the world.

Columbus was the first on deck, followed by Juan de la Cosa and every man and boy aboard. From then on it was a shouting of orders, yelling, and imprecations and labor the night through.

The *Santa Maria,* having sailed with impunity across the dreaded and uncharted "Sea of Darkness," as the Atlantic was then known, had in the languorous calm of a Christmas night of stars and setting moon, drifted to her destruction on a reef off the island of Hispaniola.

It was Pedro's first time at sea, and he had failed to recognize in the sound that had so troubled him a reverberant warning of the perils of a pounding surf on the coral reef.

Desperate efforts were made to save the flagship of the first voyage of discovery. Her mainmast was cut away, and precious stores were hurled overboard in a frenzied attempt to lighten her. The *Nina's* boat came alongside to help, but to no avail. The *Santa Maria* was driven high onto the reef, and, lying helplessly athwart the seas, was mercilessly pounded on the jagged coral by the heavy swell surging in from seaward until her seams burst and water poured into her hull.

There was nothing to be done but to abandon ship and stand by until dawn watching helplessly from the decks of the *Nina.*

As the sun rose on Christmas day Columbus sent two men ashore for help.

The people of the island of Hispaniola were Taino Indians. "A handsome people," wrote Columbus, "all of good stature," who painted their faces and their bodies red or white and gathered their coarse hair "into a hank behind that they wear long and never cut."

For all their warlike appearance, the Tainos were the gentlest of people. Their cardinal precept was the rule of charity. They were, wrote Columbus, "so free with all they have that no one would believe it who has not seen it." The man who dominated all of the northwestern region of Hispaniola at that time was one Guacanagari, "and that kind," said Columbus, "was virtuous above all."

He sent every canoe he had and "all the people of the town" to help the admiral that calamitous Christmas day. From dawn to dusk, Spaniards and Indians labored to discharge what remained of the ship's cargo and save what could be saved.

Guacanagari gave over two large houses to the Spaniards, with the promise of more if necessary. From time to time he sent his relatives to the admiral aboard the *Nina,* begging him "not to be troubled or annoyed" and assuring him "that he would give him *all he had.*"

The work done, Guacanagari went himself to the admiral. He found him as his brothers had reported, quite inconsolable for the loss of the *Santa Maria* and bitterly lamenting the insubordination that had brought her to such an inglorious end. No gold, and now no ship. The Spanish sovereigns would not be pleased.

Guacanagari stood wretchedly by with a great longing in his

heart to be able to comfort the admiral, when suddenly he was distracted by a sound he had never heard before. Quickly he turned and his eyes grew big with wonder at the sight of a thing he had never seen before.

Over the side of the *Nina* the Spanish sailors were waving at a group of Tainos in a canoe something that seemed to Guacanagari to be "solid sound." The Indians were gesticulating and shouting excitedly.

"Chuque Chuque!" they cried, trying to imitate the noise dangling from the sailors' hands.

So eager were they to possess it, they tore gold ornaments from their ears and necks and noses and threw them to the Spaniards, who pocketed them, and from a fast diminishing store flung back jingling hawk bells.

Guacanagari watched in silence as long as he could. Then, seeing the supply of bells rapidly dwindling, he could contain himself no longer. He turned to Columbus, and with excited gestures indicated that for just one bell he would give the admiral "four pieces of gold as big as his hand."

Dumbfounded, Columbus stared at Guacanagari's outstretched palm and then looked searchingly into the Indian's face. He questioned Guacanagari eagerly. By signs, the Taino king informed him that there was a place at hand where gold could be had in abundance.

And his heart was happy because the admiral was suddenly merry. He did not know that in his outstretched palm Columbus saw Jerusalem conquered.

Columbus wrote later of that first Christmas in the New World and the wreck of the *Santa Maria*, "So many things came to hand that in truth it was no disaster but great luck for it is certain that if I had not run aground I should have kept to sea without anchoring in this place."

Pedro's inexperience had, indeed, far-reaching results. It was on the Island of Hispaniola that the first settlement in the New World took place. A fortress was built with the wreckage of the *Santa Maria* at the admiral's orders and named *La Navidad* in honor of the Babe of Bethlehem, in remembrance of the day that witnessed history's most memorable shipwreck and the first Christmas in the New World.

MEXICAN MAGI [40]

A celebration of Christ's Epiphany
By Martha Murray

We were awakened at 7:30 A.M. by our host, Alejandro
Rangel Hidalgo. The old hacienda in Colima, Mexico, was a
bit damp and chilly, but the sun was beginning to shine brightly.
It looked as though we were to have a fine day for the
celebration of the *fiesta* of the Three Kings.

The feast of the Three Kings, or Epiphany, is January 6. On
that day, throughout Spain and Latin America, gifts are given
the children in memory of the gifts the Magi took to the Baby
Jesus.

The day was to start off with a special Mass in the private
chapel of the hacienda. My husband, John Creighton Murray,
the concert violinist, had offered to play; and he began to tune
his Stradivarius.

At table the night before, we had discussed the coming *fiesta*.
It was the custom to give a party for the ranch hands on
Epiphany. This year, it was to be a bazaar, with food and game
booths. The grownups were to buy the wares, and the proceeds
would go toward building a new seminary in Colima. The
children would receive everything free.

Father Conuto Barreto, who would celebrate Mass the
following day, was having supper with us. He told us that some
of the ranch children would receive First Communion at the
Mass. That was when John offered to play during Communion.

After supper, we looked at the decorations that Alejandro
Rangel Hidalgo had made for the party. For more than two
weeks, he had worked painstakingly planning and executing
the decorations.

He had hollowed out eggs, and painted some with designs.
Others he painted as clowns with cardboard hats, as peasants,
as devils, and as Chinese with long, braided, woolen pigtails.
The eggs were filled with little candies.

Hundreds of tissue paper flags had been pasted to bamboo
sticks. Each flag had a daisy painted on it. The daisy is called

Margarita in Mexico, and Alejandro's fiancee is named
Margarita. There were paper decorations in fanciful designs,
and hundreds of hand-painted paper bags had been filled with
goodies. Everything was ready and waiting for eager children's
hands.

We entered the chapel at eight o'clock. It was already filled.
The subtropical sun shone on the whitewashed walls. In the
center of the altar was an ancient image of the Christ Child.
At one side was a delicate Italian-marble statue of the Blessed
Virgin.

The little ones, dressed in white, were at the front of the
church. The girls wore white veils and looked much like
miniatures of the Virgins that Rangel Hidalgo paints. All were
clasping white decorated tapers and were looking at the altar
out of solemn brown eyes.

Father Barreto vested in view of the congregation while a
villager, who had at one time studied for the priesthood,
explained the significance of each vestment. Then he explained
the Mass as it proceeded. Father Barreto knows that instruction
must be constantly given to his people. That is one of the
reasons why, in spite of persecutions, the Church in Mexico is
stronger than ever.

Father Barreto's sermon was on the birth of Christ and the
visit of the Three Kings. He ended by telling the congregation
that, like one of the kings, a visitor had come from afar to lay
a gift at the feet of the Baby Jesus: his music.

John began to play from behind the altar. The little ones
received their First Communion, and then the people walked
up to receive. The beauty of the Mass, the absolute faith of
the people, and the splendid music made this the most moving
ceremony I had ever attended.

After breakfast, we heard the shrill and perfectly pitched
voices of Indian men singing. The house staff rushed outside
to see the singers, and we followed close behind. A procession
of brightly clad Indians carrying a small image of Jesus were
making their way down the dirt road to the chapel.

They were marching two by two. One side was dressed in
bright-blue-satin cavalier costumes of the seventeenth century.

The other line wore identical costumes of pink satin. Each Indian wore a straw sombrero that had been completely covered with pink and blue roses and little tin ornaments that tinkled merrily.

Bringing up the rear of the procession was a rowdy little group of dancers clad to represent a rancher, a friar, and several devils. All of them wore masks, and the devils carried whips with which they menaced the laughing and cowering crowd.

When they entered the chapel, those dressed in pink and blue sang their respects to the Babe at the altar. The devils gave each other playful slaps, and the rancher tried to feed the friar a tortilla through his mask. The dance is an old custom in this region, and is called *Los Pastores* (the Shepherds).

After the pink-and-blue group had finished their song and each one had knelt at the altar, they trouped out and walked back on the dirt road. The devils still cavorted behind, and their red satin and sequined costumes gleamed wickedly in the sun. Just before they rounded the corner and were out of sight, the rancher grabbed the friar, and the pair did a weird, satirical, jitterbug jig. They were a devout yet strangely grotesque group.

The *fiesta* was going to be held in the courtyard of the hacienda. The hacienda was once a sugar cane plantation, but since much of the land was expropriated the Rangel Hidalgos had planted lime trees. On one side of the courtyard is the chapel and a high, thick wall with an enormous entrance gate. Two other sides are pink and white outbuildings for the packing of lemons. On the last side is another wall, with an iron-grilled gate that leads to the hacienda patio, which is filled with tropical plants and flowers. The house, with wide veranda, pillars and arches, encloses the patio.

All afternoon, men hammered on booth frameworks. Others climbed ladders, crisscrossing the courtyard with strings of electric-lighted paper lanterns. Streamers were hung between the lanterns. The stalls were faced with palm leaves.

I went over to talk to Alejandro as he decorated the tamale booth. As he placed artificial flowers, gaily painted leaves, and paper flags, he spoke of his role as one of the owners of the ranch.

"My father and my brother Xavier take care of the work and the workers here. My brother, Juan, as you know, is an architect. He enlarged the chapel. I take care of the people's welfare and social needs."

I wondered what he meant by that.

"Did you not see the white building outside the wall? Well, it is a school. We now have a school here. This annual *fiesta* is also a part of my job. I pay for it out of the money I make from my paintings.

"Then, we instruct the people in hygiene. I see to it that we have a supply of medicine, and when someone is seriously ill, I send for a doctor or get the patient to the hospital."

"On special days, I bring a priest here to say Mass. Sometimes, priests from the city come for a vacation and rest. They want to say Mass every day; thus, sometimes we have Mass each morning for a month or two."

"My next project is to build small, model homes for the ranch hands. We have 100 people living here. I will need quite a sum to build these homes."

I marveled. Here was a family that had trained its sons to care for both the physical and spiritual well-being of the people. I began to understand why Alejandro, young as he is, has such a serene countenance and why his art seems to capture such a profound religious spirit.

At seven that night, we were ready. The lights were turned on, and the courtyard became a wonderland. The little ones' eyes gleamed and their mouths gaped.

Sparklers were given to all the children; as they ran, they filled the yard with little stars. Girls in gypsy costumes mingled with the crowd. Flower girls sold boutonnieres. Two mock policewomen with rifles took the rowdy off to jail, where freedom could be bought for a small fine. Alejandro had designed the gypsy, flower-girl, and police-girl costumes.

Lines formed at all the booths. I noticed that the children were turning in paper tickets for steaming tamales and other Mexican delicacies. Father Barreto told me that the children had received the tickets each time they had attended catechism class. Every child had a handful.

181

The *pastores,* or shepherds in all their regalia, marched into a small corral at one end of the courtyard. Here they put on a fine burlesque of a bull fight. Those in pink and blue watched with stolid calm. One of the devils, with swirled horns, stamped his feet, snorted, and charged furiously at the rancher and friar.

The rancher took a ridiculously small lace handkerchief from his pocket and made awkward passes at the bull, while the friar was butted out of the bull's way every now and then. The white-trousered men and their wives, some with babies in their arms, crowded up to see the fun. Finally, another devil leaped onto the rancher's back, and they galloped out of the corral. The *pastores* broke up, and made their way toward the food booths.

As I was watching two little boys do a take-off on the bull fight, I felt a timid tap on my arm. One of the blue-clad *pastores* removed his hat, and said, *"Señora,* you understand Spanish, do you not?"

"Yes *Señor,* I do."

"Señora, you see, there is a problem. Two young girls have journeyed here from another town. They came all this way because they had heard of your husband, and thought that he would play. Now it is almost time for them to take the last bus back home. They study the violin. Do you think, señora, that it would be possible for your husband to play a small piece? Only one? Just for them? It would mean so much to them."

The two young girls came up. Both were wearing fresh cotton dresses. Their black hair was neatly braided into a crown over their heads.

They followed John through the grilled gate to the hacienda veranda. Soon others came, and John never played to a more appreciative audience.

Earlier that day, Alejandro had made a rock terrace by the chapel. The image of the Christ Child was set on one of the levels. Now, three young men, dressed as the Magi in gorgeous robes designed by Alejandro, came up. The three stood, each on a different level, around the Child.

The people gathered near the chapel. Lights were turned off in the courtyard, and onto the tableau. Gasps of delight escaped the crowd.

"They are not real, are they?" whispered one young girl.

"What do you think?" said her companion. "That's Pedro up there in the green."

"Who would have thought it. Isn't it beautiful?"

A little child tugged at her mother's skirts, and said, "Are they saints?"

"Hush, they are the Three Kings."

The lights were turned off, and the people went home under a starry sky. Artists, Indians, peasants, townspeople, and a priest had mingled to thank God for the great gift of his Son.

MY CHRISTMAS IN ROME [41]

Seminarians at the North American College share in the traditions of the Eternal City
By Francis R. Moeslein

At four o'clock this Christmas morning—while Dasher and Prancer are transporting a thoroughly played out Santa Claus back to the North Pole, and while ma and pa are still engrossed in their long winter's nap—I and my fellow students at the North American College in Rome will be walking along the curving banks of the Tiber. The ancient, cobblestone streets will still be wet with the evening's rain, and a chilling, spongy breeze off the river will make us pull our capes closer.

When we reach the Circus Maximus, we will leave the Tiber and climb up to the Church of St. Anastasia on the slope of the Palatine hill. There, gathered around the high altar, we will hear the opening words of the daybreak Mass: "A light shall shine upon us this day, for our Lord is born to us; and He shall be called . . . the Prince of Peace."

Christmas comes to the Eternal City as quietly and as simply as that. There is no razzle-dazzle sales campaign to precede

Christmas; no daily reminder of just how many shopping days remain; no frantic, last-minute search for gifts. Romans simply cannot afford presents for all their relatives and friends. Most Romans can't even count all their relatives.

The ancient traditions of Rome are still alive; they focus attention on the essential message, the "glad tidings" that Christmas proclaims to all men who will listen. One such tradition reserves the gifts for the children, and the giving of gifts for Epiphany. Another makes Christmas Eve in a Roman seminary a day of recollection, a kind of one-day retreat designed to capture the real spirit of Christmas.

Roman seminarians, no less than American children, must hurry off to bed as soon as supper is over on Christmas Eve, but at eleven o'clock, when visions of sugar plums are just beginning to take shape in wee little heads, we seminarians awake to the sound of carols.

Our caroling is quite as practical as it is enjoyable, for it helps to shake the sleepy rumbles out of the voices of the second basses. At midnight the choir is in the loft, tuned up, and ready to present its offering to the newborn Babe as Christ comes to each of us even more humbly than He did on another winter's night nearly 2,000 years ago.

When the last notes of the *Ite Missa Est* have been swallowed up in the rafters, we head for the recreation room and cocoa and cookies. Sugar plums are all very well for children's dreams, but it is more fun to munch on reality, especially if the reality is *panettone*, the Italian version of fruitcake.

Then it's back to bed again for a nap that lasts about as long as an afternoon's siesta. At 3:30 A.M. we rise for the walk to St. Anastasia's.

The church was erected in the fifth century and dedicated to the Roman maiden who offered her life for the faith during the persecution of Diocletian. Since Anastasia entered heaven on Christmas Day, the Popes of the Middle Ages developed the custom of celebrating their second Mass in her church.

The daybreak Mass will be just that. As the choir sings the last phrases of *Stille Nacht*, the first rays of dawn will appear in the eastern sky. And while the sun is yet bobbing over the rim of the Colosseum, we will be short-cutting through the Forum on our way to Santa Maria Maggiore on the Esquiline hill.

St. Mary Major is well named: it is Rome's largest and most important church dedicated to the Blessed Virgin. The first church to be built on the Esquiline was erected in 342, just thirty years after Constantine's decree made it possible for the Christians to bring their worship out of the catacombs.

"A Child is born to us, and a Son is given to us, . . . and his name shall be called the Angel of Great Counsel." With these words begins the third Mass of Christmas. Those who are fortunate enough to be in Rome during the holy season can kneel in St. Mary's before the altar which contains a fragment of the crib in which the Child was laid.

Our Christmas joy is not entirely spiritual. We can look forward to our dinner, turkey and all the trimmings, even cranberry sauce, and a two-hour program of Christmas music presented by the Chorale.

The experience that remains longest in the memory is the one that comes at noon. The great bells of St. Peter's basilica ring out the joyous tidings, calling thousands and thousands of Christians into the embrace of the encircling arms of the huge colonnades. And then a tiny white figure appears on a balcony high above the piazza to raise his hand once again in blessing.

That is ever the highlight of our reliving of a story that began nearly 2,000 years ago, when from this same Eternal City a decree went forth from Caesar Augustus that the whole world should be enrolled, and a second decree went forth from heaven that the whole world should be redeemed.

HOLY NIGHT 42

Why did those Lord of Heaven people hold a winter festival?
By James E. Walsh

Cold, cold. The young Chinese woman stood up from her rickety stool and stamped her feet on the pavement. She pulled her padded jacket together and, using her sleeves as a muff, thrust her hands inside them. *Ai ya!* It was only a few days past the Winter Solstice, and here it was really cold already! What would the Slight Cold be like, then, that was so soon to come? And as for the Great Cold, it was better not to think about it.

She looked down at her stall: a little tray on stilts, with tiny compartments to hold her few little wares. She sold buttons mostly—when she sold anything. There were some pieces of ribbon, papers of pins, and other knickknacks. All day long sitting and standing there, and she had sold hardly a thing.

The young woman did not show her discouragement. Nor did she really feel it very deeply. Cold weather and few sales were accustomed difficulties to her. Her ruddy, moon-round face was serene and matter-of-fact.

"Well, you've got to expect some cold weather in December," she told herself. "I've often seen it worse than this. And it's a good time to sell the pickled Fukien olives, maybe. Yes, with business bad like this, I think I had better try it again tonight. Maybe Great Favor will get tired and fall asleep on me. Still, if he does, I can pick him up and go home again. That's the way it has to be, anyhow. Can't leave him there alone."

"It's good he is so sturdy and strong. I'm surprised that he doesn't mind the cold more. Of course, so far I've got him wrapped up pretty well. And when the Great Cold comes I can make another little suit for him out of my jacket, maybe, and just put it on top of the one he has. Yes, that will help. And I don't really need it so much."

"Ma!" said a voice, not very loud, a few feet away. It came from the other side of a big wooden pillar that jutted out a few feet from a shop front. She bent forward a trifle and turned her face slightly as if to peep around the pillar. Then she suddenly withdrew her face, with a faint smile.

A little face suddenly showed half of itself around the edge of the pillar, gave a slow smile, and then drew back again very much as she had done. It was the face of a year-and-a-half-old boy with chubby cheeks and big round eyes. She repeated her performance and so did the little boy, first one peeping and then the other.

She left her stall and stepped around the pillar. The little boy was standing on the top of a small wooden chest, part of a shoe-repair stand spread out on the sidewalk. A rough-looking old man, sitting with his back to the wall, had a shoe fixed on a last in front of him. He was plying a big needle.

"Old Uncle!" the young woman said. "He is bothering you. He will break something. How did he get up there?"

"No bother, Mrs. Yeh," the old man said. "He can't hurt that box. And I have an eye in the back of my head to see that he doesn't fall off and hurt himself."

She laughed. "I believe you have, Old Uncle," she said. "I just don't want him to get in your way too much."

She glanced around her at the people moving about on the street. A good many pedestrians, mostly women, were going up the street in the same direction. That seemed just a trifle odd, as the street was largely residential; it was not usually crowded around five o'clock on cold winter evenings. But she felt no particular interest; the passers-by did not look as if they wished to buy any buttons.

"I think I will pack up and go home now," she resumed. "I've hardly sold a thing all day."

The old cobbler put his needle down. "Well, that's too bad, Mrs. Yeh," he said, shaking his head. "Yes, of course, it's that way sometimes. Tomorrow it will be better, maybe." He paused. "Why not wait a little longer, Mrs. Yeh?" he added. "There's still a lot of people going and coming this evening. More than usual. You still might sell something."

"Well, I noticed that, too," she replied. "Where are those people going, I wonder? Some meeting, maybe."

"Why, they are going to that church up the street there,"

said the old man. "Those women with the flowers and things, anyhow. That is where they always go. They are Lord of Heaven people." They often go past here in the morning, and sometimes in the evening. Today is their winter festival. Or tomorrow, maybe. Holy Birthday, they call it. All over town it's like that. Those Christians, that is. A big celebration. Didn't you know that?"

"Is that what it is? Oh, I often heard about that. But I never knew any Lord of Heaven people. What do they do?"

"Well, they give presents. And wear their best clothes. And do things like that. But those people going to that church: that's to have some kind of party. It's very late at night. Men and women together. Lots of children. There's noise, music, and singing. And eating."

The old man picked up his needle. Then he thought of a way to add to his description.

"Why, it's just like honoring the Kitchen God," he went on. "The way it is at our Winter Solstice festival, you know, Mrs. Yeh. I don't know whether they write something, or say something, or what. But they do something religious. And then they have something to eat. Yes, it's about the same thing."

She nodded, and politely said "Well!" several times as she listened. She was not greatly interested. The passers-by on the street had thinned out; nobody had stopped to price any of her wares. She stooped suddenly, and scooped up the little boy in a strong right arm.

"The Kitchen God celebration is nice when there's a big family," she said. "And when you have money. Many a time— well, it's getting late. I'm going home. After supper I may come out again, and try a little peddling. See you tomorrow, Old Uncle."

She put the little boy down again and dismantled her stall. In a jiffy she had strung her tray of wares on one end of a little bamboo pole, balancing it by hanging the stand and her stool on the other end.

"Cold, not cold?" she asked, looking down at the little boy.

"Not cold," he said.

She stooped, put the bamboo pole over her shoulder, and straightened up her load. Then, taking the child's hand in her free hand, she shuffled off down the street.

She was of two minds for a while about making another venture that evening. The spot she called home, a small single room for which she paid three dollars a month rent, was not cozy. But cooking supper on the little coal stove brought just a suspicion of heat into the dingy place and made it seem comparatively cheerful. She and the child sat near the stove to eat their hot congee. It warmed them. After an hour the few briquettes she had used were ashes. Another hour saw dishes washed and everything put to rights. It was time to go to bed to get warm, or to go out on the street. But Great Favor, in the snug little suit of thick black wool which she had knitted for him, did not seem either cold or sleepy; he kept bouncing around, as full of life as if the day were just beginning.

He won't be much bother, she thought. And I shan't need to go very far. Over to Rich Prosperity St. and around that area a little, maybe.

"Great Favor tired, not tired?" she asked.

"Not," the boy answered promptly, jumping up and down.

"Does Great Favor want to go out the door with ma?"

"Want."

She reached under the bed and pulled out two small covered baskets, each full of pickled Fukien olives that people liked as a relish with an evening snack of noodles or congee. One basket would be more than enough, she thought. Still, why not take both? That way there was a better balance.

She got out her bamboo pole again, strung the two baskets on it, one on each end, and put the load on her shoulders. She took Great Favor by the hand. They went out to walk the chilly, dimly lit, semideserted streets.

"Fukien olives!" her cry went out as they trudged along. "Selling pickled Fukien olives!"

They had not walked a block when a little pigtailed girl suddenly burst out of a side door next to a closed shop front. She had a small bowl in her hands. "Olives," she said, "I want two ounces. How much?"

189

Mrs. Yeh weighed two ounces on the little scales she carried in one of her baskets. "Six cents," she said.

"All right," said the little girl. She handed over the money, took the olives in her bowl, and vanished.

Well, it's not much, but it's a quick sale, Mrs. Yeh thought. Maybe business will be pretty good tonight.

Great Favor was a toddler rather than a walker; Mrs. Yeh walked very slowly to accommodate herself to his pace. It took them almost a half hour to walk the cross-town blocks leading to Rich Prosperity St. When they reached the juncture she made the boy sit down on the curbstone for a few minutes, because she knew he was getting tircd; and she dropped her baskets and sat down with him. There had been no more sales.

But it ought to be better on Rich Prosperity St., she reflected. And then we can cross over and come back on Tranquil Peace Road.

When they stood up, she made the child climb on her back and put his arms around her neck.

There were some other hawkers about: a few old men selling shelled peanuts and a few old women selling oranges, some of them walking, others crouched in corners. But there seemed to be little trade. She walked and walked, and nothing happened.

She saw, with some surprise, that she had reached the Little Dragon Gate Park, the juncture where she had intended to strike off cross-town again. "My goodness," she thought, "did we come that far already? It must be late."

She unslung Great Favor and her two baskets from her shoulders and sat down on the curbstone again hugging the little boy to her side.

"Cold, not cold, Great Favor?"

"Not cold."

"It just isn't my day," she thought. "Why, it's exactly like this morning—one little sale. Well, let's go home."

Lights. Chatter. Bustle. A big open gate with some little knots of people passing in, coming out, clustering in front of it. All women and children, apparently. What could that be? She was already close to home, slogging along under her double load with head down, when she suddenly became aware of an animated scene down the block. She knew exactly where she was. Three blocks more and she and the little boy would be home.

Seeing the lights and the people, her hawker's call went out on the air instinctively. "Selling olives! Selling pickled Fukien olives!" She felt little hope. Whatever was going on there, it was now pretty late for people to be doing any eating.

Then her memory stirred. "Why it's that little church," she thought. "The one Old Uncle was talking about. And he said they had some kind of party late at night, didn't he? That must be it."

"Selling olives! Selling pickled Fukien olives!"

She had scarcely got the words out of her mouth for the second time when two women came tripping toward her, both with aprons tied around them.

"You have olives? Fukien olives?" The two women were both talking at once. "What's the price? How many have you got? Are they pickled olives? The price is high. Two baskets full!"

"Well, they don't look very musty. Yes, they might be all right. Well, it doesn't matter about a little more or less—no need to talk price."

"That's a nice little boy. Well, come along with them and we will take the lot. Yes, all of them. Right in here. No, don't put them down—just bring them right into the kitchen."

Great Favor slid off her back, and they walked into the church compound, the two women leading the way and still chattering. "Well, wasn't that lucky? There's not a shop open anywhere now—and it's just the thing for the congee! Well, wouldn't you think Father Ling would take another look? And that old sacristan always forgets everything!"

They skirted the church and went to a smaller building directly behind it. There they entered a narrow passageway, pushed open a small door at the end, and plunged into a big, warm, brilliantly lighted kitchen, where five women were fluttering around two gas stoves and a big table full of dishes.

"We found some olives, Mrs. Lee," announced one of the

191

women.

An elderly woman of Junoesque appearance helped to ease the baskets of olives to the floor. Her face was mild and pleasant. She did not even glance at the olives. She looked at the young woman who had brought them. Then she gave Great Favor a good scrutiny.

"Is he your child?" she asked. "It's late for him, isn't it?"

"Yes, it's very late. I hardly ever bring him out like this. But when business is bad . . . ."

"Oh, the money! Wait and I will get it for you. Sit a minute. You must be tired."

Mrs. Lee spoke a word to one of the women who had bargained for the olives. Then she picked up a handbag from the table and took out a roll of bills. She counted out the money and tendered it to Mrs. Yeh with an openhanded gesture, more or less as if glad to see the last of it. Young Mrs. Yeh received the wad of bills with her two hands. She had not handled that much money in a long time. Well! It had been a good idea to venture out this evening, after all.

Just as she stood up to go, one of the women walked over from the stove with two bowls of hot rice congee in her hands. "Maybe you could eat this," she said. "And here is one for the little boy. It's cold tonight. And this will do you good. We don't eat until later on."

"Oh, it's late. I haven't got time. I must be—what time is it, please?"

"It's a quarter after eleven," Mrs. Lee said, looking at her watch. "Eat a bowl before —."

"What? After eleven? Oh, he will fall asleep on me! It's too late! I must hurry! I didn't know!"

Mrs. Lee smiled. "Wait until he eats one, anyhow," she said, motioning toward Great Favor, who was already eating away. "It won't take long. Where is your home, may I ask? Have you far to go?"

"Not far. I live in Supreme Harmony alley. You know it, maybe—a few blocks down, that's all. Only, it's so late."

"Why, that's very near. But maybe your family will be worried."

"I haven't got any family, I came from Ningpo. And I got married here. And my husband died last year. And his family belongs in Wuhu. So there's just myself and the child."

"Oh! Is that the way it is?" Mrs. Lee nodded. She looked again at Mrs. Yeh, who had now started on her bowl of congee simply out of politeness. She also took another good look at Great Favor.

"Listen," she said. "If you live that close, why don't you just stay here a while? You and the little boy. We are going to have a party for the children pretty soon. We are getting ready now. And you are a neighbor. So we would be glad —."

"Oh, he's too sleepy!"

Mrs. Lee smiled. "Lots of the children fall asleep before it's over," she said. "And some are asleep now. Inside, in the assembly room where we are going to have the party, you know. My own two small ones are in there."

"It's a bother, but we like to bring them because tonight is Holy Birthday. That's the best time of all the year for us Lord of Heaven people. So we go to church and have Mass, and we say prayers and have singing. And then we have a little party for the children. Just something to eat. And some prizes and presents, maybe. It doesn't take long."

Mrs. Yeh was mystified by much of what she heard. But the children's party might be nice, she thought. Great Favor had never been to one. Time seemed less important, too, after the relief of receiving the good sum of money. The kitchen was warm and cozy. And the attitude of the women around her, especially that of Mrs. Lee, added a certain warmth of its own. She had never before met people so full of friendliness at first sight.

"Well, if I had some place to put him," she said, "it might be —."

"Let's take him in with the others," Mrs. Lee said. She pushed Mrs. Yeh and Great Favor into the passageway, opened another door, and led them into a bigger room blazing with lights. The room was full of women and children.

"This is where we have the party," Mrs. Lee said.

A dozen tots and babies were asleep on settees and on thick

quilts on the floor, while a dozen more small children were scattered about the room, some romping, some just sitting, and very nearly all, it seemed, prattling and shouting.

A few women and some little girls were bustling about. The room was not nearly as warm as the kitchen. But Mrs. Lee promptly got an extra quilt, and spread it on the floor, placing it near a small coal stove at the end of the room. Great Favor was installed in the improvised bed. He was asleep almost by the time one end of the quilt had been folded over him.

Mrs. Yeh hesitated for a moment when the time came to wake him to go into the church with the others. But he would have to be awakened soon for the party in any case. And it was nice to have a child of your own when so many of the others were taking one, and some even two or three. Mrs. Lee woke up her own two little boys. And Mrs. Lee had invited her to go into the church with the rest and see what it was like, so she thought it was good to stay close to her and follow her example.

She picked up the sleepy Great Favor and carried him in her arms, feeling a little hesitant and bewildered still, but also a little proud. He was as fine-looking a little fellow as any of them had, she felt.

> *Silent night, holy night . . .*
> *Songs of angels fill the air . . .*
> *Strains of heavenly peace.*

What were they singing? The words were Chinese, all right, but she could not make head or tail of such a jumble. Something about "holy night," it seemed; she caught that expression repeated over and over.

She watched the little procession that wound slowly across the space before the altar. She could see it plainly from the front pew where she sat beside the friendly Mrs. Lee. Men, women, and children were packed together everywhere. Many of them stood in the aisles. And not all of them wore good clothes, she noted with a little relief. Many were dressed as poorly as she.

The procession took only a minute or two to pass. A half-dozen small altar boys marched at its head, and a half-dozen more brought up its tail. In the very middle of it came four very small boys balancing a small litter with a life-sized replica of a newborn infant lying on it. The infant, with arms outstretched, looked realistic and appealing.

Two larger altar boys, the tallest in the whole group, walked beside the litter, one on either side of it, and put out a hand to steady it now and again.

The wobbling procession crossed the front space to the opposite corner. It was dark there; but some extra light suddenly spotlighted the corner nook which had been fitted out to resemble the interior of a cave. Inside the cave a scene of life in a poor family was crudely represented. A small statue of a bearded old man was at one side. A little wooden box, open and filled with rough straw, occupied the central space. In front of it squatted a tiny plaster lamb. Above it, pinned somehow to the cave ceiling, hovered two small paper angels.

The procession halted. Then, by precarious juggling, the figure of the infant was taken off the litter by two of the altar boys and placed upon the straw in the box.

Silent night, holy night. The strains went on to the accompaniment of a small harmonium. Some singers stood around the harmonium in the rear part of the church, but the whole congregation seemed to join in the singing. The little hymn evidently was familiar to all. It was beginning to seem a little familiar, by force of repetition, to Mrs. Yeh, and to sound soothing and pleasant in her ears, when it suddenly ceased.

Mrs. Lee leaned over and whispered to her. "It's the birth of the Saviour of the world," she said, "come down from heaven. And that's his Mother standing there."

She nodded, and said nothing. "Well, I wonder what that means," she thought. "Holy night? Maybe that child is just born—yes, that must be it. There's something pretty about it in a way, really. What kind of a family is that? Poor maybe."

She understood even less, indeed nothing whatever, of the low Mass that followed. Almost everybody in the packed little church struggled up to the sanctuary rail for Communion. It was almost 1:00 A.M. when she and Great Favor found themselves back in the assembly room where the party was to be.

Most of the congregation promptly went home. The party

was for children particularly, though not exclusively. Those who stayed for it were the children themselves, and a flock of women and girls, who had undertaken to look after them. When all these had crammed themselves into the assembly room, the congestion appalled the only two men who ventured into it, one of them being Mr. Lee, the husband of Mrs. Lee, and the other being Father Ling, the pastor, who had celebrated the Mass.

Mr. Lee was an elderly, fat, sleepy-looking man dressed like a businessman. After one look around, he wished happy returns of the day to all and hastily withdrew. Father Ling was squeezed into one of the few chairs available. He apparently felt obliged to carry on awhile, although he looked sleepy.

Nobody else seemed to mind the congestion. Most of the children squatted on the floor. The party began at once. Amid a babble of chattering and laughing and shrieking, of pushing and squeezing, everybody was served a steaming bowl of congee and a procelain spoon with which to eat it—or, in some cases, a bowl of noodles with chopsticks. All the food was liberally sprinkled with the Fukien olives, now minced into small slivers, which had been purchased from Mrs. Yeh. Mrs. Yeh herself was glad to see that, and to hear a little chorus of complimentary remarks about them.

Each child also got a handful of small cakes and candies and two mandarin oranges. Most of them put this little store into their pockets. As Great Favor had no pockets, Mr. Yeh put his handful into her own jacket pocket for him.

Great Favor was not a bit sleepy any more. He ate his bowl of congee quickly and with relish. He was restless, even excited.

The distribution of presents was in grab-bag style. The children filed up to a big table where mysterious packages were spread out: some very small, some medium-sized, some quite large, all neatly wrapped in fancy paper and tied with ribbon. Some of the smaller children reached up and took two or three or four packages with one swoop of both hands, whereupon a lynx-eyed lady took the extra loot away. Some very small ones could not decide what to take, but just stood and looked, where-upon the same lady selected something from the table for each of them.

The smaller children usually took the large packages. The older children almost invariably preferred the small ones. They knew that the large ones usually had nothing much in them, paper flowers or a big cardboard picture, maybe, useless things like that, whereas a small package might contain a shuttlecock, marbles, a top, knife, or even a fountain pen. Yet there was nothing certain, either. Sometimes a large package disclosed something pretty good.

Great Favor was pushed forward in his turn by Mrs. Lee. And Mrs. Lee now had three sons in tow; her two small boys had been reinforced by another larger one. He had been among the altar boys who carried the infant in the procession. He was six years old and was called World Treasure. The three little Lee boys and Great Favor filed along together, and got their presents.

Great Favor took the first package he saw, a medium-sized one, opened it at once, and took out a little pair of mittens. His mother was glad to see the mittens, but Great Favor showed no enthusiasm. He just held them in his hand and looked around to see what the other packages were disclosing.

Excited Oh's and Ah's were going up; there was laughter and banter as children disengaged some inconsequential little presents from a lot of wrapping.

"Oh, look!" a cry sounded. "Look at what World Treasure Lee picked! Isn't that a good one!"

The altar boy had taken one of the larger packages; on opening it, he had found himself owner of a handsome imitation goose, of soft white plush. He held up his prize for all to see.

Great Favor looked at the goose. Then he dropped his mittens on the floor and began to cry.

Mrs. Yeh blushed. Mrs. Lee smiled, and beckoned to her six-year-old son. "He wants your goose," she said.

"He does?" World Treasure hesitated. "Well . . . well . . . all right, then. I give him my goose—for half a day. He can have him all morning. I want him back after that."

Mrs. Yeh did not want to let Great Favor accept the goose at all. Unthinkable! But Father Ling came over and interposed, and he and Mrs. Lee together persuaded Mrs. Yeh to change her

197

mind and take the goose home.

They would get one just like it for World Treasure, they said, and nobody would be the loser. And no need to bring it back. They wanted the little boy to keep it as a souvenir of the party.

After much pressing Mrs. Yeh consented. The goose stayed in Great Favor's arms, where World Treasure Lee had already placed it.

"This will help to balance your load," Mrs. Lee said, as Mrs. Yeh picked up her empty baskets and bamboo pole. "It's a little outfit we get ready for some of the children around here every Holy Birthday. And there are some extra ones, so you might as well take this one. It's clothes. There's a little padded suit and a woolen cap and stockings and felt shoes. For a small boy like him. The things will just about fit him, and they will be useful, maybe, when the Great Cold comes."

Young Mrs. Yeh protested again out of politeness, but not very long or determinedly, because this particular provision was the very thing she had been worrying about. Besides, she now looked on Mrs. Lee as a friend. Yes, a good friend. So she did not feel obliged to refuse it more than three or four times. After that she stammered some thanks, and strung the little bundles of clothing on her pole.

"It's awfully late," she reflected as she and Great Favor set out to cover the short distance to Supreme Harmony alley. "He must be very tired, although he really doesn't look it from the way he walks along with the goose. Well, it's all right, anyhow. We can just sleep a little late tomorrow, maybe, because we did pretty good today and, oh my, much better than I ever expected that we could do."

"What makes those people so friendly, I wonder? Well, it was nice anyway—all that Holy Birthday business. And the party. And everything. But I don't think it's exactly the way Old Uncle said, about honoring the Kitchen God and all that. It didn't seem that way to me at all!"

ONE HOLY NIGHT IN JAPAN [43]

Ten-year-old Debbie springs a "s'prize"
By Tats Blain

Christmas? I'd been postponing thought of it. How
could we celebrate Christmas properly in postwar Japan?

When my husband, Cmdr. Jack Blain, was assigned to naval
duty in Sasebo, I took our ten-year-old daughter Deb out of
school, gathered up our belongings, and went along. After our
long separation while Jack was busy fighting in the second
World War, I felt that we were mighty lucky to be a family
again. But now with Christmas coming on, I had to admit to
some homesickness for the States.

"It's going to be a little difficult this year, darling,"
I explained to Deb. "The shops in Sasebo haven't much for
sale. I don't think we can get a tree —" My voice trailed off.
"I've already got a tree," Deb replied. Years of living with her
have taught me never to be surprised at anything she manages.

Next morning her task force invaded our living room. Led
by Deb, it consisted of Si and Meatball, two sailors off duty;
Speedy, Chesty, and Gus, GI's from the Military government;
and our Japanese gardener with an unpronounceable name.
We always called him Hoe, because he owned one but never
used it. Among them, they carried a plump pine tree.

"Where'd you get it?" I asked in alarm. "Debbie, you know
you're not allowed to cut trees here in Japan." Wood was
scarce and badly needed for fuel.

"Don't worry, mom," Deb answered. "I got permission from
my friend, the head of Military gov'ment. I just told him
I thought red tape on a Christmas tree was pretty silly, and
he did too. Besides, I need it for my s'prize."

Sherry dropped in to see what the excitement was about.
She was an army wife who had recently arrived. She didn't care
much for Japan, dirty, smelly Sasebo, or us. She spent her days
whining for the U.S., plumbing, beauty parlors, night clubs, and
smart shops. She was pretty, and had red hair, but we liked her
husband. We often invited them in because they were newcomers.

She was full of Christmas, too. "We just have to have a party," she announced, "to get through Christmas Day in this hole. Have you anything planned?"

"No, Debbie's in charge of our Christmas." Deb guffawed.

"Kid stuff," said Sherry, ignoring them. "I mean something for grownups. Gay. Glittering. I'll wear my new dress."

"I don't want to give a party, Sherry. Jack wants a family Christmas."

"That's fine for you. You're older." Sherry has a habit of implying that I'm too old to expect any more fun. "And you have Debbie," she added hastily as I gave her a look. "But I get so lonely and homesick." Tears overflowed her big, mournful eyes.

"What did you have in mind?"

"Open house," she promptly replied, forgetting to cry any more. "Here, of course. Your house is bigger. And something traditional, not the usual macaroni salad and tuna." That was our usual party food in Sasebo. "I have it. Eggnog and Christmas cookies. You bake the cookies."

I reminded her we had neither fresh cream nor rum for eggnog.

"You can make it out of whisky and vanilla ice cream."

It probably takes like whisky and vanilla ice cream, I thought, but who wants to be a crab at Christmas?

"Come on," she coaxed. "All you'll have to do is bake the cookies. I'll help decorate. We can start on the tree. We'll paint it silver."

Deb and her assistants roared at this awful suggestion. "Put paint on my tree?" Deb cried shrilly. "Never!"

Meatball put down the hammer he was using to nail the stand. "Sure would spoil it, ma'am," he said, "Smells purty the way it is."

"The tree is Deb's. Let it alone," I decreed, wishing Sherry would go home.

"Now, we've got to think up trimmings," Deb announced, setting her cap over one eye.

"Tin foil offa smokes," Si suggested.

"Cotton for snow," offered Chesty.

"And paper chains and red berries," agreed Deb. Meatball

200

and Chesty adjusted the tree in its stand.

"What iss thiss Kreesmuss?" asked Hoe as I crushed foil from cigarettes into ornaments.

"Mom, don't they know about Christmas?" Deb's blue eyes were big with unbelief. I'll have to tell them about baby Jesus and Santy." And she did.

"Pure corn," sneered Sherry, looking up from the guest list she was compiling.

"Baby in clib, stockings on fiahplace, man coming down cheemney? Iss not good, getting burned, yiss? Iss Deb keeding, or iss it really, modom?" Hoe's shoe-button eyes twinkled at me.

"It's real in our hearts, Hoe," I answered, realizing that it was true.

"We helps," Hoe decided, politely shelving our crude efforts with tinfoil and bringing out a package of varicolored paper. His nimble fingers soon folded the sheets into a flock of birds, tiny yellow ones no bigger than a bumblebee and perky red-and-gold ones the size of a robin.

"Joy to the world," we hummed, as we pasted a final paper chain. Deb approved of our efforts.

"Those big wreaths look just keen on the front door," she said. "Isn't it Christmasy? This is all working out just dandy for me." She giggled, looking mysterious.

"What are you talking about, Deb?"

"You'll find out, mom. I can't tell you yet. But me and Mrs. Sherry are on a collision course."

Deb ran in and out of the house, busy on mysterious errands. Awkwardly tied bundles appeared at the base of the tree, and a big "Off-Limits" sign was posted on her closet door. Once I was sure I caught a flash of her red bedroom curtains going by under her overcoat as she pranced through the living room.

Once the clerk from the PX phoned. "Is it all right to sell Debbie ten cartons of chocolate bars? I don't want her to make herself sick."

Debbie came to the phone. "Mom, they're not for me; they're for Christmas." So I had a hunch what Santy was going to bring me. Deb is very fond of chocolate. "D'ya think daddy will like this pink kimono? It has a gold dragon."

This holiday commotion was fun. In the U.S., I would be in a flurry of Christmas programs at school, choir practice at church, last-minute Christmas cards. In Sasebo, the Japanese went stolidly about their business, bundled in nondescript garments against the sullen winter cold. Here were no gaily decorated shop windows. The glass had been shattered by bombs, and not replaced. No electric trains nor cuddly baby dolls. Bowls of rice were more important to Japanese mothers. No fat, jovial Santas were on street corners ringing bells. Just the click-clack of wooden clogs as the Japanese trod the uneven cobblestones.

Christmas Day dawned murky, with bone-chilling dampness. After church, we opened our boxes from the States, and Jack and I pushed away thoughts of home: Christmas with all our family assembled; excited nieces and nephews running up and down our big hall; carolers crunching on the snowy path. But Deb wasn't troubled by any such memories. Opening and shoving aside the sweaters, socks, and pajamas Aunt Edwina sent, "'Cause they're clothes, and I don't count them as presents," she dressed her dolls and drew a bead on a vase with her air rifle. "Oh boy! Am I glad to get these. They got here just in time."

"In time for what, Debbie?"

"I can't tell you yet, mom. You'll see."

Our Japanese servants thanked us politely for the presents we gave them, but I was disappointed. They had a furtive, hurried air, and the Christmas spirit seemed noticeably lacking.

"No use getting droopy-mouthed, honey," Jack comforted, gingerly putting on his pink kimono. "Just what I've always wanted, Deb." He settled down by the fire with some new books. I twanged a couple of sour notes on the samisen Deb had given me, wondering what she had done with all the chocolate bars.

Deb put on her overcoat. "Deb you're not going out on Christmas, are you? Where?"

"Just out that's all," she replied with that same mysterious air that was beginning to get on our nerves. "I'll be back pretty soon, and then you'll know. But don't ask questions."

"What's this 's'prize' that Deb hopes we'll pry out of her?" Jack asked petulantly.

"I don't know, Maybe the marines have made her an honorary

general. About the party, probably no one will show up, anyway. Merry Christmas, dear."

But every officer in the area converged on us, including those from the destroyers in the harbor and two Australian cruisers. Fifty men came, and half a dozen women, the only wives then in residence. I got the old nightmarish feeling I always get at such parties, that I'd blundered into a men's smoker. After one sip of the whisky ice cream, a look of horror came over the guests, and they made a beeline for the highballs. The kitchen was neat and empty except for an island of ice-cream cans and a mountain of surplus cookies.

The open house, not too cheery in the beginning, quickly descended to melancholy and gloom. Our guests were drawn together by herd instinct against the loneliness of Christmas in a foreign land that did not know happiness. The country offered only rain, mud, and inscrutable kimono-clad fingers slipping by in the half-light of winter. The guests lapsed into a depressing silence.

Suddenly the outer door slid back with the crash that usually presages Deb's entrances. She marched in. "Merry Christmas, everybody. Here's my s'prize."

She stepped aside to let in a crowd of ragged Japanese children. A gaunt boy about Deb's age was first. He was dressed in the tatters of a cast-off uniform; his eyes were wary, darting, unsure of his welcome. A group of younger boys edged nearer him for guidance. Then came hollow-cheeked little girls in faded cotton overalls, some with babies strapped to their patient backs, and trembling with terror. Toddlers with runny noses and scabby sores stared openmouthed at the happy little pine tree with its gay birds and paper chains and red berries.

Our dejected guests turned to them, their highball glasses halted in mid-air. They stared as if turned to statues. Suki, our cook, appeared, in a red pajama suit made from Deb's bedroom curtains. Pillows rounded out his flat figure, and his almond face was swathed in a frame of white cotton. So he was Santa Claus!

"Merrily Kreesmus," he chortled thickly through his cotton beard.

"Where in the world did you get these children?" asked Sherry. "Are they orphans, Deb?"

" 'Course not. Orphans always get looked after. The Red Cross is giving them a party. These are just kids I found around. Kids who didn't even know what Christmas is. Imagine that!"

Wham Green, a naval officer, said, "You're a great girl, Deb," and blew his nose hard. A bearded Australian captain reached out to pat one awkwardly on the head. "I say, the little nippers are cute, what?"

"Get me some cardboard and scissors," said Colonel Blair. "I'll show them how to pin the tail on the donkey."

"Let me do my card tricks," begged Major O'Brien, our toughest marine.

When five gallons of ice cream and mounds of cookies had been eaten, and when we had all done parlor tricks no one usually cared to watch, the children's shyness and fear had vanished. The lonely adults who had been bolstering their sagging spirits with highballs were relaxed and content, each surrounded by a chattering group of Japanese children.

With a box of paper handerchiefs in one hand, Sherry was maternally wiping Japanese noses. "They're really sweet when you get the dirt off," she said, catching my eye. "They're little dolls."

Suki gave out the games and puzzles Deb had brought with her from the U.S., and ribbons, shoelaces, tennis balls, and vitamin pills "from my friends, the navy doctor and the army doctor, to make the children full of pep," Deb said. And there was chewing gum from the army, oranges from the navy, and chocolate bars (at last!) from the PX.

As the party drew to a happy close, Deb stood under the Christmas tree and led her kids in song. Their sweet, true voices began, "Si-rent Night, Ho-ree Night, All iss carm, all iss bright." Our voices blended with their as we sang the finest Christmas carol of all.

A CHRISTMAS IN NORTH DAKOTA [44]

A first Noel for the Indians
By Helen C. Califano

It was Christmas Eve in 1810 in the wilderness of what is
now Minot, North Dakota. Father Lougain stepped from behind
a clump of alders so stricken by wind and snow it had lost its
identity. In a pause in the gale he could see the Indian village
in the clearing ahead. He had reached journey's end. The village
consisted of fifty tepees and a crude hut. The priest headed for
the hut; it was closest and would prove more spacious than a
tepee. Progress was hampered by his equipment, consisting of
medical kit, Mass kit, and parcels, and by the fact that he had
a small child with him.

Father Lougain knocked. Snow all but smothered the shelter;
wind howled through its walls. An old squaw with a gourd-shaped
head and pocked face opened the door. She asked no questions,
for she spoke no tongue other than her own; and the situtation
was evident.

As the Father entered, she pointed to a small bunk along the
far wall. Then she knelt by the fire. Satisfied all was well with
the evening meal, she looked over her shoulder. Concluding that
a woman's services were needed, she lurched upright; the next
moment she was bending over Father Lougain's patient. The
child was still wrapped in blankets, only now it was possible to
see her limp head, covered by masses of purple-black hair. It
was possible, too, to see her sweet olive face, and eyelashes so
long they rested like corn silk on her tired cheeks.

Suddenly the squaw squeaked recognition and surprise. Her
body began to quiver with excitement and a torrent of gutturals
rose from her wrinkled throat. Father Lougain understood some
Indian, though he had been working among the Dakotas less than
a year. Wanda was the name of the little girl.

"I was right, then," he said with satisfaction; "she is one of
yours. I found her almost frozen to death in a stretch of
woodland." He moved towards the fire. The cold had entered
his blood and chilled his heart; his feet and hands were awkward

with pain. The squaw followed the course of his tall, youthful form with dusky gratitude, her face like a patch of lit earth on the forest floor. Father smiled the smile of peace. He had trudged twenty miles off the beaten path in a terrifying blizzard, the like of which he could not have even imagined in sunwashed southern France, where he had been born, to bring an Indian girl back to her people.

He had been a good shepherd, who not only brings back his own sheep but all sheep that are lost. He recalled with pleasure an inspired passage from a volume on foreign missions, his constant companion. He had memorized it because it described so well what he felt in his heart concerning his priesthood. It read: "The missionary priest will come closer than any man to the common denominator of all humanity. He will see hope where other men see blackness and will find God where others see nothing but evil. Sparks from the fires of his sacrifice will light souls living in darkness, and they will see the cross and the way to eternal life. Rightfully to fulfill his destiny, he must cut the Gordian knot that ties him to his people, and cast himself upon the Lord. And it will be his badge of merit that when he has realized his calling his countenance will be as the Lord's."

Aware that now the old crone was swaying and croaking her concern for the little one, Father Lougain reached for his medical kit to administer restoratives. Wanda was even frailer than most Indian girls of ten, and dangerously languid from exposure and fatigue. He worked with that minimum of effort characteristic of men who know what they do. The study of medicine had been a requisite at his Jesuit seminary at Toulon and again at Rome. He had brought to that study, as he had brought to all his seminary work, the penetrating analysis and the academic point of view of a well-born Frenchman. He had brought, too, the high seriousness of a man reared in sanctity who at an early age experienced the sense of vocation. Watching him, the squaw relaxed. She knew nothing about the white man's medicine, but her instincts concerning men were correct. She looked at the cook pots, then at the Father, enacting a pantomime to indicate that the food was ready. A moment later she disappeared through the drafty doorway to become part of the icy swirl beyond.

Alone with the child, Father Lougain's natural humility asserted itself. Whatever the moment of expansion he had so recently experienced, now he felt inadequate and young, and overwhelmingly homesick. A sense of unworthiness that had haunted him as far back as he could remember and had shadowed moments of personal triumph claimed him with fresh vigor. Memories of teachers and prelates who had watched him go forth on his North American mission with joy in their souls and prayers on their lips returned to sadden him. They had believed that from his sowing could come much good fruit. But he had failed to vindicate their high trust. He had made no converts.

Moreover, thirty-five miles away at an Indian mission where he had expected to spend this Christmas Eve and the morrow as well, a group of faithful was waiting his arrival. They would have to do without him. Nor would they have the holy crêche in the chapel, as he had promised, since the figurines were with him: some owl and loon wings hanging from the ceiling, a beaver skull at his feet, frames for stretching hides covered with torn skins in various stages of decay. France was far away.

Darkness was falling when the old squaw returned, accompanied by a younger woman and three braves. They entered on a gust of congealing wind, stamping their feet. The young squaw ran over to Wanda. Motherhood claimed her and made her soft; the far reaches of the firelight rendered her heavy face appealing. "Wanda," she said softly.

The braves, the rightful occupants of the hut, slouched over the fire to their supper. With great dispatch they crammed duck and squash down their hungry throats. They milled around at their end of the cabin, staring curiously now and then, but without hostility, at the priest, who, in turn, was making covert appraisal. Aroused by the general disquiet and her mother's mournful crooning, Wanda stirred, upsetting a parcel the Father had placed on the bed. Father Lougain pushed it gently out of sight under the balsam bunk. It was a Gesu Bambino which had been carved by a master craftsman for the Lougain family 400 years before the good Father had been born. Father Lougain had always regarded the Babe with reverence and affection; tonight, he identified it with all that was a good report in his past. The Gesu was dressed in a sweeping infant dress of white satin his mother had sewn with exquisite stitches for the Babe's first Christmas in America. Father Lougain wished to keep it by his side to stand between him and loneliness.

Turning to him very shyly, Wanda's mother endeavored to make white man's conversation with the mixture of jargon, gestures, and English she told him she was grateful. Her lips attempted an explanation of what had taken place. "Wanda hears story of Babee called 'Jeesou.' White lady at trading post tell Wanda. Wanda go find Jeesou. She tink that Jeesou give her present. I tell her dere is no Jeesou but she no believe me. She go away to find heem." She paused for breath, shrugging her shoulders hopelessly at Wanda's quest and its amost tragic consequences. Then she laughed the primitive, full-throated laughter of a woman long disillusioned, who can still be amused by the vagaries of childhood.

The braves and the old squaw joined in the mirth; the braves because they had understood and agreed, the squaw because her men were laughing. Outside was the fury of winter; both inside and out there was utter desolation. The brittle quality of the rude laughter against the background of the storm grew disconcerting and pregnant with evil. A sputtering log in the fireplace became a heinous hiss. From out of the sum total of sound emerged successive waves of mockery that filled the cabin with cries of pagan victory. Christ was being crucified with zest on the very night of His birth. Legions of an unseen foe were grimly gathering around a believing white man and his little friend. Father Lougain knew a crisis was imminent. He prepared to meet it. Like a soldier on the eve of battle, he was fearful and weak and at the same time impregnable and unafraid. The blood drained from his face. He rose to full height and placed his hand upon a crucifix at his side. The gesture was that of a warrior drawing his sword. He was now the most important figure in the room.

When finally the laughter had subsided, Father Lougain began to speak. He waived difficulties of the moment with newly-found mastery. His words reflected all the gifts of birth and training, all the grace of prayer, and spiritual discipline. "There is a Jesus," he declared. "He was born in a country called Judea more than 1800 years ago. Yet He still lives and will live forever. Angels announced His birth, and Wise Men came to worship, and bring gifts of gold, incense, and myrrh. He was born in a stable over which hung a star, and his mother was called Mary. He was the Christ, the Son of God; He came to earth to live and be crucified that man might have eternal life." In his earnestness, the young priest lifted his face as if addressing a congregation, and it rent the gloom like a white fire.

The braves listened with puzzled interest, the squaws with statuesque immobility. Only Wanda smiled knowingly, her thin hands nervously picking deep irregular furrows in the blanket fold. Some of this she had heard before. Father Lougain capitalized upon this fact by training the rest of his defense where it would do the most good. Taking one of Wanda's restless brown hands in his, he went gravely on: "He sent me all the way from France to you here tonight, Wanda. He sent me because He loves you very much and wants you to know Him."

With the spotlight upon her, Wanda was overcome by alternate spasms of shyness and childish delight, but her only sound was to squeak like a little mouse. Her eyes roved from face to face to measure her triumph. Then she found her voice.

"Do He geeve present?" she asked excitedly. The manner of her asking implied confirmation. There was a Jesus; He had sent Father Lougain to her, then surely there must be the gift. Father Lougain stopped to claim the parcel which but a short time before he had sought to conceal. "Yes," he assured her smilingly, "He sent you a present. It's an image of Himself called 'Gesu Bambino.'" He removed the doll from its wrappings with tenderness, and adjusted its rich robe and gold ornaments. He cupped the cuffs of heavy lace protecting the Infant's clutched hands. Squaws, and braves moved, as if magnetized, to where he stood holding his Christ on high like a banner, the shining glow of the white satin dress matching his face. For a moment he might have been the angel on the first Christmas Eve, and the Indians the lowly shepherds. With one last caress he placed the Gesu reverently into Wanda's outstretched arms. "Keep it, Wanda," he said kindly, "and love it always."

Thus Father Lougain cut the Gordian knot with his past and on a night when only the past made the present tolerable. For the first time as a missionary priest he had fully realized his calling and cast himself upon the Lord. In a moment of revelation he saw that never again would he greatly long for home, for whatever was best of the culture and faith from which he had sprung was embodied in his way of life, and could not be restricted to some particular plot of earth. The knowledge that this was so made the night holy and blessed as no Christmas Eve had ever been. Redeeming compensation descended upon him and happiness so abundant that one heart could not wholly contain it. Some of it spilled over into the soul of the little girl and some into the dull lives of her elders. Christmas had come to an Indian village, and Father Lougain had brought his first Indians to Bethlehem. Then the Lord, lavishly as is His wont, laid one last token of divine favor as a Christmas gift at the feet of His child and priest.

The little Wanda, fondling the luminous white of the infant dress, immediately associated it with the color of her benefactor's face and his shining manhood. "I will luve Jeesou always," she said ecstatically. "He look just like you."

Chapter VI
Poetry and Legend

It was inevitable that around the great figures of the world legends and poetic fancies should spring up to fill out for the imaginations of men the starker truths of history. It is a commonplace teaching in the schools of journalism that in the case of really extraordinary news events there is no limit to what the public will read, the only limit is available space. Something like that happened about the birth of Christ. After the known facts were retold and for the most part known by heart, people still thirsted for more, and "more" was supplied by the writers of legends and fables. Almost every new writer tries his hand with a new fictional story about Christmas. In ancient times there were many apochryphal gospels written which never got any official sanction from the Church. Since most of them were written out of devotion with no specious intent to deceive we should not be too ready to condemn the writers. Poets of the Nativity were attempting something of the same thing—to develop into full orchestration the thin themes of the true Gospels. There is little danger from poets or legends as long as children learn them after they have learned the plain, and forever unsurpassable, story of the Babe of Bethlehem.

THE DONKEY'S EARS [45]

The legend says he heard the first Christmas carol
As told by the donkey of Bethlehem to June A. Grimble

I, too, was at Bethlehem on the first Christmas Eve. But
perhaps you already know that, because I have a mark on my
back, the mark that makes me go. Listen, and I will tell you
the story of how I got that mark, and how I came to have
long ears.

Bethlehem is where we first met, you and I. I first met you
when you first met God-made-Man. And it was you children
who gave me my long ears, at Bethlehem that night, for a
Christmas present.

On the evening that is now called Christmas Eve, I was in a
stable that was once the house of Jesse, in Bethlehem. It was
quite early, but dusk already had fallen and it was mightily cold.
A great white ox was in the stable with me, and we stood,
huddled together for warmth, in a dark corner behind the manger.
We were nodding and almost asleep when the door opened and
a tall man walked in. He carried a staff in one hand and his arm
was around the gentlest, loveliest lady that you ever saw. The
man was troubled; he kept muttering the words *Caesar,* and
census, and *taxes,* and adding, "And now no room at the inn!"
We did not understand, the ox and I—but perhaps you do—so
we just looked on.

The woman's name was Mary and she called the man Joseph.
She bade him hurry out and get some sticks for a fire. The ox
stayed to keep watch over the woman, but I ran out after
Joseph, thinking that perhaps he could find a basket so that
I could carry the sticks for him. But he was too troubled to
think of baskets.

He ran straight for a faint red glow on the hillside below the
stable. It came from the fire of some shepherds keeping a night
watch over their flocks. Joseph rushed up to them; I trotted
behind.

A little shepherd boy was fanning the feeble glow for all he
was worth, crying all the while, because his father was scolding

215

him.

"Oh, stupid one!" the father was shouting. "Green ash sticks for the night watch! Wretched boy! How many times must I tell you that green sticks will not burn. But blow, boy—blow and bawl! And well you may, for we shall have no supper tonight."

The poor lad blew with all his might and main, but could manage to keep alive only the tiniest flicker of a flame.

Joseph looked at the pitiful glow and then looked up at the sky in desperation. Following his gaze, I saw a star, marvelously bright, shining splendidly right over our stable. It was very beautiful, but this was no time for star-gazing. Joseph turned to the boy's father. "Good shepherd," he burst out, "I beg you to give me of your fire. There is a Babe to be born this very night in a stable in Bethlehem. There is no room at the inn and the cold is bitter."

"My fire I would gladly share with you, master," answered the shepherd. "But alas! the sticks are green, and do what you will—they will never burn. This wretched boy . . . ."

Joseph did not wait for more. He picked up the smoldering sticks and put them in his cloak. And they burst into flame. But the cloak did not burn.

It must have been a miracle, because you know and I know that the shepherd was right. Green sticks won't burn easily. And cloaks always will. But to this day the ash is the only wood that will burn when it is green, because it was the ash tree whose sticks made the fire that gave warmth for God's lady in the stable at Bethlehem.

Back in the stable, Joseph placed the sticks carefully on the ground. They blazed bravely, but not without difficulty (they were really very green), Joseph did not have time to notice their struggle.

Mary had swept the stable and was now pulling fresh hay from the manger and arranging it in a pile beside her. But Joseph had a better idea. He found one of our clean troughs and stuffed it full of hay, fresh and sweet smelling, and placed it at her feet. She was pleased, and she did a lovely thing that I have often seen humans do—she smiled at him. And it was as if another miracle had happened. Joseph suddenly looked like a man whose heart is singing. He took courage, and set about doing other things for the lady's comfort.

First he put a fresh pile of hay in the middle of the cave (the stable was a cave), away from the damp walls. Having placed Mary thereon, he made the gentle white ox lie down behind her back so that she had something to lean against. Me, in my thick winter coat, he made to lie between the draughty door and the lady, like a kind of screen. We were blissfully happy, the ox and I. True, we couldn't watch her any more because Joseph had placed us with our backs to her. But we could watch for her, and this is what we saw.

Joseph moved to a place just beyond us, and knelt there, leaning on his staff. And he watched and he prayed. Never have I seen a man watch so tenderly or pray more fervently. His heart was in his eyes and his eyes never once left the lady. So even he did not see what we saw.

He did not see the green ash fire struggle valiantly for life and almost fail. But we saw it, and the little brown bird who nested in the manger saw it. And out he flew from the safety of his home and round and round those dying embers he fluttered, fanning them. As the flames rose, still he fanned, to make them strong for the lady's sake.

Every time he stopped to rest, the flames faltered. So he fluttered and he fanned until his breast was so cruelly scorched that his heart was almost burned out of him. He fanned until he fell at my feet. And then a wondrous thing happened. As he lay there, feathers sprouted and completely covered the little fellow's fire-scorched breast. But they were not brown like the rest of him. They were red—bright red. And to this day he wears his fire-bright finery and is known as "robin redbreast." But only a very few know how he came by it.

It was a cry that woke the robin—a feeble cry, the cry of the Newborn. But I tell you it was a sound that pierced heaven and roused the world. And all the angels and all the creatures in creation heard it, and it echoed where their hearts beat.

Joseph leaped toward the woman who was the Mother of God, and they both knelt, and together they adored, because the Word was made flesh and dwelt amongst us, and God was now Man.

At that moment of perfect love when a man and a woman first offered the gift of two hearts big with faith to the Babe of Bethlehem there was of a sudden a great and golden blaze of light and all the world was mystery-filled and glorious with wonder, because the splendor of God shone round about. And a voice there was, as golden as the light, which sang, "Behold! I bring you good tidings of great joy, that shall be to all the people; for this day is born to you a Saviour who is Christ the Lord." And suddenly there was with the angel a multitude of the heavenly host praising God and saying, "Glory to God in the highest; and on earth peace to men of good will."

And that was the moment that we first met, you and I. You were all around me. All the children ever to be born were round about me, loving God in Bethlehem. Because, whether you know it or not, your guardian angels were there, and together we bowed down, and together we adored Him. And then it was that I got the mark upon my back. You saw it happen, but perhaps you cannot remember.

At the first sound of the Infant's cry, I fell upon my knees and put my face against the trough that was the crib of God, and with all my donkey being I did love Him. But my heart was sad because I had no soul to love Him with as well, and in that moment of sadness, the Babe reached out and touched me. God touched me! And where God had touched, there came a mark upon my back.

It is there yet for you and all the world to see. It is a cross. His sign—a sign of love, and a symbol of salvation, and I, the donkey, am marked with it. And in that sign there lies a secret of how to make me go! There is no need to beat me. But touch the very center of my Mark of God, and see how I will go!

The ox, too, received acknowledgement that night in Bethlehem. Because he was the first four-footed creature to kneel in adoration of his God (it was his example that I followed) he is now the one creature in creation that kneels before he lies down to sleep. Watch him, and you will see— and watching, remember that he is a king, king of the kine, a symbol of St. Luke the Evangelist and of the priesthood, and an emblem of the sons of Israel, as I am of the Gentiles.

But to the story of my ears, your Christmas gift to me and my descendants. There was, let me tell you much fidgeting and jostling among the heavenly hierarchy that night! The six-winged seraphim, the four-winged cherubim, the thrones, the dominations, the virtues, the powers, the principalities, the archangels and the angels, ten thousand times a hundred thousand of them, clamored and clustered round the crib to pay homage to the Baby Jesus, tiny and laughing in his crib.

The guardian angels had the hardest time, because they were the littlest, and they could not see over that host of shimmering wings. You try peering through the six wings of just one seraphim, or the four wings of one cherubim and you'll see what I mean.

I was nosing over the crib with the ox and we were breathing on the Infant to keep Him warm—all those angels in front of the fire, you understand—when all at once a group of guardian angels started to cry because they could not see God. I was sorry for them, so I moved back and give them my place. And then *I* couldn't see the Christ Child any more, and I couldn't even hear Him above the fluttering of wings. So I began to cry, and the guardian angels saw me. Down they swooped upon me, comforting and singing:

> *Because of us you cannot see,*
> *Because of us you'll crowned be*
> *With ears to catch the smallest sound,*
> *With ears tremendous and renowned.*

And then they started pulling. The whole heavenly choir of them took hold of my short, pointed ears (the kind donkeys wore in those days) and they pulled. And when they stopped pulling, I had the two big ears you see on me now. Long they were, and fur lined, and every syllable of sound they caught for me. What's more, I could waggle them. So if the sound was high I raised them up; if the sound was low I dipped them down. They were perfect, and I was happy, and right now I want to thank you—and your guardian angels—for them.

Soon after my ears had been made long, and just as Mary had

finished wrapping the Babe in swaddling clothes, there came a
knock at the door. The angels vanished, Joseph called, "Come
in," and in walked the shepherds from the hills around
Bethlehem. Some of them we had met already; they had given
us their fire. But now they were joined by others. They came,
they said, at the bidding of an angel, to see a Baby he had told
them about. Each one had a present for Him—fruits and
vegetables and lambs and pigeons and rabbits and wood doves
for the Baby Jesus.

The father and son who had given us the fire were there.
But the father wasn't angry and the son wasn't crying any more.
They were excited and filled so full of good will that it was
shining in their eyes.

Their gifts were different from the others. The old man,
having no faith in green ash sticks that should not and cloaks
that do not burn, had brought a quilt.

It was a feather quilt—large, soft, warm, cozy—the finest a
heart could desire. He had saved his coins for it for so long,
he was not likely ever to own another. It was his most treasured
possession, and he brought it for the Babe.

Jesus smiled as if to thank him, and Mary and Joseph looked
at each other, and then at the shepherd, and back to the quilt,
and finally toward the fire. Then Mary whispered something
to Joseph, and Joseph led the shepherd over to the fire to show
him what a splendid fire it was, and he said, "Good shepherd,
fear not. The Child does not suffer from the cold. See! The
green-ash fire burns brightly now. Therefore, keep, we beseech
you, your fine feather quilt. But know, that because of the
great kindness in your heart, you will one day sit by the side of
this same Babe in heaven, and when his birthday dawns you
will be privileged to scatter the feathers from your quilt upon
the earth below."

. The shepherd was filled with joy. And so are you children
filled with joy when you wake on Christmas to find the world
all white with feathery flakes tumbling from heaven as the
happy shepherd strews about the snowy contents of his quilt.

The shepherd's boy was very poor. He had nothing of his
own to bring to Jesus. But on the way to the stable, he found

a little white flower that had pushed its head above the earth as if it, too, wanted to share the wonders of that night. This flower the boy offered shyly at the crib side. The Babe of Bethlehem received it, and He touched it to his mouth, and where his lips had touched, a crown of gold sprang forth. And from that day to this the daisy wears its yellow crown to celebrate the night that it was kissed by God.

The shepherds left. Days passed, and the kings came, the ones that are called the Magi. They, too, brought gifts for the Christ Child.

Melchior, king of fabulous Arabia, brought gold; Balthasar, dusky king of Ethiopia, land of spices, brought frankincense; and Caspar, king of Tarsus, land of merchants, brought myrrh.

> *And the gold was for a King—*
> *that was Jesus.*
> *And the frankincense for a*
> *High Priest—that was Jesus.*
> *And the myrrh for the Great*
> *Physician—that was Jesus.*

The kings received gifts in return, and the gifts that they received were perfect: perfect charity for gold; perfect faith for frankincense; perfect truth for myrrh.

Melchior brought also a pure white ass for the Holy Family. Strong and beautiful and fit it was, he said, to carry king or queen.

And the white ass did carry a king and queen, because a few days later the Magi had a dream, and Joseph had a dream, and there was much murmuring about a man called Herod. Because of him, the Magi returned to their homes by a different way from the one they had taken to Bethlehem, and because of Herod, Joseph set Mary, with the Baby Jesus nestling safe against her heart, on the ass's back. Me, he set before them on the road, and taking his staff in his hand, he bade me lead the Holy Family into Egypt. I did, and we arrived safely.

But I must tell you that one day in the very midst of the desert it rained hard, and my fine ears proved weatherproof— they did not shrink at all. So I was happy. And I am still happy, because, as you know, I have them to this day.

221

CAROL

Villagers all, this frosty tide,
Let your doors swing open wide,
Though wind may follow, and snow beside,
Yet draw us in by your fire to bide;
Joy shall be yours in the morning!

Here we stand in the cold and the sleet,
Blowing fingers and stamping feet,
Come from far away you to greet—
You by the fire and we in the street—
Bidding you joy in the morning!

For ere one half of the night was gone,
Sudden a star has led us on,
Raining bliss and benison—
Bliss tomorrow and more anon,
Joy for every morning!

Goodman Joseph toiled through the snow—
Saw the star o'er a stable low;
Mary she might not further go—
Welcome thatch, and litter below!
Joy was hers in the morning!

And then they heard the angels tell
'Who were the first to cry Noel?
Animals all, as it befell,
In the stable where they did dwell!
Joy shall be theirs in the morning!'

THE FOX AT THE MANGER [46]

Only a fable, but a true lesson
By P. L. Travers

It was late at night. Silence had dropped like a stone into
the stable. The stillness spread out ring on ring, away to the
fields and the farthest hills. A faint glow came from the center
of the stable, but beyond that, all was shadow. Near by, the
shepherds, with their fleecy cloaks drawn around them,
leaned heavily on each others' shoulders and nodded their
heads. Outside, the angels, poised in the air above the roof top,
were resting from their songs of praise. Even after great wonders,
perhaps particularly after great wonders, there must be sleep.

The Child Himself, like a shadow in the midst of His own
glow, slept in His manger-crib. And the beasts of the farmyard
stood quietly with drooped heads, their hoofs planted solidly
in the stable straw, very still, like furry statues. Looking at
them you would have thought they were far away in the deepest
slumber, beyond dreams, aware of nothing. But animals sleep
with one ear pricked. They are creatures of earth and it is their
nature to listen for the smallest of earth's tremors.

Presently each of those listening ears gave a little twitch. For
the beasts, as they dozed, had caught the vibration of an almost
soundless sound. Even the young lambs which the shepherds
had brought heard it, and one of them struggled uncertainly to
his feet and listened with his head turned inquiringly to one side.

The sound, too delicate to be perceived by any human ear,
came slowly nearer. A cautious, deliberate padding became every
second more audible as it approached the stable. Soft, discreet,
determined paws were walking the earth. And soon the watchful
creatures in the stable discerned, picking his way through the
spangled fields with one foot after the other making a flowerlike
imprint in the frost, a small red fox.

They stiffened in their places as he came on, pointing his
sharp nose along the earth as though following a scent. And as
the shine from the manger fell on him he lifted his head and
paused in the doorway. Without glancing to right or left, his

yellow, far-apart eyes took in the scene and brightened as though he had found what he was seeking. For a long time he stood there looking at the crib. Then, without attempting to come farther into the stable, he sat down on his haunches and went on gazing.

The flanks of the farmyard animals quivered and the straw rustled under their hoofs. But the fox took no notice. He seemed not to know—or if he knew, not to care—that there was any creature in the place except himself. He swept his tail like a great red feather round his body and kept his eyes on the Child.

The hoofs shuffled warningly. Again the straw crackled. But the fox did not move. At last the ass tossed his head. "Out, fox!" he said sternly to the intruder. "This is no place for you!"

"Be off!" warned the cow, the sheep, and the dove from his place in the rafters.

The fox twitched an ear. Slowly as though he were fetching his attention from a great distance, he turned his head. His eyes blinked as they took in the group of animals tensely watching him from the shadows. He shrugged his shoulders. "On the contrary," he said quietly, "it is the only place for me."

The ass's tail switched ominously and his hind legs stamped in the straw. "Do not try our patience too far, Renard! We should be loath to use them on such a night, but I warn you our hoofs are hard!"

The fox, without stirring, looked thoughtfully at the switching tail and the stamping hoofs. "Will you tell me," he inquired mildly, "why this should be a place for all of you," his glance measured them, "for cow, for ass, for sheep, and dove, and not a place for me?"

"We are here to protect Him!" said the ass proudly.

"And because we love Him," added the cow, with a gentle glance at the crib.

The fox appeared to consider this, bending his head sideways as he turned it over in his mind. "Of love," he said thoughtfully at length, "I can say nothing. It is always better not told. But as to protecting Him, why should I not do that as well as you?"

"Because we are the friends of man," the cow answered. "You are his enemy!"

224

"When was man ever a friend to me?" demanded the fox. "Not this side of Eden, I assure you! If I am his enemy, he is mine. And yet," a shadow darkened the yellow eyes, "I shall be His friend when the time comes. I shall be His friend only, though He is not yet grown."

"You are a cheat!" the sheep cried shrilly. "Remember how you tricked the crow! Remember the goat! Remember the stork!"

At that the fox smiled. "Foolish creatures, I remember them well! They never troubled to think for themselves. They deserved what they got."

"Chicken thief!" the dove screamed down, flapping his wings in the rafters.

"Chickens were born to be stolen," the fox answered calmly. "There are millions of chickens in the world and none of them of any more use than to have his bones picked. But there are very few foxes."

"You live by cunning!" the ass accused him.

"What else should I live by?" demanded the fox. "How else should I distinguish, on a spring evening, the false leaf and the crossed sticks that show me where the trap is set? What else will tell me, as I hunt the furrow in summer, that the hare's body stretched there has a heart packed with poison? What warns me on an autumn morning, that the shadow of the branch is the huntsman's bow? What takes me off down wind in winter, away from the ravening hounds? Only my cunning!"

His gaze, without guilt or shame, moved tranquilly from one animal to another. "Have you anything else against me?"

"You have a strong, red-foxy smell," said the dove, sniffing the air disdainfully.

"You hunt rabbits," the sheep accused him.

A dreamy look came into the fox's eyes and he ran his tongue over his lips as though the very words were delicious. "I have to eat to live," he said smiling.

"You cannot be tamed!" said the cow reproachfully.

"If you mean," the fox answered, "that I would not willingly wear a halter, you are quite right. Nor do I like living in barns. When they put me in a cage I waste away, running from corner

to corner. I bite the hand that feeds me when that hand puts
a chain on my neck. No one tames a fox. And yet," his yellow
eyes darkened again, "the time is coming when a fox shall be
tamed."

Each animal looked at him disbelievingly. They made jeering,
throaty, angry sounds. "When will that be?" they all demanded.

The fox was silent for a moment. Then he turned his head
towards the manger and gave a little nod.

"When I have given Him my gift," he said quietly.

"Oho, Renard! Have you suddenly learned to share?" laughed
the ass. "What gift could you give him?"

"Is it your coat?" demanded the sheep. "If so, it is far too
coarse and prickly. Besides, I have already given Him my wool
to keep Him warm."

"It is not my coat," the fox assured her.

"Your lair," asked the cow, "for Him to sleep in? I fear a
fox hole would smell too strong. Anyway, as you will have
observed, I have already given Him my manger."

"It is not my lair," replied the fox.

"You are not assuming, Renard," inquired the ass, "that you
could carry Him about? That is my job. I have already brought
His Mother a long way, and my back is broad enough for any
journey He is likely to take."

"No such thing was in my mind," said the fox.

"You don't imagine you could sing to Him, surely?" said the
dove, preening his wing. "I have already cooed Him to sleep and
I intend to go on doing so."

"I am no songster," said the fox smiling. But the smile faded
as he looked from one to another. And he shook his head sadly.
"Do not be disturbed," he reassured them. "What I have for
Him is mine alone. It will not take away from any of your gifts."

"What is it?" they all cried at once. "Let us judge of that
for ourselves!"

The fox regarded them for a moment in silence. Then he gave
a little shrug. "My cunning," he said quietly.

The animals stared. And the fox calmly returned their gaze.

"Good!" said a voice from the manger.

As though there were but one mind among them, they turned

quickly from the fox to the crib and saw that the Child had waked up. He was looking at them with His bright, shadowy eyes and smiling with great kindness.

"That is a good gift," He said gently, glancing toward the fox.

"Why is it good?" cried the ass. "You are young and true and innocent. You do not have any need for cunning!"

"It is good," said the Child, "because it is not half a thing. It is whole. Who else will give Me as much? The kings," he smiled "will bring Me many gifts. But they are wise men and rich men and their presents are inexhaustible. They can never give away all they have. The shepherds have brought Me their young lambs. But in the spring there will be many more for the ewes to suckle. There are always lambs abounding. The cow has given Me her manger, but soon I shall have grown too big for it and she will eat her oats from it again. The ass, indeed, carried My Mother uphill and down and he will carry Me, too. But for all that, his back is not broken: it is strong enough for other burdens. When the dove sang Me his lullaby it was not the end of his singing. There will be other children to coo to sleep, and brood after brood of nestlings. The sheep has given Me her warm coat but she will grow others as the seasons pass. All of you—and, lovingly, I thank you—have given Me gifts that still remain your own. That is as it should be, for in this way we can share them together. But the fox . . .."

The Child paused and the light about Him glowed more brightly. "The fox has given Me all he had. Without his cunning how will he find food or escape the snare? How will he live now, alone in the woods? His cunning is his strength; his cunning is his life. It is the only thing he has and he has given it away."

"But what will You do with such a gift?" cried the ass in a troubled voice, wrinkling up his brow. "I am puzzled. I am full of doubt. What is this cunning? There is something here I do not understand."

"Nor I!" echoed the sheep, the cow and the dove, shaking their heads in bewilderment.

"It is not necessary to understand. It is only necessary to love," said the Child with a quiet smile. Then He turned His head toward the door and raised His hand and beckoned. "Come!" He commanded.

Delicately lifting each paw and putting it down without a sound, the fox stepped up to the manger. And the Child put out His hand and laid it on the red head in the broad space between the ears.

"Stay with Me. Be My friend. I shall need you," the Child said urgently. "Stay with Me. Let it be you and Me together!"

But the fox, his eyes glistening, let his head rest for a moment only beneath the Child's hand, then he bent it sideways away. "You know I cannot do that," he said. "That would make two of us. You have come from beyond the world and You know well that what You have to do can only be done by one. Do not tempt me! I am Your friend and for that reason I must refuse to be Your friend, no matter what it costs me. Let me be. I have given You my cunning, and much good may it do You. You are the fox now—alone, against the world."

"You are right," whispered the Child. "That is how it must be. Alone when the wind rises and when the rain comes down."

"And under the snow," the fox added. "I will go and live in the hedgerows." As he spoke, he moved his body away, slowly, inch by inch, so that the Child's hand slid down the length of his red back and along the brush to the last hair. It seemed as though neither could bear to let the other go.

Then the fox flung up his head abruptly and thrust himself away from the crib and padded with deliberate, delicate steps over the straw toward the farmyard animals. He chose a place between the cow and the ass and lay down, curling his pointed mask along his paws.

The young lamb, who had watched the scene in silence, left its mother and staggered clumsily across the stable and lay down beside him.

But the fox took no notice. His yellow eyes were fixed unblinkingly upon the Child, and the Child's eyes glinted brightly back at him. Long and long they gazed at each other with a look that seemed to be unwinding time. What they said in that look no one can tell. They might have lived a lifetime in it; thirty-three years of life, perhaps, stretching away from this winter night to a far-off day in spring.

The other animals, without knowing why, felt their anger melt away. Flooded with a humble joy they pondered on the night's events, and drew nearer to the fox as they pondered. "We are too simple to understand," they thought to themselves. "All we can do is love." And after a while, for they were unused to thinking things out, they nodded drowsily and then awoke to ponder again and nodded again and slept.

Outside, the great star above the stable spun on its axis with a steady hum. The angels and archangels, in a trance, swung like pendulums in the air and rested their cheeks on their harps. The town slept, ringing the stable round; and all that ringed the town about lay in a tranquil slumber.

But the Child and the fox were both awake, gazing at each other. Silently, sleeplessly, without stirring, as though they two were alone on the earth, they looked at each other and kept their watch all through the turning night.

THE BIRTHPLACE OF SANTA CLAUS [47]

St. Nicholas comes from a town in Turkey
By Marcus Brooke

"Evet Markus, Noel Baba vardir" is Turkish for "Yes, Marcus, there is a Santa Claus." And who, if not the Turks, should know this?

Santa Claus, or Saint Nicholas, comes, not from the Holy Land nor from Lapland, but from Patara on Turkey's southern shore. Patara and the nearby village of Myra, where St. Nicholas became bishop in the fourth century, lie in that region of Turkey which, in Homer's time, was called Lycia.

I visited this homeland of Santa Claus. A very comfortable ship of the Turkish Maritime Lines took me, in two days, from Istanbul to Fethiye on the southwest coast. Early the next morning I boarded a bus which left Fethiye by a broad divided highway. Soon, this gave way to a wide, fairly straight, graded, dirt road. The countryside was rich in timber, especially eucalyptus, and the journey was uneventful except for the many flocks of guinea fowls which we disturbed. After several hours we reached Patara. A few miles away, scattered among the sand dunes between the road and the Mediterranean, were some ruins. This was where St. Nicholas was born.

He was the son of wealthy parents who died when he was young. With the money left him he made a practice of giving secretly to the poor. In Patara lived a nobleman who had lost all his wealth. This man had three very beautiful daughters who could not marry for lack of a dowry. One day Nicholas heard of the plight of his impoverished neighbor's daughters. He knew that if he offered to give him money, the proud nobleman would be insulted. So, that very evening, he threw a bag of gold into the nobleman's home through a window.

Thinking about this the next day, Nicholas decided that one bag of gold was insufficient, so that night he threw another bag through the window. Next day he thought, "Three daughters, so why not three bags of gold," and on the third night he prepared a third bag of gold. However the windows were repaired by now and firmly locked. Undaunted, Nicholas climbed onto the roof and threw the third bag down the chimney.

The nobleman's daughters became suddenly very much sought after, and were soon married. Patara being a small town, everyone guessed from where the dowries came and soon the secret was out and it became the custom in Patara to give presents secretly just as Nicholas had done.

St. Nicholas died on December 5, and in ancient times this was the date that was kept as his day. On the eve of St. Nicholas Day, children hung up their stockings, and because St. Nicholas especially loved children, there would be presents in the stockings the next morning. In some European countries such as Belgium, Holland, and Luxembourg, especially in the Catholic communities, the evening of December 6 is still celebrated. Children are exhorted to be good, say their catechism, and be thankful for their gifts. When Protestants came from the Netherlands to New Amsterdam (New York) they brought the festival of St. Nicholas with them. The Dutch word for St. Nicholas, which is "Sinterklaas," was soon corrupted to Santa Claus.

On leaving the bus at Patara I set off for the ruins on foot. My way was soon blocked by a recently irrigated field. The waters were from the Xanthus River, and although the thought of wading into them should have thrilled me, it did not. It was in these very waters, that, according to Lycian legend, Leto bathed her two newborn children, Apollo and Artemis.

But I found a way, and a couple of miles later marched through a triple triumphal Roman archway and was among the Patara ruins. Sadly there remains nothing to be seen to connect St. Nicholas with Patara. However, in the southwest, hidden in heavy shrubbery and partly sitting in a marsh, was an unusual large gray building. It turned out to be a splendid granary built for the navy during the reign of the Roman Emperor Hadrian. Bullfrogs croaked in the marsh and I recalled more of the legend which has it that Leto attempted to drink of the waters of Patara to assuage her thirst. Because the inhabitants would not permit this, she turned them into frogs and announced that if they valued their water so highly they could remain in it.

I caught the next bus for Demre, the modern name of Myra, which is about four hours and fifty miles east of Patara. The road got worse and worse, and as it climbed and fell, twisted and turned, the grading deteriorated. It was more suitable for the exotic camel trains we passed than for the bus. Still, as compensation, there were enchanting views of the turquoise Mediterranean and the countryside covered with cedar, oak, and pine. After two hours I broke the journey at the small port of Kas.

The next day in Demre, helpful villagers indicated the way to the church of St. Nicholas. It was only 600 yards up the road but I located it only at the third attempt. It is below the level of the road and the neighboring fields and sits in a kind of quarry. This is the result of the deposition, over hundreds of years, of enormous quantities of rich alluvial soil which, with its glorious climate, make Demre one of the richest market gardens in Turkey.

A fine bird's-eye view of the church could be had from the ground above. The exterior of the building is undistinguished, and indeed, nondescript. Its appearance is not enhanced by the corrugated tin roofs which protect part of it. At the west end is a somewhat incongruous three-tiered belfry. The most attractive features of the church are the clean white masonry and, in the forecourt at the southern side, old columns topped by ancient Corinthian capitals.

It was in this church that Nicholas, on returning from a pilgrimage to Jerusalem, was greeted with the cry, "Hail to our new bishop." Nicholas, who was but a young man, was stunned. He was told that the previous evening while deliberating, the priests had heard a voice telling them to choose as bishop the first man who entered the church the next morning. That man was Nicholas.

Within the church, the nave was long and lofty and ended in a semicircular apse. In the apse, stretching from the floor to just below the three windows were ten semicircular rows of stone seats arranged like a tiny Roman theater. I had seen a similar arrangement in the Church of St. Irene in Istanbul and in the Church of Mount Nebo in Jordan, from where, some claim, Moses saw the Promised Land.

In the Aisle to the south was a large stone sarcophagus with intricate bas-relief work. Although obviously early Roman, it is in this sarcophagus that, it is claimed, St. Nicholas was buried. This part of the story is clearly apocryphal.

The relics of St. Nicholas are no longer in this church but in a silver cask which sits in the crypt of the Church of St. Nicholas in Bari in southeast Italy. In 1087, a band of seamen from Bari delivered a cargo of wheat in Antioch. There they learned about the relics of St. Nicholas at Myra from a Venetian crew who intended to steal them and bring them to Venice. The Bari crew reached Myra before the Venetians and, after their offer of gold for the bones of the saint had been righteously spurned, they broke into the sarcophagus and stole the remains. The sailors believed that they were "rescuing" rather than stealing the relics, for in that very year Myra had been captured by the infidels, though the Christians of the town had been left their freedom to tend and guard their shrine.

The Venetian crew, not to be outdone, also returned home with some bones which they pretended to be those of St. Nicholas. All other relics of St. Nicholas were later taken in a Russian frigate to St. Petersburg at the time of the Greek War of Independence in the nineteenth century.

To this day, the shrine of St. Nicholas in Bari is one of the most popular in all southern Italy. Each year from May 7 to 9 there is a celebration during which the saint, in the shape of a life-sized seventeenth century wooden statue, is taken out to sea for the day, since he is also the patron saint of sailors and fishermen.

In the Church of St. Nicholas at Demre the attendant had led me to the gallery, and while complaining that most precious items had been removed to the museum in Antalya, the main city of the region, showed me a small collection with various architectural fragments, pieces of glass and pottery and a ship's bell. I later visited Antalya and found in the museum a gaudy picture of Nicholas and some relics which are claimed to be his.

And so my pilgrimage to the land of St. Nicholas was over. I was off to dream, not of Lapland reindeer, but of Turkish donkeys, pulling cartloads of Christmas presents. *"Cok mutlu bir Noel gecirmenizi dilerim,"* which is Turkish for "Have a very Merry Christmas."

SILENT NIGHT [48]

The story of the Christmas song
By Hertha Pauli

As you sit around the Christmas tree and sing "Silent Night, Holy Night," children and grownups all over the world are singing that same song, in Mexico, England, Germany, and in far-away Japan.

They sing the same song even though the words are in different languages: Silent Night; *Stille Nacht; Douce Nuit.* But in each language the words bring the same gladness.

Some songs aren't just words and a tune. They have been on so many lips and in so many hearts that they have come to life. "Silent Night" is just such a song, and many people think of it as a folk song. But it isn't. The story of how it came to be was lost for a time, but it was later found by a king, which is as it should be, because it is no ordinary tale but a true and wonderful Christmas story.

Our story begins in an old village in the Austrian Alps. In the whole place, there were but two educated persons: Father Joseph Mohr, the priest, and Franz Xavier Gruber, the schoolteacher. Both were young and both came from "outside," so they became fast friends.

Every Sunday they would meet to make music. Gruber would sing the basso parts to Father Mohr's tenor, and play the accompaniment on the guitar. The children of the village would gather outside the window to listen.

On December 24, 1818, Father Mohr sat in his study, working on his Christmas sermon. The sun had set behind the mountains, and the valley looked like an enormous Christmas tree. That was because hundreds of people were coming to the village for midnight Mass, and they carried candles to light their way along the mountain paths. The priest worked on, scanning his Bible for the appropriate text, "Behold, I bring you good tidings of great joy, that shall be to all the people. For this day is born to you a Saviour."

Just then, someone knocked at his door. He opened it to a

peasant woman, wrapped in a coarse shawl. "Praised be Jesus Christ," she greeted him, in the manner of the country, and then went on to tell him of the birth of a child earlier that day to a poor charcoal maker's family. Would the priest come and bless the infant, that he might live and prosper?

Father Mohr got up, put on his hat and coat, and followed the woman through the knee-deep snow. At last they came to a ramshackle hut. A big, awkward man greeted the priest and asked him to enter. The low room was filled with wood smoke, and poorly lighted, but on the crude bed lay the young mother, smiling happily. In her arms she held her baby, now peacefully asleep. Father Mohr gave them both his priestly blessings.

The young priest felt strangely moved as he went down the mountain again, alone. The smoky shack, with its crude bed, did not really resemble the stable in the City of David. Yet, somehow, the last words he had read in his Bible seemed suddenly to be addressed to him, Joseph Mohr. He forgot all the gayer holidays he had known elsewhere. It seemed to him as though the Christmas miracle had just happened before his eyes. He felt the promise of peace and good will in the forest silence and in the brilliance of the stars. He saw deer, rabbits, and foxes between the trees, standing quite close to the trail and fearlessly watching him. Even the forest creatures seemed to know and keep the peace of Holy Night. From all the mountain villages, near and far, bells began to ring and echo from the mountain walls: "Jesus Lord at Thy birth."

Father Mohr offered midnight Mass and then went home. But he found no sleep. He went into his study and tried to put down on paper what had happened to him. The words kept turning into verse, and when dawn broke, he had written a poem.

On Christmas Day, Father Mohr took his poem to Franz Gruber. Thought of fame never entered his mind. He had quite simply put his own wonder on paper, and he wanted to give it to his friend for Christmas.

The teacher read it once, then a second time. Greatly moved, he said, "Father, this is just the Christmas song we need. God be praised."

235

"But without the right tune, the song will be pretty lonely," answered Father Mohr.

So Franz Gruber agreed to compose the music; he would go right to work on it. Soon, long before Father Mohr expected him, he was back, a broad smile on his face and a sheet of music in his hand. "It was easy," he exclaimed, "your words sang themselves. Let's play it."

"But how? The church organ is broken," the priest objected.

Gruber chuckled. He had thought of that, too, and had jotted down the notes for what was at hand, two voices and a guitar. And so, on Christmas Day, 1818, as the children gathered outside Father Mohr's window, they heard, as usual, the priest and his friend singing to the accompaniment of an old guitar. But the song they heard was destined to be heard in all the lands where there is Christmas. "Silent Night, Holy Night . . .."

A few days after Christmas, one of the most famous organ builders of the district, Karl Mauracher, stopped at the village. He was a friendly man with a long, bushy beard, dressed in Tyrolean clothes on which silver buttons winked. Father Mohr and Gruber were both happy to see him, and watched anxiously as his gray head disappeared into their sick organ. But Mauracher presently reassured them. Mice had eaten a hole in the bellows. In an hour, he had the organ going.

Franz Gruber seated himself on the bench and began to play. He slipped into the new Christmas melody. It sounded much better than on the guitar, and suddenly Father Mohr was singing it and so was Gruber. "Silent Night" rang out as sweetly and as fittingly as if this were Christmas, and not an ordinary working day.

The organ builder listened quietly, and then said, "I'd like to hear that again, Mr. Gruber." So Father Mohr and Gruber sang the words again; old Mauracher listened, and his twinkling eyes became uncommonly serious.

"Where did you get that song?" he asked. "I've never heard it."

The priest and the teacher smiled at each other, but said nothing.

"Would you mind if I took it with me?" Mauracher asked. "Folks back where I live would greatly appreciate it."

Father Mohr and Gruber both assured the organ builder that he was welcome to their song, and Gruber began writing down the words and notes. But Mauracher shook his head, and told them not to bother. He already had a hundred songs in his head; one more would not make any difference. He said good-by to the two friends and set off across the mountains, not knowing that he carried with him a Christmas gift for the entire world.

Mauracher went on about his job building and repairing organs in large towns and small all over Austria. And because he liked to sing, the new Christmas song spread quickly from valley to valley. The children learned it first, then the grownups, and in no time at all, the mountain folk were singing "Silent Night." Because Father Mohr and Franz Gruber had been too modest to claim the song for their own, Mauracher could not say who had written it. It became known as the "Song from Heaven."

Of all those who came to know and love "Silent Night," none knew it better nor loved it more than four little children named Strasser—Caroline, Sepp, Anderl, and Maly. Their parents and older brothers and sisters were glovemakers, but these children weren't big enough to do the exacting work of turning the skin of the native mountain chamois into gloves. But they could sing, and they could sell gloves. The time came when, like nightingales, every spring the four traveled northward. With their baskets filled with fine gloves, they would leave their native mountains for Germany.

In the big markets of Leipzig and Berlin, the little merchants felt lost. Nobody, they thought, would pay any attention to their gloves. And they were homesick. So they did just what they did at home when their spirits needed lifting: they sang together. They sang all the songs they knew, and the one they sang most, for it was their favorite, was "Silent Night."

Its charm worked even in the busy city. Passersby stopped to listen, stepped closer to look, and ended by buying gloves. One day an elderly gentleman spoke to them. Would they care to appear in a concert? They would, even before they knew that the concert was to be given in a royal palace, before the king and queen of Saxony. The man who had accosted them was Herr Pohlenz, the royal director-general of music.

The evening of the concert arrived. The great hall of the palace was filled with a distinguished company. The queen wore a dainty gown; the king, the uniform of a general. Herr Pohlenz had chosen a very loud program for the evening. There was much drumming and trumpeting. The Strassers loved it. They thought it perfect from the first note to the last.

Suddenly, Herr Pohlenz raised his hand for silence, and announced that there were four children present. "Not singers by profession, but merchants. Yet they have the finest voices it has been my privilege to hear in years," said Herr Pohlenz.

He took the youngsters' breath away. A hush fell on the audience, and all eyes were on the children. Their first song was "Silent Night." They sang it exactly as they did at home. At the first note, their stage fright vanished, and to the listeners it was as though the young voices were carrying the peace of a mountain winter night into the glittering hall. When they had finished there was a moment of almost reverent quiet. Then applause broke loose; it went on and on. It was twice as loud and twice as long as that for the orchestra, but Herr Pohlenz didn't mind. The audience shouted for more. The youngsters sang all the songs they knew, and then they sang "Silent Night" again. Before they left, the queen had made them promise that they would sing their song on Christmas Eve that year in the royal Saxon court chapel at Pleissenburg. It was the first Christmas the children had ever spent away from home.

The fame of the children and of their song spread. The king of Prussia commanded a performance in Berlin. He found the song as pleasing as had the king of Saxony, but, not satisfied with the explanation that the author of the song was unknown, he ordered his royal concertmaster, Ludwig Erk, to find out who had written it.

Erk's search took many years. Everywhere he went throughout the Austrian Tyrol, people knew the song but knew nothing of the authors. By now, many of those who might have given him a clue were gone. Even Father Mohr, who had left the village

238

to become vicar of Wagram in Pongau, had died six years before.

But Franz Gruber was still living. He was now the choirmaster and organist of Hallein. One evening, Erk stopped for the night at St. Peter's abbey near Salzburg. The choir inspector there, who was no monk but a simple townsman named Prennsteiner, listened sympathetically to Erk's weary account of his search.

Now, one of Herr Prennsteiner's choir boys, a young lad named Felix Gruber, seemed to know more about "Silent Night" than anyone else in the district. So Prennsteiner questioned the boy about it. "How did you learn so much about that song?" he asked.

"Why, from my father, of course," replied young Felix. "He made it up."

"Come along, Felix," said Herr Prennsteiner excitedly, "we're going to visit your father."

Old Gruber was greatly honored to receive a visit from the distinguished choir inspector of Salzburg. "I hear that you have written a famous song," Herr Prennsteiner greeted him.

"A famous song?" Franz Gruber was puzzled.

"Yes, indeed. We've had quite a little excitement about it, at St. Peter's. There was a man down from Berlin, a Prussian, who had come there specially to look for the composer. Your son tells me that you wrote it, 'Silent Night.' "

"Oh, that," said Gruber. "Why, I wrote that when I was just a village schoolteacher, over thirty years ago."

"Well, it has come a long way," replied Prennsteiner.

"Does the Prussian know the right words?" Gruber asked his guest. "Because the words aren't mine; they are by the late Father Mohr, God rest his soul. There are six beautiful stanzas."

"All that our Prussian knew was four," replied Prennsteiner.

Before he left, Prennsteiner had commissioned old Gruber to write the authentic story of "Silent Night." When Gruber had finished his account, he dated it, like the methodical man he was: "F. Gruber, Town Church Choirmaster, Hallein, December 30, 1854."

For years, on each holy eve, "Silent Night" was sung at Hallein in the house where Gruber lived and died, to the accompaniment of his own original guitar. Later, the song was carried from

Hallein round the world by radio until a day in 1938 when Hitler wiped Austria off the map, and the little song of peace was proclaimed "undesirable."

But the great land of music from which it comes knows no frontiers. And the "Song From Heaven," like the Christmas message itself, still rings for all men of good will.

THE POETRY OF CHRISTMAS[49]

The wonder and paradox of the Incarnation have inspired some of the world's most beautiful verse

By John Druska

Poetry suits Christmas. In accounts of the first Christmas, light clashes with darkness and overcomes it. Spring appears in the midst of winter's night, releasing the earth from Adam's curse. A virgin gives birth, God enters human life as a child, in order to die. And animals join a motley few in honoring the Babe happily born under deadly edicts, human and divine. Such paradox and wonder offer a natural field for poets.

In medieval times, Christmas poetry tended to revive and hallow the event of Christ's birth and all that attends it. Many of these poems were set as carols, and their tradition continued.

In a sixteenth century carol, French shepherds give the Child a lamb, a redwing, and milk. An old Spanish carol adds "one small fish from the river" and "one wild bee from the heather" to the family of animals at the manger.

Robert Herrick in the seventeenth century sends a "pretty child" to visit "his Saviour, a Child," bearing a flower to place on "his bib, or stomacher" and "a whistle new, made of a clean straight oaten reed."

The first American carol, *Jesous Ahatonhia*, is credited to the seventeenth century Jesuit martyr Jean de Brébeuf and written in the Huron language. In it God the Father appears as "Gitchi Manitou," sending choirs of angels to sing over his Son, who is wrapped in a "ragged robe of rabbit skin." Chiefs replace Magi in the song, bringing "gifts of fox and beaver pelt."

These poems and many others, on into our time, show an awareness of the paradoxes innate to Christ's birthday. English poet and martyr Father Robert Southwell posed the riddle: *Patrem Parit Filia* ("The daughter gives birth to the Father") John Donne wrote of Christ as "Immensitie" who yet makes Himself "Weake enough, now into our world to come." And Christopher Smart hailed the Nativity's "magnitude of meekness."

Before such wonders, awe and rejoicing are in order. Some poets have Chanticleer singing long before dawn to herald Christ's appearance. Shakespeare alludes to this legend in the first scene of *Hamlet,* where Marcellus invokes the season.

> *Some say that ever 'gainst that*
> *season comes*
> *Wherein our Saviour's birth is*
> *celebrated,*
> *The birds of dawning singeth all*
> *night long . . .*
> *No fairy tales, no witch has*
> *power to charm;*
> *So hallow'd and so gracious is*
> *the time.*

In William Drummond's *The Shepherd's Song,* "springs ran nectar, honey dropped from trees." Milton's *On the Morning of Christ's Nativity* hymns the beginning of man's redemption, an end to the "old Dragon's" sway. Longfellow translates a Neapolitan carol that shows the earth turning to paradise at Christmas. E. A. Robinson addresses *A Christmas Sonnet* "to one in doubt," reclaiming for the twentieth century at least a trace of wham received millennia ago:

> *Something is here that was not here before,*
> *And strangely has not yet been crucified.*

Poets of celebration have been prey to doggerel at times. But they have nevertheless managed to produce some genuinely

241

good Christmas poetry. And poems like Gerard Manley Hopkins'
The Blessed Virgin Compared to the Air We Breathe illustrate
the vitality of the tradition beyond its medieval sources. Hopkins
asks in his poem that the mother who "came to mould" Christ's
limbs be "my atmosphere."

> *If I have understood,*
> *She holds high motherhood*
> *Towards all our ghostly good*
> *And plays in grace her part*
> *About man's breathing heart,*
> *Laying, like air's fine flood,*
> *The deathdance in his blood*
> *Yet no part but what will*
> *Be Christ our Saviour still.*

The joyful wonder in much of this Christmas poetry is strong.
But so is the sense of evil at work in the world and challenged
by the Christ Child. The celebratory poets are optimistic. As
long as Christ has moved earth and men and can keep doing so
through their poems, there is reason to hope and have faith.

After the seventeenth century, though, Christmas poetry, at
least in the English language, loses a good deal of its religious
vigor. The feast seems to attract fewer genuine celebrants.
In early America, Puritan churchmen discouraged Christmas
festivity, although many Puritan churchgoers did their utmost
to ignore the ban. In Europe, folk traditions were responsible
for many carols. But these traditions themselves had long been
waning. Soon an age of reason and satire reshaped English
letters; and an age of machines followed hard upon it. Christmas
had always insisted on the simplicity of its origins. Now, in a
world growing more complex, it suffered.

Nevertheless, poets somewhat isolated from their society or
closer to the folk (and so perhaps to the source of medieval
faith), could still catch something of the ancient impulse to
celebrate Christmas. The peasant poet John Clare, after a long
evocation of old Christmas customs in *Christmas Time,* realizes
how isolated he is in his appreciation: ". . . soon the poet's song
will be/ The only refuge they (the customs) can find." Thomas
Hardy, likewise, recalls in *The Oxen* an old legend of the animals

kneeling before Christ, related to him by an "elder" one
Christmas Eve. "So fair a fancy few would weave/ In these
years!" he laments.

Modern times have done more to Christmas than just change
its appearance. Christmas has been forcibly altered, hemmed
by massive commercialism, wars, and worldwide alienation.

War, of course, isn't unique to our century. Longfellow, in
Christmas Bells, rails against the Civil War; but the bells persist
and bring him back to his faith in peace on earth. Later, after
the first World War and Irish civil strife, W. B. Yeats is less
hopeful. He declares "the ceremony of innocense . . . drowned,"
and envisions as *The Second Coming* a "rough beast" that
"slouches toward Bethlehem to be born."

A war later Robinson Jeffers looks at "veils under veils of
the vanished England" and discovers the "seas netted with
ambushes/and the skies falling." But he recalls how "dark was
that first Christmas Day" and he implies, though faintly, that
there still is hope.

The second World War made such hope in the Christmas
promise of good will and peace more difficult than ever to
summon. In *Holy Innocents* Robert Lowell symbolizes the
armistice year 1945 as an oxcart laboring up hill:

> *If they (the oxen) die*
> *As Jesus, in the harness, who*
> *will mourn?*
> *Lamb of the shepherds, Child,*
> *how still you lie.*

The skeptical tradition of Christmas poetry ranges from
intimations of futility to outright despair. It suggests that the
event of Christ's birth has lost its effect on man's personal and
communal histories. Christmas, once regarded as miraculous,
is now merely ironic. By its old hope we gauge our losses.
Indeed, our losses may demoralize us more because of what
Christmas once led men to expect. James Wright expresses
this sort of sadness in a poem he titles *Having Lost My Sons,*
I Confront the Wreckage of the Moon: Christmas 1960.

Some modern poets, however, have given new life to the
celebratory tradition of Christmas poetry. W. H. Auden's long

Christmas oratorio, *For the Time Being,* is undercut by his knowledge that it's just a seasonal ceremony, ineffective on the world's stage. But Auden still believes in a love that surpasses human understanding, that makes what little we have sufficient for the time being.

Patrick Kavanagh manages, if only for the moment, to return himself to *A Christmas Childhood,* where his father plays the melodeon and mother milks the cows. Kavanagh admires the unwordly beauty of this common Irish landscape:

> *One side of the potato-pits was white with frost—*
> *How wonderful that was, how wonderful!*
> *And when we put our ears to the paling-post*
> *The music that came out was magical.*

In our world it's probably worth recalling that words can offer us a source of miracle. The modern poet may not be George Herbert shepherding his thoughts, words, and deeds; singing to a sun whose beams he wishes would twine with his breast, "till beams sing and music shine." Perhaps he is not Milton hastening his Muse to beat "star-led wizards" to the child "and lay (thy humble ode) lowly at His Bless'd feet." He may not even be Clare, creating in his song a "refuge" for Christmas' ancient rites. Few poets today agree on what Christmas means.

Yet men of good will and all faiths, or no faith, still respond to Christmas in their poetry. Maybe poetry can't do without Christmas. After all, John tells us, Christmas is a form of poetry, the Word's coming to life. Christmas, by its nature, requires attention, whether from the skeptical or faithful. And it could force poets to perform miracles.

As he regards Christmas, the modern poet still may find it necessary to speak of the Child as a center of men's hopes and fears, a miraculous source of poetry in a prosaic world. This is what Kenneth Patchen does in *I have Lighted the Candles, Mary.* In a "bitter world" he sees "the cold, swollen face of war lean in the window." The poet speaks to his wife ("the taste of tears is in her mouth") and to Christ's mother. And the words reveal that Christmas may have been betrayed by the world, but still must be kept alive in it. Otherwise, Patchen implies, we (and poetry with us) risk madness:

> *They are blowing out the candles, Mary . . .*
> *The world is a thing gone mad tonight,*
> *O hold Him tenderly, dear Mother.*
> *For He is a kingdom in the hearts of men.*

THE BURNING BABE [50]

The Christmas poem Father Southwell wrote in the Tower of London
By Francis Howard

One of the world's great religious lyrics was written by a Catholic priest awaiting execution under Elizabeth I, during the yuletide of 1594.

He wrote it in the Tower of London, where so many persons, both famous and obscure, had been confined, later to suffer death by execution, that the surroundings would seem to have made for melancholy and despair.

But Father Robert Southwell, S.J., was able to rise above the dismal environment. During his Christmas devotions in 1594, stirred by love for the Child of Bethlehem, he poured forth his soul in *The Burning Babe.* It was in anticipation of his own martyrdom that he pictured the Christ Child bringing to earth a heart burning with cleansing fire for the souls of mankind.

Ben Jonson paid Father Southwell the supreme compliment when he confessed that he would gladly destroy all his own poems if only he could say he had written the Christmas poem.

In Queen Elizabeth I's day Catholic priests were not permitted to remain in England more than forty days. If they overstayed this limit, they were charged with treason and put to death.

Father Southwell knew this when, in 1586, he came from France in disguise. He had heard about Catholic families, scattered through the countryside, that had no priest to minister to them. For six years he carried on his mission without detection, moving from one Catholic household to another, celebrating Mass and giving religious instruction to the children.

His arrest in 1592 was sudden and unexpected. He had become a close friend of Richard Bellamy, whose kinsman had been hanged for sheltering Anthony Babington, the head of a conspiracy against the queen. The other Bellamys were still suspect. They were not aware of it, but the chief of the queen's officers, the notorious Richard Topcliffe, had them under close surveillance.

Father Southwell had frequently visited this home, celebrating Mass and giving instruction to the sons and daughters. He was not present when Topcliffe's men suddenly showed up, but the daughter, Anne Bellamy, weakened and broke down under the officer's ruthless questioning.

A trap was then sprung. Word was sent to the unsuspecting priest in London that Richard Bellamy wanted him to come at once. After his arrival, the queen's men, with Topcliffe in the lead, broke in as he was celebrating Mass.

Amid a great hue and cry the prisoner was brought back to London. He was lodged in the chief officer's own house in Westminister churchyard. The officers subjected him to torture but could not break his spirit nor gain any information on other priests hiding in England. One of the tortures was hanging by the wrists for hours at a time.

Topcliffe then had the prisoner moved to the Gatehouse at Westminister, to a cell swarming with vermin. Father Southwell's father came there to see his son, and when he discovered his pitiful condition, he dispatched a petition to the queen, begging her that the accused be brought to trial at once even if it meant his execution, rather than that he be left another day "in that filthy hole."

For once the queen seems to have been moved by compassion, for Father Southwell was soon lodged in the Tower of London. There his father was able to supply him with clothes and reading matter. It was three years before he was brought to trial.

He was taken from the Tower to Newgate, and confined in

the dungeon known as "Limbo." On February 21, he was hauled before the King's Bench at Westminster. When the indictment was read, Southwell replied, "Not guilty of any treason." He admitted, however, that he was a Jesuit and was prepared to die. The jury brought in a swift verdict of guilty, and the prisoner was sentenced to a traitor's death.

Sentence was carried out the next day. Father Southwell was drawn on a sled to the gallows at Tyburn. When he was lifted onto the scaffold, this gentle man, his auburn hair blowing in the winter breeze, proudly proclaimed that he was "a priest of the Catholic and Roman Church and of the Society of Jesus." He solemnly denied that he had attempted, contrived, or imagined any evil against the queen.

The hangman bungled his job. The rope had been so clumsily wound about the prisoner's throat that some time elapsed before life was extinct.

When the head was severed from the body and held up before the crowd, there was a strange silence. No cry of "Traitor!" was raised by any of the onlookers, for those times, an almost unheard-of occurrence.

Less than two months after his martyrdom, a book was published, *St. Peter's Complaint and Other Poems.*

The volume carried no author's name, but all London knew who the author was. It attracted so many readers that it was reprinted a dozen time in the next forty years. The most popular poem in the collection was *The Burning Babe.* That Christmas poem of the fearless missioner is still cherished after three and a half centuries. As reproduced here, the spelling has been modernized.

THE BURNING BABE

As I in hoary Winter's night
    Stood shivering in the snow,
Surprised I was with sudden heat,
    Which made my heart to glow;

And lifting up a fearful eye,
    To view what fire was near,
A pretty Babe all burning bright
    Did in the air appear;

Who, scorched with excessive heat,
    Such floods of tears did shed,
As though his floods should quench his flames,
    With which his tears were fed;

Alas (quoth he) but newly born,
    In fiery heats I fry,
Yet none approach to warm their hearts,
    Or feel my fire, but I;

My faultless breast the furnace is,
    The fuel, wounding thorns:
Love is the fire, and sighs the smoke,
    The ashes, shame and scorns;

The fuel Justice layeth on,
    And Mercy blows the coals,
The metal in this furnace wrought
    Are men's defiled souls

For which, as now on fire I am
    To work them to their good,
So will I melt into a bath,
    To wash them in my blood.

With this he vanished out of sight,
    And swiftly shrunk away,
And straight I called unto mind,
    That it was Christmas Day.

Chapter VII
Modern Twists

A good many young school children, if you have never brought the subject up before, will tell you the song the angels sang around the Crib was Silent Night. These would not be stupid children; they would only be responding to an emphasis we put on certain songs and customs in our own culture. A person visiting our shopping centers for the first time from a completely non-Christian country might well think our Christmas season is basically commercial, with our chief energies and thoughts devoted not to religion but to business. A visitor from some pagan starving Third World country might be most impressed by our feasting, and think the Christmas dinner the center of all observance. Silent Night, gift shopping and cooking are late comers to the Christmas scene, but they have become such integral parts of it that it would be unthinkable folly to try to do away with them. Just as in the case of Santa Claus, for us Christmas wouldn't be Christmas without them.

ANNIVERSARY OF A GUITAR MASS [51]

When the organ broke down, the organist set the priest's poem to music

By Dan Madden

When a guitar was used one Christmas Eve in the village church of Oberndorf in the Austrian Alps, there were no scandalized mutterings about "Folk Mass."

It seemed quite natural to the townspeople. The organ had unexpectedly collapsed. Since music was needed for the Midnight Mass the organist saved the day by bringing along his guitar. He also brought along the music he had just composed for the Christmas poem the assistant pastor had written. With a guitar as accompaniment, priest and organist sang their Christmas song for the first time.

That was in 1818 on Christmas Eve. The song was *Silent Night*.

Today, the words of *Silent Night* are sung in all languages. In a real sense it has become an international folk song, handed down from generation to generation by people everywhere.

Its authors obviously never thought their song would reach beyond the church door. Joseph Mohr, the twenty-six-year-old priest who wrote the words, was new to the parish. Franz Gruber, the thirty-one-year-old composer, taught school in a neighboring hamlet and rounded out his week at the church organ in Oberndorf.

Like a folk song, *Silent Night* passed from place to place and person to person without its authors even being aware of it. The song traveled from the Salzach valley westward into the Tyrol and north into Germany. In 1854, thirty-six years after its debut, *Silent Night* had reached Berlin. A member of the Imperial Orchestra took it upon himself to trace the song's beginnings.

By that time Father Mohr was dead. Gruber had given up teaching but was active as organist and choirmaster in the village of Hallein on the outskirts of Salzburg.

Gruber wrote a letter to the Berlin musician relating the origins of *Silent Night* and included a copy of the way it had

253

been written. This is the only record of the song's birth.

Oberndorf was an ideal setting for the creating of a Christmas folk song. Rimmed by snow-covered mountains, it lies a dozen miles north of Salzburg on a narrow river. The word *salt* in Salzburg and the river Salzach explains the area's ancient economics. Almost half the people of Father Mohr's Oberndorf hauled salt from mine to market along the Salzach. Most of the others were farmers.

The guitar was part of everyday life in Oberndorf. It set the tune at happy gatherings in the home on a snowbound winter night and in a wine garden on a soft summer evening.

Christmas Eve in the village church was the happiest gathering of the year. It still is. The townspeople bundle up in warm clothes and walk along the snow-filled roads to the village church of St. Nicholas. Women wear dark velour hats. The black fedoras of the men have high green bands to show that they are Alpine people. The blouses of the women are edged with delicate lace which they, or their mothers, or their grandmothers made. Some men, and almost all the young boys, wear leather knickers to church.

Voices of the townspeople singing *Silent Night* filter from the church through the hushed village. After midnight Mass village families exchange Christmas greetings on the church steps. The men retrieve long pipes from the deep pockets of their green coats and solemnly pack them with tobacco. Some pipes are treasured meerschaums. Puffs of smoke silently link up in the dark over the heads of the chattering townspeople.

Throughout the Salzach valley, the midnight quietness brings the bells from many villages close together in a unified salute to Christmas Day.

The pattern of life of an Austrian village changes slowly. Just the same, the years have brought some changes to Oberndorf. For one thing, the town's population has more than doubled. When *Silent Night* was written, Oberndorf had 1,203 inhabitants and 190 houses. The latest census counted 513 houses and 3,083 inhabitants.

Many of Oberndorf's families still farm. But farming has changed, too. Burgermeister Raimund Traintinger notices this.

When not at the town hall he makes farmhouse calls as a veterinarian. Most of his animal patients nowadays are cows and pigs. Few horses are left, he says.

The mayor's car is outfitted with a mobile telephone. His wife Inge acts as dispatcher. Via house-to-car radio she passes on to her husband emergency calls from the town hall, from irate citizens, and from worried farmers with sick animals on their hands.

Salt is no longer a basic source of the town's income. The *Schifferscheutzenkorps* has celebrated its anniversary for 700 years, but its purpose has changed with the times. It was founded to protect the salt-carrying river boats from pirates. Now, its function is mostly ceremonial.

In their red coats and white trousers descendants of the old-time ship-protection men form a guard of honor at midnight Mass on Christmas Eve and on other festive occasions.

But the river at Oberndorf's doorstep is still a main concern of the *Schifferscheutzenkorps*. They keep an eye on the river level and sound the alarm when floods threaten. Floods destroyed the original St. Nicholas church in which *Silent Night* was introduced as well as two dozen houses. Foundations of the original St. Nicholas church were so waterlogged that it was decided to build a new one a few hundred yards from the river-bank.

On the site of the original church a commemorative chapel was built. One stained-glass window shows Father Mohr with a quill in one hand and a scroll in the other. In the opposite window, Franz Gruber is pictured strumming a guitar.

Masses are celebrated in the chapel on the anniversaries of the two authors, both of which fall just before the Christmas season. Franz Gruber's birthday was November 25; Father Mohr's, December 11.

The guardian of the Silent Night chapel is a friendly retired Vienna policeman named Adolf Muksch. For the 150th anniversary of *Silent Night* the Austrian post office issued a commemorative postage stamp featuring a guitar. Herr Muksch has made an artistic contribution, too. He has designed a rubber-stamp for his correspondence which pictured the continents of the world banded together by the musical message of *Silent Night*.

Christmas Eve, of course, is the busiest time at the Silent Night chapel. At 5:00 P.M. the mayor, village notables and townspeople crowd into the chapel for Mass. The village choir sings Christmas carols, climaxing with the song born on the spot where they stand.

Many visitors to Oberndorf like to include in their pilgrimage the neighboring hamlet of Arnsdorf, two miles away. Its two-story school has changed but little since the days when Franz Gruber was schoolmaster. Frau Ottilia Aigner, a pleasant woman in her late twenties is the teacher. Her husband Joseph is principal.

Franz Gruber held both jobs, often for as many as eighty boys and girls, aged from six to fourteen. They sat six in a row in the large room on the first floor. Today, fifty-eight children in eight grades study in two classrooms.

Schoolmaster Gruber used to live with his wife and children on the second floor of the schoolhouse. This has been preserved as a memorial.

School parties are as informal as they were when Franz Gruber staged them. In farm clothes, parents line the sides of the main classroom and applaud as the children recite, sing, and dance.

The Arnsdorf church a century and a half ago had three daily Masses and four on Sundays. Franz Gruber played the organ for most of them. On Sundays, however, his oldest son would usually substitute for him while he went to Oberndorf.

Oberndorf at the time was a brand new town. It is only two years older than *Silent Night*. Since it was a new parish, St. Nicholas's had no organist of its own. Franz Gruber, therefore, was asked to help out. Father Mohr was assigned as assistant pastor the year before he and Franz Gruber wrote *Silent Night*.

Several years after the birth of *Silent Night,* the two young authors went their separate ways. Father Mohr was transferred to another village. Eventually he was appointed pastor in Wagrain, the town where he died. Meanwhile, Franz Gruber took the job of teacher-choirmaster in the neighboring Berndorf.

He had applied for a similar post in Oberndorf but for some reason was turned down. He was so disappointed that he decided to move from the town with which he is now so closely associated.

The district school inspector, in rating him first among the five applicants for the Berndorf job, gave him very high marks. "He knows very much (can paint and is a musician). He is industrious . . . handles children very well. People like him. He is very specially trained in every sense."

Whether the paths of the teacher and the priest ever crossed again, no one knows. For years after the birth of *Silent Night,* few people gave any sign that they knew either one of them even existed.

The memorials and museums came later. On the wall of the house where Franz Gruber died, across the street from the parish church in Hallein, Los Angeles teachers placed a plaque in 1934. "In honor of a teacher for his universal message of peace and goodwill."

Some fifty miles away, in the tiny churchyard of Wagrain, ornamented wrought iron decorates the grave of Father Mohr. The inscription reads, "Dedicated to the writer of the unforgettable Christmas song."

The guitar which accompanied the priest and the teacher when they sang their Christmas song for the first time is preserved in the Hallein museum.

MERRY CHRISTMAS COOKING [52]

When Christ is in the kitchen and at the table
By Florence S. Berger

Of all the rooms in a house, the friendly, comforting kitchen is mother to us all. It is the source of our food, our learning, our virtue. Here the first pale gray streaks of dawn find a woman grinding coffee; the aroma wakes the family. Here the baby spills his milk with impunity. All during the day little helpers find new adventure here in tasks which teach and amuse—even though it means sifting flour on the cat. Here the older children run, after school, to raid the apple bin or cookie jar. Even the high-school gang prefer to kick off their shoes in the kitchen rather than any other room. At night there are lessons to do here, while debate and philosophizing split the ceiling. When the rest of the rooms are asleep at last, the light in the kitchen remains first and last in our affections and memories.

There is, I believe, a reason for this, and it lies in the woman who is mistress of that kitchen. Cook, you may call her. I prefer to call her Christian in Action. She herself is Christ-centered because she brings Christ home to her kitchen and, in corollary, her kitchen reflects the Christ within her.

To some it may seem sacrilegious to connect cookery and Christ, but if I am to carry Christ home with me from the altar, I am afraid He will have to come to the kitchen because much of my time is spent there. I shall welcome Him on Easter and He shall eat new lamb with us. I shall give homage to Him on Christmas and Epiphany and shall cook a royal feast for Him and my family. I shall mourn with Him on Holy Thursday and we shall taste the bitter herbs of the Passover and break unleavened bread. Then the cooking we do will add special significance to the Church year and Christ will sanctify our daily bread. That is what is meant by the liturgical year in the kitchen.

Perhaps mothers and daughters can lead their families back to Christ-centered living and cooking. Foods can be symbols which lead the mind to spiritual thinking. After Christ preached to the multitude, He fed them. If our family is to hear the Gospel, I shall first feed them on symbols and then on more substantial meat. The one will help the digestion of the other.

At the very first Sunday of Advent, we women hear the warning to get busy, "Stir up Thy power, we beseech Thee, Oh Lord, and come." It is the time to hurry home and stir up your plum puddings. In England even today this is known as Stir-up Sunday. The more you can stir a pudding the better. Each member of the family should come and give a good stir. Plum puddings are deliberate affairs. It takes a bit of gathering and garnering before we begin.

Perhaps I could introduce our family to you while they collect the ingredients for the pudding. Mary, the eldest, with all the importance of her eleven years, is telephoning her father to please bring home some raisins, currants, citron, and almonds. These are things which won't grow on our Ohio farm. Ann, our nine-year-old, is a natural-born cook. She has been saving the orange and grapefruit peel for several days and now at last, after two parboilings, the peel is bubbling in a thick syrup. Freddie, our only boy, has been sent to the root cellar for carrots, potatoes, and apples. I can hear him banging around among the tin cans in which we will steam the pudding. Kathy, who will soon be three, has her chubby fists full of suet and bread crumbs. She plans to put them on the bird tray, but they are making a fine Hansel-and-Gretel trail across the kitchen floor and out on the hall rugs. Christine, not quite a year, is crawling after an orange.

Each year, as we assemble all those ingredients, the children want to hear the plum-pudding story. It is a tale which goes far back into pagan times when the Celtic god, Dagda, lived in the hills of Britain. Dagda was the God of plenty. When he saw the sun turn in its course to come closer to the earth with each lengthening day, he decided to hold festival. So he built a great fire under an enormous black cauldron called Undry. In the cauldron he placed the most delicious fruits of the earth and all other good things. Slowly he cooked it, spiced it, tasted it. Dagda was pleased with his plum porridge and he was ready to rejoice at the yuletide.

The recipe was passed down through the years. When Christianity came, the recipe was not changed. The dish of honor, though, was dedicated, not to the sun, but to Christ, "the true Light who comes to enlighten the world."

Family cooperation is well taught in the making of the pudding. Everyone lends a helping hand. At times a coin or thimble or doll are stirred in, too, just for luck. So good luck to you with the list of proportions which follows:

PLUM PUDDING

1 pound suet
3 cups brown sugar
2 cups stale bread crumbs
6 eggs
Juice of 10 oranges
4 cups sifted flour
1 teaspoon ginger
1 teaspoon salt
1 teaspoon cinnamon
1 teaspoon nutmeg
1 fresh lemon peel
1 fresh orange peel
1/4 pound candied orange peel
1/4 pound candied grapefruit peel
1 1/2 pounds raisins
1/2 pound currants
1/2 pound citron
1/4 pound blanched almonds

To stretch your pudding add:
2 medium-size raw potatoes
2 medium-size raw apples
2 medium-size raw carrots

Grind the suet and bread. Moisten with beaten eggs and orange juice. Add sifted dry ingredients. Grind fresh and candied peel with the raw vegetables. Add these to the batter. Stir in raisins, currants, citron and almonds. If the pudding is dry or lumpy, add wine or fruit juice. Pack in buttered tins, and steam.

Our grandmothers would steam their plum puddings for eight or ten hours, but I put mine in the pressure cooker at fifteen pounds pressure for eighty minutes. After steaming, the pudding will keep indefinitely. Time only improves the flavor. I have kept some an entire year. If you have brandy, pour it over the top of the pudding to age, and your dessert for Christmas dinner is ready.

The children of the house have smelled the good smells of spices, and they are dancing around the table with mixing spoons and cookie cutters in their hands. "Don't forget St. Nicholas, mother. He comes tomorrow night."

There is no forgetting St. Nicholas (December 6) at our house. That is the eve when we all hang up our stockings. Most of the real sport, though, comes the day before, when we make the treats to fill those stockings.

You will find traditions very easy to begin again with children. When they are grown men and women, they will be loath to cast them aside. Most American families threw their spiritual and social traditions into the sea when they left Europe. They no longer wished to appear Dutch or French or Swedish, so they left you and me without a background.

Several days later we begin to plan our Christmas cookies. Sometimes our cookies are good enough to end up as Christmas gifts. But they're always good enough to serve at parties, and to keep in a little basket that hangs on the front door for visiting children. Our four favorite cookie recipes come from Switzerland, Moravia, Holland and Germany.

One of the saddest complaints I ever heard came from a mother at a Family Life conference. She couldn't stand her daughter messing in the kitchen. The daughter had her own ideas of preparing food, and she was just in the way. As a result, the mother's kitchen was very tidy, but her daughter's emotions were in a clutter. Christ means parents to be teachers. A child can learn best by doing. If our homes were real workshops, with Christ as manager, the parents foreman, and the children as workers, we could educate more mature Christians.

If you would ask which cookie spells Christmas to me, I

would vote for the sweet, honeyed *Lebkuchen*. Some modern writers have explained the name *Lebkuchen* or Life Cake as a cookie hard and heavy enough to have a long life. That sounds like utter foolishness to me. They are too good to live long in anyone's cookie jar.

The Life Cake is, rather, a religious symbol of the new life which we find at Christmas. When we Catholics receive the consecrated Host at Christmas Mass, we pray: "May the new life derived from this sacrament ever revive us, O Lord: since it is His sacrament whose wonderful birth hath overcome the old man." The *Lebkuchen* is a perfect carryover of the Bread of Life to a special feast day cake. Anyone who is sensitive to symbolic language can understand its Christmas message. We do not hold Christmas merely as a memory of the Lord's birth, but each year we, too, are reborn into Christ and die to the old man of sin so that we might be a "people acceptable."

LEBKUCHEN *(Life Cake)*

- 1 cup honey
- 1/4 cup water
- 2 cups brown sugar
- 2 eggs
- 8 cups flour
- 1/2 teaspoon soda
- 1/4 teaspoon salt
- 1/4 teaspoon nutmeg
- 1/4 teaspoon cloves
- 1 1/2 teaspoons cinnamon
- 1 1/2 cups shredded orange peel
- 1 1/2 cups chopped citron
- 2 cups chopped blanched almonds

Boil honey, sugar and water for five minutes. Beat in the eggs. Add sifted dry ingredients. Stir in fruit and almonds. Cover, and let stand overnight to ripen. Roll one-fourth inch thick. Cut into rectangles one inch wide by three inches long. Give cookies plenty of room on greased sheet. Bake in moderate oven (350°) for 15 minutes.) When cool, ice with:

- 1 cup confectioners' sugar

5 teaspoons boiling water
1 teaspoon lemon juice

December days pass by before we realize it. There is a smell of sweet wood smoke in the air because our fireplace is always glowing. White hoar-frost hangs upon the trees as the fog rises from the river.

By December 17, both the Church and the children become increasingly impatient for Christmas. This holy impatience has found expression in the beautiful antiphons which call Christ to come and to come quickly. It is very natural for children to use the *O Antiphons* for their daily prayer at this time. We say them at the evening meal when the Advent wreath is lighted.

Another old custom which we revived is the giving of family treats. In the monasteries long years ago, the monks furnished extra treats on those days before Christ's birthday. The gardener gave the Community some of his finest dried or preserved fruits on December 19, when he called on Christ, "O Root of Jesse, come to deliver us and tarry not." The cellarer unlocked the best wine for his treat as he called, "O Key of David, come, and come quickly." Finally, on December 23, the abbot gave his extra gift to the brethren. Expense accounts which are still extant show how generous and extensive a list of foods were used on the abbot's "O day."

Each one in our family keeps his gift a secret until supper time. We begin with the smallest child. His treat may be only a graham cracker for dessert. Freddie cracked and picked some black walnuts for us. All the pounding didn't give it away, because little boys are so often pounding. Ann made some Advent-wreath cookies and used up all the cinnamon drops for decoration—on the cookies, and her face and fingers. Mary made a big casserole of baked beans, and we couldn't quite decide whether she was treating herself or the family. Finally, it was mother's turn, and then, at last, father's turn to produce something really outstanding.

When dessert time came, he got up from the table without a word, put on his hat and coat without a smile, and left us sitting at the table with our mouths open in amazement. After

five minutes which seemed like hours, he stamped back into
the house, with a big bowl of snow ice cream. The squeals of
delight would have pleased an abbot.

At last the vigil of Christmas is here. Most of our cooking
and baking is done on this day so that we may be Marys and
not Marthas on the holy day. For Christmas breakfast we
bake a sweet nut bread which the Bretons made. It is as
wholesome as it is good.

BRETON NUT BREAD

2 cups whole wheat flour
1 cup white flour
1/2 cup brown sugar
3 teaspoons baking powder
2 teaspoons baking soda
1/4 teaspoon salt
2 cups sour milk
1 cup chopped nuts
1/2 cup raisins
1/2 cup currants

Mix sifted dry ingredients in a bowl. Add sour milk slowly
and stir to a smooth dough. Mix in nuts, raisins, currants.
Bake in a hot oven (400°) for about 60 minutes.

Another cake, which tastes even sweeter after early morning
Mass, is made from a Greek recipe. In Greece it is customary
to make this cake at Christmas and hide a silver coin deep in
its crust. The one who receives the coin in his piece of cake
is honor man for the day.

MELACHRINO *(Spice Cake)*

3/4 cup butter
1 cup sugar
3 eggs
3/4 cup milk
1 3/4 cups flour
1/4 teaspoon mace
1 1/4 teaspoon cinnamon
1/4 teaspoon ground cloves
1 1/2 teaspoons backing soda

1/4 teaspoon salt
1 1/2 tablespoons lemon juice

Cream butter and sugar. Beat in eggs. Add milk alternately
with sifted dry ingredients. Stir in lemon juice. Pour batter
into a greased 9 by 14 loaf pan. Bake in a moderate oven
(350°) for 45 minutes. While the cake is still hot, ice with:

1 1/2 cups confectioners' sugar
5 or 6 tablespoons water
1/2 teaspoon lemon juice.

To my mind, the ultimate in Christmas breads is the famous
German *Stollen*. If you were French, you would choose
brioche or *galette*. If you were Scotch, you might long for a
yuletide bannock. If you were Bohemian, you would want
vanocka. But, since you are American, you may have all five.
I advise that you use one sweet bread one year and another
the next.

The shape of the German *Stollen* is supposed to represent
the Christ child. The folds in the dough on the top of the loaf
should remind you of swaddling clothes. When you bake your
Stollen, give it plenty of room in the pan so the shape will be
sure.

STOLLEN

1 cake yeast
1 teaspoon sugar
1/4 cup luke warm water
6 cups flour
1 teaspoon salt
1/2 teaspoon nutmeg
2 cups scalded milk
1 cup shortening
1-1/4 cups sugar
2 eggs
1 cup raisins
1 cup currants
1/2 cup blanched almonds
1/2 cup chopped citron
1-1/2 teaspoons lemon extract

Dissolve yeast and teaspoonful of sugar in water. Sift flour
and salt and nutmeg. Add to yeast mixture. Knead until
smooth. Cover and let the dough rise to double in bulk.
   Cream shortening and sugar. Add eggs and milk. Stir in
fruit and flavoring. Combine this mixture with the raised dough.
Knead dough again. Shape dough into ropes about one and
one-half inches in diameter. For each large *Stollen,* make one
rope three feet long and two that are two and one-half feet long.
Braid the dough. Bring the braid to a point at either end. Place
the braid on a greased cookie sheet. Let rise until double in size.
Bake in a hot oven (400°) for 25 minutes, or until brown. This
recipe will make two large or three small *Stollen.*

   Our Christmas dinner is served at night. Nothing is quite so
welcome in the afternoon as a glass of English eggnog and some
German cinnamon stars. That blend of nationalities, at least
during our lifetime, has spelled dissensions; but on Christmas
Day when "the King of Peace is magnified above all kings of
the whole earth," all nations are reconciled. "All flesh shall
see the salvation of our God."

   Being American Catholics, we can choose the best of the
culture of all the nations of the world and make them ours in
Christ. We can call the songs, stories, dances and foods of all
peoples our own because in our American heritage there is blood
and bone and spirit of those different men and women. If
America is a melting pot, it can also be a cooking pot from
which we can serve up a Christian culture.

ENGLISH EGGNOG

12 eggs
2 1/4 cups sugar
   1 quart brandy
   1 pint rum
   3 pints cream
   2 quarts milk
   1 cup powdered sugar

   Beat egg yolks with sugar. Add brandy and rum slowly so
eggs will not coagulate. Beat in milk and two pints of cream.
Fold in six stiffly beaten egg whites. Beat remaining egg whites

very stiff; add powdered sugar and one pint cream. Float this egg-white mixture on the eggnog. Chill overnight.

Almonds have always been associated with childhood. The Christ child was often honored by some kind of almond cookie. During the Middle Ages, almonds were used lavishly, even though they were never notably cheap. Almond milk was made by grinding blanched almonds in warm, honeyed water. This was eaten by dipping sops or toasts of bread in the milk. It was considered a safe and sane dessert for children. Almond-milk-flavored *blanc mange* was often the sweet served at a Baptism party. In France the godparents of the infant Christian still throw *dragees* (like the English Jordan almonds) to the village children who wait on the church steps or under the windows of the home where the party is held. The same *dragees* are packed in fancy white boxes and given as favors to intimates and members of the family. That is why we use so many almonds at Christmas when the infant Christ has His birthday party.

We have tried many recipes for dressing, those with corn bread or oysters or chestnuts, but we always return like prodigals to the one my grandmother used. We like whole-wheat bread for dressing because it eliminates that pasty whiteness which you sometimes see.

STUFFED TURKEY

    10 pound turkey
    2 loaves whole-wheat bread
    1/2 cup milk
    2 beaten eggs
    2 chopped onions
    2 tablespoons butter
    1 cup diced celery stalks
    1 teaspoon dried sage
    1 cup raisins
    Salt
    Pepper
    1 teaspoon dried rosemary

Break the bread. Mix in milk and eggs. Fry onions in butter. Add onions, celery, sage and raisins to the dressing. Season with salt and pepper. Fill the salted turkey. Roast uncovered in hot oven (500°) for 30 minutes. Baste with butter and dust with flour. Lower heat to 400°. Baste three or four times during the roasting period. At the last basting, sprinkle rosemary over the turkey. Cover after the bird is well browned. A 10-pound turkey will take about three hours.

Preparations for Christmas dinner are ended now, except for the plum-pudding sauce. In England after 1644, plum puddings were forbidden and declared fit only for heathens. I am sure those reformers would have changed their minds if they had had enough of this sauce. I have often doubled and tripled this recipe, so use your own judgment.

PLUM PUDDING SAUCE

  1 egg white
  1 teaspoon rum
  1/2 lemon juiced
1 1/2 cups confectioner's sugar
  1 tablespoon butter
  3/4 cup whipped cream

Beat egg white, rum, lemon juice and sugar. Add butter and beat hard. Fold in whipped cream. Serve cold.

As the minor notes of the French carol, *Christmas Eve Is Here*, cut through the frosty air into our hearts, a dozen traditions await retelling. Many good and holy customs have been lost from one generation to another. Our old folks grow forgetful and the young ones are inattentive. As a result, our homes become modern, but our children lose touch with the good things of the past. Not that the here and now is bad. God forbid. The present, however, is enriched by a knowledge of the past and the future will be great only if our contribution of good is great. That is why we gather and reteach Catholic traditions.

Christmas Eve was not only the time to "deck the halls with boughs of holly." It was a day on which each country contributed something to Christ's cookbook. Since Christ was the Bread of Angels, men made special breads in His honor. In Germany, bread which was baked on Christmas Day was holy bread. The Introit of the Golden Mass of the Wednesday of

Advent Ember week was recited as the bread was baked. "Drop down dew, ye heavens, from above, and let the clouds rain the just; let the earth be opened and bud forth a Saviour." The dew of Christmas sanctified the loaf while the charity of the Advent Ember days mounted right to the vigil of Christ's birth night. This was to be bread for the poor.

With all this talk of cakes and cookery, you will think that Christmas Eve is to be nothing but a "night of cakes," as the Scotch used to call it. This, however, is not true, for the honest Christian must see first things first.

Although there be "no Christmas without flesh," the feast we prepare is but a shadow of the heavenly banquet which Christ prepares for those who love Him. Never forget that all our earthly bread is but a symbol of the Bread of Angels, which Christ serves this night at midnight.

A feast day is a day of joy, so by all means plan to use your day for higher things. A feast day is a day of family gathering, so gather your dear ones at Mass, at prayers, at the table, around the Christmas tree.

There is nothing quite so unliturgical as a mother stewing over a hot stove most of Christmas Day while her family waits to eat and sleep like pagan Romans. What if most of the crowds do go to midnight Mass? Why not try a quieter, more prayerful time? This is a day on which to lead a higher, more perfect life. Your work is finished, so enjoy your leisure.

You have called on Christ to come all during Advent. Now He is here; run to meet Him. This is the day your family has been waiting for; now enjoy it as a family. The food you have prepared will help to bind them to your table, and the love you have given them will bear fruit. Here again, cookery and Christ are united.

BLESSED ARE THE CHRISTMAS SHOPPERS [53]

For they shall find true bargains
By Daniel Durken, O.S.B.

One December afternoon on my way to a parish assignment I stopped at a crowded shopping center. I came away with a free lesson on the meaning of Christmas.

I chose a shopping center for my Advent adventure because of the abundance there of the very material that gives meaning to Christmas—flesh. "The Word became flesh and dwelt among us." That sentence is still the simplest and clearest description of the Incarnation. Indeed St. Luke describes the Christmas event in terms of that same flesh.

"All the world," Luke writes, went to be enrolled in Caesar's census. And they must have done more than just sign the official roster and pay the registration fee before they returned home. Joseph and Mary probably mingled with the crowd on the Bethlehem mall. Before they looked for a room at the local inn they must have searched for bargains in swaddling cloth, carpenter tools, and household essentials.

Jesus enjoyed that first incarnational interaction with shoppers, bargain hunters, and browsers. And for the rest of his life He went on a kind of shopping spree, searching for what He could save. "The Son of man came to seek and save . . . ." Jesus is not even out of his crib before He encounters shepherds, who can only afford to look, not buy; and kings, big-time spenders who don't even have to see price tags to decide whether they can like the merchandise. Jesus is not off his cross before He encounters two common shoplifters, the thieves who are put to death with Him.

Between crib and cross Jesus brought joy to local merchants, for wherever He went a standing-room-only crowd was sure to follow. At the start of his preaching and healing ministry, the good news got out that Jesus had cured the mother of Peter's wife. Soon "the whole city was gathered together about the door."

Sometimes there wasn't even room to stand. The time Jesus

270

went to his own home in Capernaum "many were gathered together so that there was no longer room for them, not even about the door." No wonder that soon afterwards Jesus moved from shop to shore. "Jesus withdrew his disciples to the sea, and a great multitude from Galilee followed."

Jesus would enjoy a Christmas rush. He loved crowds. He was no leg-weary and footsore clerk aching for the last customer to leave. "When He saw the crowds, He had compassion for them, because they were harassed and helpless, like sheep without a shepherd," like shoppers without a salesperson. He tells his disciples, "I have compassion on the crowd because they have been with Me now three days and have nothing to eat; and I am unwilling to send them away hungry, lest they faint on the way."

Only once did Jesus disperse a crowd of shoppers. "Jesus entered the temple of God and drove out all who sold and bought in the temple, and He overturned the tables of the money-changers and the seats of those who sold pigeons. He said to them, 'It is written, "My house shall be called a house of prayer"; but you make it a den of robbers.' " Zeal for his Father's house prompted this outburst of anger. But in a calmer moment Jesus said, "In my Father's house are many rooms." I think He has prepared a special place in that house for those who shop.

The Kingdom of God has been revealed in such human activities as a planter's sowing and a woman's baking bread. Surely the shopper can give us another symbolic glimpse of that kingdom. In fact, Jesus likens the kingdom of heaven to "a merchant in search of fine pearls, who, on finding one pearl of great value, went and sold all that he had and bought it."

As a parable, shopping changes from vulgar commercialization to an expanding celebration of sound, sight, and touch. It is with these very same senses that we know the Word of life "which we have heard, which we have seen with our eyes, which we have looked upon and touched with our hands."

Heard. Seen. Touched. These elements can make prayer so much more than mere concentration on words. Prayer, like life, is hearing, seeing, and touching, not just thinking. Christmas gives us the Word of life. And the Word of life is the Word made *flesh*. Prayer is an incarnational exchange, between God and us or between one person and another. Prayer that is hearing, seeing, and touching can be as full of grace and truth as the Word made flesh.

Watch a shopper approach a counter. Here is total involvement: the object is touched, handled, squeezed, unwrapped, stretched, held up for size, shaken. Here is identification between buyer and object: if the item does not reflect, extend, enhance, or fit the shopper, it remains unsold. Here a price is paid to satisfy a need, and every shopper gets exactly what he pays for. Here patience and perseverance can be practiced, for not every counter or rack carries what is being sought. Here another's help can be asked without embarrassment, and received as graciously as that help is given. To hear, see, and touch these realities around us is to make a den of robbers into a house of prayer.

So there need be no conflict between those who count the paying days before Christmas and those who count the praying days left in Advent. In Advent the whole world waits again, while God shows us once more that He cares enough to send the very best, "the perfect gift from above, coming down from the Father of lights."

Advent also offers us the one thing missing from a shopping center—joy. With prices what they are, I hardly expected to see people laughing and skipping behind their shop carts. But I had hoped to see a few more than the two beaming faces that I did see. Those were the faces of two young lovers who obviously had found what everyone else was still looking for; the pearl of great price—the hidden treasure of each other.

The Advent liturgy provides us with the paradox of already possessing the One whom we still seek. So we can afford to "break forth together into singing" with "abundant joy and great rejoicing." For Jesus has come, and Jesus will come again and again to seal our searching with delight. No matter how many times the price of other items is marked up, Jesus' gift of Himself to us is always free. And it makes us free. "If the Son makes you free, you will be free indeed." From now on we can spend ourselves for others with generous abandon, as if we had a credit card with all the charges being paid by someone else.

Advent's shopping celebration does not end with the last ring of a cash register late on Christmas Eve. It never leaves us frustrated, tired, or angry at having spent much and gotten little. Jesus makes certain that one good shopping celebration deserves another. And since his own birthday began with a surge of shoppers He arranges the same sort of setting for the birthday of his Mystical Body the Church on Pentecost.

For when Jesus sent the Holy Spirit, the shops and streets were filled again with folks "from every nation under heaven." Parthians, Medes, Elamites, Cretans, and Arabians milled around the mall. And with Peter and his troop acting so strangely, it may really have looked, sounded, and felt like the prelude to a world-wide, cosmic clearance sale.

It's a long time from Christmas to Pentecost. But we can start making our shopping list now. We have just begun to see the bargains, for it is written, " 'The things that no eye has seen and no ear has heard, things beyond the mind of man, all that God has prepared for those who love Him'—these are the very things that God has revealed to us through the Spirit." That's the Spirit of Christmas.

GIVE A GIFT OF TIME 54

It is perhaps the most precious—and personal—offering you can make
By Peg Kehret

The most personal gift you can give is the gift of time. Your time.

Bob Arneson, a busy executive who frequently works evenings often regretted that he wasn't able to do more things with his two young sons. For Christmas last year, Bob decided to give his children a gift of time.

He gave each boy a book of coupons redeemable on any Sunday afternoon. One coupon read, "Good for one game of Monopoly." Another said, "Good for a long hike in the woods." Still others were, "Good for making something together in my workshop," and "Good for a game of badminton."

The boys were delighted. Each week they carefully deliberated over which coupon to turn in. Bob found that, although he might have said No if the boys had merely interrupted his reading with a vague request to "play with us," he thoroughly enjoyed redeeming the coupons.

The real reward came two months later on Valentine's Day. Both boys bubbled with excitement as they presented their valentines to their dad: two coupon books decorated with crayoned hearts and containing coupons good for, "Shine your shoes," "Wash the car," and "Bring you the Sunday paper in bed."

Another man, a bachelor professor in his fifties, says the best present he ever received came on his birthday last year from his newly married niece. The gift: and invitation to dinner with spaces to be filled out and returned.

The professor, who eats most of his meals in restaurants or pops frozen dinners into the oven, claims that he deliberated a full two hours over which home-cooked dishes he should choose. After carefully considering meat loaf, fried chicken, pot roast, and a host of other favorites, he finally decided, "There's just nothing like homemade beef stew and biscuits."

On the appointed day his niece followed the menu choices

exactly, and she couldn't have had more compliments if she had served her uncle pheasant-under-glass and baked Alaska.

In these days when catalogues offer us gift choices of everything from mink-trimmed water beds to sterling silver egg timers, Christmas can become a nightmare of indecision and overspending. A gift of time is not only easy on the budget but it is personal as well. It is a rare commodity, a present planned especially for one person only, the recipient.

It has the added virtue of spreading Christmas out, of making other days special, too. A promise to someone out-of-state to send "a letter every Monday, all year" will be anticipated and enjoyed fifty times over. Few things you purchase can make that claim.

Betty Jo, a pretty teen-ager, had been asking her mother for over a year to teach her how to knit. "It was one of those things I kept putting off," her mother explained. "It just never seemed to be the right time. Finally it dawned on me one day that I would have to make the right time happen."

One of Betty Jo's birthday gifts that month was a little card from her mothing saying, "This Saturday I'll show you how to knit."

On Saturday, Betty Jo and her mother spent most of the day selecting a soft gold yarn, choosing an easy pattern, and going over the basics of knitting. "I enjoyed it as much as she did," Betty Jo's mother said later. "Maybe more. It was the first time in several months that we had talked to each other as friends, not just as mother and daughter." Knitting became a hobby that they shared together for years to come.

That's the nice thing about gifts of time. They have a way of offering bonuses that the giver cannot anticipate. One young mother, for example, received a call from her neighbor, a white-haired grandmother whose own children were grown and gone, offering to baby-sit free of charge any day of the following week from nine until three. It was a treat for her, she explained, to spend an occasional day caring for little ones again.

It was certainly a treat for the young mother, too. She had a whole day free to shop, get her hair cut, and simply read quietly with no interruptions from her busy toddlers.

"But I couldn't spend that whole precious day entirely on myself," she told her neighbor when she got home. "I also took an hour to call on my great-aunt who is in a rest home. I try to go every Saturday, but she was pleased by an unexpected mid-week visit."

The grandmother's unselfish gift of her time had started a happy chain reaction that affected not only her young neighbor and the children (who were delighted to have a familiar, competent sitter to entertain them) but extended even to an elderly widow on the other side of town.

The professor mentioned earlier decided to take a cue from his niece and do something original for her birthday. Knowing that she was a devotee of crossword puzzles, he made up a large puzzle containing many family names and private jokes. Getting all the words to fit properly took hours of his time, but it was worth it. His niece was so thrilled with the gift that she and her husband had it framed (after she worked it, of course). It now hangs in their den, one of their most treasured possessions.

A gift of time, though kind to the pocketbook, is never cheap. In 278 B.C., a wise man named Diogenes said, "Time is the most valuable thing a man can spend." To share this treasure with someone else is perhaps the highest compliment we can pay.

CHRISTMAS IN STAMPS [55]

The most popular Yuletide stamp ever issued showed a painting of Christ's Nativity
By M. W. Martin

In 1971, an incredible 1.2 billion copies of a single postage stamp were printed by the U.S. Postal Service. It was the largest stamp printing order in the world since postage stamps were first introduced in 1840. It was almost ten times larger than the usual printing of an American commemorative stamp. The stamp was one of two Christmas stamps issued that year. It depicted a Nativity scene by the Italian painter Giorgio Giorgione, *Adoration of the Shepherds,* and portrayed Mary, Joseph, the Christ Child, and two shepherds.

The enormous demand for this stamp shows the great popularity of Christmas stamps. But it also points out the demand for stamps that directly reflect the Christian significance of the holiday. The other Christmas stamp issued that year featured a secular Christmas design, *A Partridge in a Pear Tree.* Its sales were far below those of the Giorgione design.

Christmas stamps are a fairly new idea. *Xmas 1898* appeared in the design of two-cent stamps issued by Canada. But these stamps were issued to commemorate a secular event, the introduction of the Imperial Penny Postage scheme on Christmas Day, 1898. The Canadian post office never thought they might be used on holiday greetings.

The first stamp intended to be used on Christmas greetings was issued by Austria in 1937. Its motif was a rose, a Christmas symbol peculiar to that country. In fact, for the first thirty years of their use, Christmas stamps around the world tended to show Christmas symbols. Some nations showed universally accepted Christmas designs; a star, for example. Others displayed symbols that were special to their country; the U.S. had used a poinsettia.

Still others showed the joy of children, their toys, the tree decorations, and pictures of St. Nicholas, or Santa Claus, or Father Christmas. It's hard to think of a Christmas motif that has been omitted from stamps. Even "Silent Night, Holy Night" found its way onto a stamp.

The first Christmas stamp to portray part of the story of Christ's birth was issued by Brazil in 1939. It showed the Magi and the Star of Bethlehem. The first full set of stamps devoted to the Christmas story appeared in Hungary in 1943. Over the next fifteen years Christmas stamps appeared only sporadically.

The number of Christmas stamp-issuing nations slowly grew from 1958 to 1961. During those four years, Costa Rica, Spain, New Zealand, Norfolk Island, Peru, and several others joined; the Christmas story largely replaced secular symbols. In 1959 appeared the first set of Christmas stamps from the Vatican, three beautiful reproductions of Raphael's *Nativity*.

The issue of a U.S. Christmas stamp in 1962 no doubt helped to popularize the idea. This first American offering was a small green and red stamp showing a Christmas wreath and candles.

The stamp caused a lot of controversy. Many people objected to it on the grounds that the government was mixing business and religion. But its acceptance was so overwhelming that the critics simply disappeared. Since that year, the U.S. has issued Christmas stamps annually, and several times has offered more than one. Four were issued in 1964, and five in 1970.

In 1964, Canada issued its first "real" Christmas stamp. It was so popular that within six years she was issuing a dozen different Christmas designs. In 1966, twenty-two countries issued Christmas stamps.

By 1968, the list had doubled, and since 1970 some 50 nations have annually issued stamps recalling Christ's birth. The designs of Christmas stamps are now predominantly religious. Much emphasis is placed on ancient stained glass windows and paintings by old masters. The Nativity scene has appeared on stamps of Spain, Antigua, New Zealand, Great Britain, Australia, and many other countries.

The Magi have appeared on stamps from all corners of the globe; some designs have been traditional, others modern. The two extremes can be seen in 1971 issues of Great Britain and New Zealand. The British set depicted the Wise Men as shown in the three upper panels of the window in the North Choir Aisle of Canterbury Cathedral. These stained glass windows are

about 800 years old. The New Zealand design was a symbolic
Three Kings, by the contemporary artist Enid Hunter, a
telephone operator who paints in her spare time.

Christmas stamps have been issued by countries from which
they would hardly be expected. Jordan has issued one, and so
has Korea. The Arabian sheikdoms of the Trucial States have
poured out a deluge of Christmas stamps in magnificent designs.
These were strictly a money-making deal for the government,
as export products that never saw any postal service in their native
their native countries. Egypt has issued "greeting card" stamps
in December during various years. They show different motifs;
in 1969 it was the American poinsettia.

Chapter VIII
The Early Life

Almost anyone who follows Christ at all could write an essay or give a speech on the "true meaning" of Christmas. But this effort would usually be only a complaint about how Christmas has been commercialized or how the religious content of the feast has been eroded. To get a really "truer" meaning there has to be reflection and meditation on passages from Scripture that are concerned with Christ's coming, on the dogmatic background of the events in His life, and on the meaning of the historical happenings we know of in His early life and of those in the time just preceding His coming. Archbishop Sheen has done this in his work on the life of Christ, a running commentary on the marvels and beauties forever associated with the Birth at Bethlehem.

THE EARLY LIFE OF CHRIST ON EARTH[56]

By Fulton J. Sheen

1 The Only Person Ever Pre-announced

History is full of men who have claimed that they came from God, or that they were gods, or that they bore messages from God—Buddha, Mohammed, Confucius, Christ, Lao-tze, and thousands of others, right down to the person who founded a new religion this very day. Each of them has a right to be heard and considered. But as a yardstick, external to and outside of whatever is to be measured, is needed, so there must be some permanent test available to all men, all civilizations, and all ages, by which they can decide whether any one of these claimants, or all of them, are justified in their claims, These tests are of two kinds; reason and history. Reason, because everyone has it, even those without faith; history, because everyone lives in it and should know something about it.

Reason dictates that if any one of these men actually came from God, the least thing that God could do to support His claim would be to pre-announce His coming. Automobile manufacturers tell their customers when to expect a new model. If God sent anyone from Himself, or if He came Himself with a vitally important message for all men, it would seem reasonable that He would first let men know when His messenger was coming, where He would be born, where He would live, the doctrine He would teach, the enemies He would make, the program He would adopt for the future, and the manner of His death. By the extent to which the messenger conformed with these announcements one could judge the validity of his claims.

Reason further assures us that if God did not do this, then there would be nothing to prevent any imposter from appearing in history and saying, "I come from God," or "An angel appeared to me in the desert and gave me this message." In such cases there would be no objective, historical way of testing the messenger. We would have only his word for it, and of course he could be wrong.

If a visitor came from a foreign country to Washington and

said he was a diplomat, the government would ask him for his passport and other documents testifying that he represented a certain government. His papers would have to antedate his coming. If such proofs of identity are asked from delegates of other countries, reason certainly ought to do so with messengers who claim to have come from God. To each claimant reason says, "What record was there before you were born that you were coming?"

With this test one can evaluate the claimants. (And at this preliminary stage, Christ is no greater than the others.) Socrates had no one to foretell his birth. Buddha had no one to pre-announce him and his message or tell the day when he would sit under the tree. Confucius did not have the name of his mother and his birthplace recorded, nor were they given to men centuries before he arrived so that when he did come, men would know he was a messenger from God. But, with Christ it was different. Because of the Old Testament prophecies, His coming was not unexpected. There were no predictions about Buddha, Confucius, Lao-tze, Mohammed, or anyone else; but there were predictions about Christ. Others just came and said, "Here I am, believe me." They were, therefore, only men among men and not the Divine in the human. Christ alone stepped out of that line saying, "Search the writings of the Jewish people and the related history of the Babylonians, Persians, Greeks, and Romans." (For the moment, pagan writings and even the Old Testament may be regarded only as historical documents, not as inspired works.)

It is true that the prophecies of the Old Testament can be best understood in the light of their fulfillment. The language of prophecy does not have the exactness of mathematics. Yet if one searches out the various Messianic currents in the Old Testament, and compares the resulting picture with the life and work of Christ, can one doubt that the ancient predictions point to Jesus and the kingdom which he established? God's promise to the patriarchs that through them all the nations of the earth would be blessed; the prediction that the tribe of Judah would be supreme among the other Hebrew tribes until the coming of Him Whom all nations would obey; the strange yet undeniable fact that in the Bible of the Alexandrian Jews, the Septuagint, one finds clearly predicted the *virgin* birth of the Messias; the prophecy of Isaias 53 about the patient sufferer, the Servant of the Lord, who will lay down his life as a guilt-offering for his people's offenses; the perspectives of the glorious, everlasting kingdom of the House of David—in whom but Christ have these prophecies found their fulfillment? From an historical point of view alone, here is uniqueness which sets Christ apart from all other founders of world religions. And once the fulfillment of these prophecies did historically take place in the person of Christ, not only did all prophecies cease in Israel, but there was discontinuance of sacrifices when the true Paschal Lamb was sacrificed.

Turn to pagan testimony. Tacitus, speaking for the ancient Romans, says, "People were generally persuaded in the faith of the ancient prophecies, that the East was to prevail, and that from Judea was to come the Master and Ruler of the world." Suetonius, in his account of the life of Vespasian, recounts the Roman tradition thus, "It was an old and constant belief throughout the East, that by indubitably certain prophecies, the Jews were to attain the highest power."

China had the same expectation; but because it was on the other side of the world, it believed that the great Wise Man would be born in the *West*. The Annals of the Celestial Empire contain the statement: "In the 24th year of Tehao-Wang of the dynasty of the Tcheou, on the 8th day of the 4th moon, a light appeared in the Southwest which illumined the king's palace. The monarch, struck by its splendor, interrogated the sages. They showed him books in which this prodigy signified the appearance of the great Saint of the West whose religion was to be introduced into their country."

The Greeks expect Him, for Aeschylus in his *Prometheus* six centuries before His coming, wrote, "Look not for any end, moreover, to this curse until God appears, to accept upon His Head the pangs of thy own sins vicarious."

How did the Magi of the East know of His coming? Probably from the many prophecies circulated through the world by the Jews as well as through the prophecy made to the Gentiles by

Daniel centuries before His birth.

Cicero, after recounting the sayings of the ancient oracles and the Sibyls about a "King whom we must recognize to be saved," asked in expectation, "To what man and to what period of time do these predictions point?" The Fourth Eclogue of Virgil recounted the same ancient tradition and spoke of "a chaste woman, smiling on her infant boy, with whom the iron age would pass away."

Suetonius quoted a contemporary author to the effect that the Romans were so fearful about a king who would rule the world that they ordered all children born that year to be killed— an order that was not fulfilled, except by Herod.

Not only were the Jews expecting the birth of a Great King, a Wise Man and a Savior, but Plato and Socrates also spoke of the Logos and of the Universal Wise Man "yet to come." Confucius spoke of "the Saint"; the Sibyls, of a "Universal King"; the Greek dramatist, of a savior and redeemer to unloose man from the "primal eldest curse." All these were on the Gentile side of the expectation. What separates Christ from all men is that first He was expected; even the Gentiles had a longing for a deliverer, or redeemer. This fact alone distinguishes Him from all other religious leaders.

A second distinguishing fact is that once He appeared He struck history with such impact that He split it in two, dividing it into two periods: one before His coming, the other after it. Buddha did not do this, nor any of the great Indian philosophers. Even those who deny God must date their attacks upon Him, A.D. so and so, or so many years after His coming.

A third fact separating Him from all the others is this: *every other person who ever came into this world came into it to live. He came into it to die.* Death was a stumbling block to Socrates— it interrupted his teaching. But to Christ, death was the goal and fulfillment of His life, the gold that He was seeking. Few of His words or actions are intelligible without reference to His Cross. He presented Himself as a Savior rather than merely as a Teacher. It meant nothing to teach men to be good unless He also gave them the power to be good, after rescuing them from the frustration of guilt.

The story of every human life begins with birth and ends with death. In the Person of Christ, however, *it was His death that was was first and His life that was last.* The Scripture describes Him as "the Lamb slain as it were, from the beginning of the world." He was slain in intention by the first sin and rebellion against God. It was not so much that His birth cast a shadow on His life and thus led to His death; it was rather that the Cross was first, and cast its shadow back to His birth. His has been the only life in the world that was ever lived backward. As the flower in the crannied wall tells the poet of nature, and as the atom is the miniature of the solar system, so too, His birth tells the mystery of the gibbet. He went from the known to the known, from the reason of His coming manifested by His name "Jesus" or "Saviour" to the fulfillment of His coming, namely, His death on the Cross.

John gives us His eternal prehistory; Matthew, his temporal prehistory, by way of His genealogy. It is significant how much His temporal ancestry was connected with sinners and foreigners! These blots on the escutcheon of His human lineage suggest a pity for the sinful and for the strangers to the Covenant. Both these aspects of His compassion would later on be hurled against Him as accusations: "He is a friend of sinners"; "He is a Samaritan." But the shadow of a stained past foretells His future love for the stained. Born of a woman, He was a man and could be one with all humanity; born of a Virgin, who was overshadowed by the Spirit and "full of grace," He would also be outside that current of sin which infected all men.

2 Early Life of Christ

A fourth distinguishing fact is that He does not fit, as the other world teachers do, into the established category of a *good man.* Good men do not lie. But if Christ was not all that He said He was, namely, the Son of the living God, the Word of God in the flesh, then He was not "just a good man"; then He was a knave, a liar, a charlatan and the greatest deceiver who ever lived. If He was not what He said He was, the Christ, the Son of God, He was the anti-Christ! If He was only a man, then He was not even a "good" man.

But He was *not only* a man. He would have us either worship Him or despise Him—despise Him as a mere man, or worship Him as true God and true man. That is the alternative He presents. It may very well be that the Communists, who are so anti-Christ, are closer to Him than those who see Him as a sentimentalist and a vague moral reformer. The Communists have at least decided that if He wins, they lose; the others are afraid to consider Him either as winning or losing, because they are not prepared to meet the moral demands which this victory would make on their souls.

If He is what He claimed to be, a Savior, a Redeemer, then we have a virile Christ and a leader worth following in these terrible times; One Who will step into the breach of death, crushing sin, gloom and despair; a leader to Whom we can love even unto death. We need a Christ today Who will make cords and drive the buyers and sellers from our new temples; Who will blast the unfruitful fig-trees; Who will talk of crosses and sacrifices and Whose voice will be like the voice of the raging sea. But He will not allow us to pick and choose among His words, discarding the hard ones, and accepting the ones that please our fancy. We need a Christ Who will restore moral indignation, Who will make us hate evil with a passionate intensity, and love goodness to a point where we can drink death like water.

THE ANNUNCIATION

Every civilization has had a tradition of a golden age in the past. A more precise Jewish record tells of a fall from a state of innocence and happiness through a woman tempting a man. If a woman played such a role in the fall of mankind, should she not play a great role in its restoration? And if there was a lost Paradise in which the first nuptials of man and woman were celebrated, might there not be a new Paradise in which the nuptials of God and man would be celebrated?

In the fullness of time an Angel of Light came down from the great Throne of Light to a Virgin kneeling in prayer, to ask her if she was willing to give God a human nature. Her answer was that she "knew not man" and, therefore, could not be the mother of the "Expected of the Nations."

There never can be a birth without love. In this the maiden was right. The begetting of new life requires the fires of love. But besides the human passion which begets life, there is the "passionless passion and wild tranquility" of the Holy Spirit; and it was this that overshadowed the woman and begot in her Emmanuel or "God with us." At the moment that Mary pronounced *Fiat* or "Be it done," something greater happened than the *Fiat lux* (Let there be light) of creation; for the light that was now made was not the sun, but the Son of God in the flesh. By pronouncing *Fiat* Mary achieved the full role of womanhood, namely, to be the bearer of God's gifts to man. There is a passive receptiveness in which woman says *Fiat* to the cosmos as she shares its rhythm, *Fiat* to a man's love as she receives it, and *Fiat* to God as she receives the Spirit.

Children come into the world not always as a result of a distinct act of love of man and woman. Though the love between the two be willed, the fruit of their love, which is the child, is not willed in the same way as their love for one another. There is an undetermined element in human love. The parents do not know whether the child will be a boy or a girl, or the exact time of its birth, for conception is lost in some unknown night of love. Children are later accepted and loved by their parents, but they were never directly willed into being by them. But in the Annunciation, the Child was not accepted in any unforeseen way; the *Child was willed.* There was a collaboration between a woman and the Spirit of Divine Love. The consent was voluntary under the *Fiat;* the physical cooperation was freely offered by the same word. Other mothers become conscious of motherhood through physical changes within them; Mary became conscious through a spiritual change wrought by the Holy Spirit. She probably received a spiritual ecstasy far greater than that given to man and woman in their unifying act of love.

As the fall of man was a free act, so too the Redemption had to be free. What is called the Annunciation was actually God asking the free consent of a creature to help Him to be incorporated into humanity.

Suppose a musician in an orchestra freely strikes a sour note.

The conductor is competent, the music is correctly scored and easy to play, but the musician still exercises his freedom by introducing a discord which immediately passes out into space. The director can do one of two things: he can either order the selection to be replayed, or he can ignore the discord. Fundamentally, it makes no difference which he does, for that false note is traveling out into space at the rate of more than a thousand feet per second; and as long as time endures, there will be discord in the universe.

Is there any way to restore harmony to the world? It can be done only by someone coming in from eternity and stopping the note in its wild flight. But will it still be a false note? The harmony can be destroyed on one condition only. If that note is made the first note in a new melody, then it will become harmonious.

This is precisely what happened when Christ was born. There had been a false note of moral discord introduced by the first man which infected all humanity. God could have ignored it, but it would have been a violation of justice for Him to do so, which is, of course, unthinkable. What He did, therefore, was to ask a woman, representing humanity, freely to give Him a human nature with which He would start a new humanity. As there was an old humanity in Adam, so there would be a new humanity in Christ, Who was God made man through the free agency of a human mother. When the angel appeared to Mary, God was announcing this love for the new humanity. It was the beginning of a new earth, and Mary became "a flesh-girt Paradise to be gardened by the Adam new." As in the first garden Eve brought destruction, so in the garden of her womb, Mary would now bring Redemption.

For the nine months that He was cloistered within her, all the food, the wheat, the grapes that she consumed served as a kind of natural Eucharist, passing into Him Who later on was to declare that He was the Bread and the Wine of Life. After her nine months were over, the fitting place for Him to be born was Bethlehem, which meant "House of Bread." Later on He would say:

God's gift of bread comes down from heaven
And gives life to the whole world

John 6:33

It is I Who am the Bread of Life;
He who comes to Me will never be hungry.

John 6:35

When the Divine Child was conceived, Mary's humanity gave
Him hands and feet, eyes and ears, and a body with which to
suffer. Just as the petals of a rose after a dew close on the dew
as if to absorb its energies, so too, Mary was the Mystical Rose
closed upon Him Whom the Old Testament had described as
a dew descending upon the earth. When finally she did give
Him birth, it was as if a great ciborium had opened, and she
was holding in her fingers the Guest Who was also the Host of
the world, as if to say, "Look, this is the Lamb of God; look,
this is He Who takes away the sins of the world."

THE VISITATION

Mary was given a sign that she would conceive by the Holy
Ghost. Her elderly cousin Elizabeth had already conceived a
son in her old age, and was now in her sixth month. Mary,
now bearing the Divine Secret within her, journeyed several
days from Nazareth to the city of Hebron, which, according
to tradition, rested over the ashes of the founders of the people
of God—Abraham, Isaac, and Jacob. Elizabeth in some
mysterious way, knew that Mary was bearing within herself the
Messias. She asked:

How have I deserved to be
Thus visited by the Mother of My Lord?

Luke 1:43

This salutation came from the mother of the herald to the
mother of the King Whose path the herald was destined to
prepare. John the Baptist, still cloistered in his mother's
womb, on his mother's testimony leaped with joy at the
mother who brought the Christ to her home.
Mary's response to this salutation is called the *Magnificat*,
a song of joy celebrating what God had done for her. She

looked back over history, back to Abraham; she saw the activity of God preparing for this moment from generation to generation, she looked also into an indefinite future when all peoples and all generations would call her "Blessed." Israel's Messias was on His way, and God was about to manifest Himself on earth and in the flesh. She even prophesied the qualities of the Son Who was to be born of her as full of justice and mercy. Her poem ends by acclaiming the revolution He will inaugurate with the unseating of the mighty and the exaltation of the humble.

THE PREHISTORY OF CHRIST

The Lord to be born of Mary is the only Person in the world Who ever had a prehistory; a prehistory to be studied not in the primeval slime and jungles, but in the bosom of the Eternal Father. Though He appeared as the Cave Man in Bethlehem, since He was born in a stable hewn out of rock, His beginning in time as man was without beginning as God in the agelessness of eternity. Only progressively did He reveal His Divinity; and this was not because He grew in the consciousness of Divinity; it was due rather to His intent to be slow in revealing the purpose of His coming.

St. John at the beginning of his Gospel relates His prehistory as the Son of God:

> In the beginning was the Word,
>> And the Word was with God;
> And the Word was God.
>> The same was in the beginning with God.
> All things were made by Him,
>> And without Him was made nothing that was made.
>
> *John 1:1-3*

"In the beginning was the Word." Whatever there is in the world, is made according to the thought of God, for all things postulate thought. Every bird, every flower, every tree was made according to an idea existing in the Divine Mind. Greek philosophers held that thought was abstract. Now, the Thought or Word of God is revealed as Personal. Wisdom is vested in Personality. Prior to His earthly existence, Jesus Christ is eternally God, the Wisdom, the Thought of the Father. In His

292

earthly existence, He is that Thought or Word of God speaking to men. The words of men pass away when they have been conceived and uttered, but the Word of God is eternally uttered and can never cease from utterance. By His Word, the Eternal Father expresses all that He understands, all that He knows. As the mind holds converse with itself by its own thought, and sees and knows the world by means of this thought, so does the Father see Himself, as in a mirror, in the Person of His Word, Finite intelligence needs many words in order to express ideas; but God speaks once and for all within Himself—one single Word which reaches the abyss of all things that are known and can be known. In that Word of God are hidden all the treasures of wisdom, all the secrets of sciences, all the designs of the arts, all the knowledge of mankind. But this knowledge, compared to the Word, is only the feeblest broken syllable.

In the agelessness of eternity, the Word was with God. But there was a moment in time when He had not come forth from the Godhead, as there is a moment when a thought in the mind of man is not yet uttered. As the sun is never without its beam, so the Father is never without His Son; and as the thinker is not without a thought, so in an infinite degree, the Divine Mind is never without His Word. God did not spend the everlasting ages in sublime solitary activity. He had a Word with Him equal to Himself.

> All things were made by Him,
> And without Him was made nothing that was made.
> In Him was life and the life was the light of men.
> And the light shineth in darkness;
> And the darkness did not comprehend it.
> *John 1:3-5*

Everything in space and time exists because of the creative Power of God. Matter is not eternal; the universe has an intelligent Personality back of it, an Architect, a Builder, and a Sustainer. Creation is the work of God. The sculptor works on marble, the painter on canvas, the machinist on matter, but none of them can create. They bring existing things into new combinations, but nothing else. Creation belongs to God alone.

God writes His name on the soul of every man. Reason and

293

conscience are the God within us in the natural order. The Fathers of the early Church were wont to speak of the wisdom of Plato and Aristotle as the unconscious Christ within us. Men are like so many books issuing from the Divine press, and if nothing else be written on them, at least the name of the Author is indissolubly engraved on the title page. God is like the watermark on paper, which may be written over without ever being obscured.

BETHLEHEM

Caesar Augustus, the master bookkeeper of the world, sat in his palace by the Tiber. Before him was stretched a map labeled *Orbis Terrarum, Imperium Romanum*. He was about to issue an order for a census of the world; for all the nations of the civilized world were subject to Rome. There was only one capital in this world: Rome; only one official language; Latin; only one ruler: Caesar. To every outpost, to every satrap and governor, the order went out: every Roman subject must be enrolled in his own city. On the fringe of the Empire, in the little village of Nazareth, soldiers tacked up on walls the order for all the citizens to register in the towns of their family origins.

Joseph, the builder, an obscure descendant of the great King David, was obliged by that very fact to register in Bethlehem, the city of David. In accordance with the edict, Mary and Joseph set out from the village of Nazareth for the village of Bethlehem, which lies about fives miles on the other side of Jerusalem. Five hundred years earlier the prophet Micheas had prophesied concerning that little village:

> And thou, Bethlehem, of the land of Juda,
> Art far from the least among the princes of Juda,
> For out of thee will arise a leader who is to be
> The shepherd of My people Israel.
>
> *Matthew 2:6*

Joseph was full of expectancy as he entered the city of his family, and was quite convinced that he would have no difficulty in finding lodgings for Mary, particularly on account of her condition. Joseph went from house to house only to

294

find each one crowded. He searched in vain for a place where He, to Whom heaven and earth belonged, might be born. Could it be that the Creator would not find a home in creation? Up a steep hill Joseph climbed to a faint light which swung on a rope across a doorway. This would be the village inn. There, above all other places, he would surely find shelter. There was room in the inn for the soldiers of Rome who had brutally subjugated the Jewish people; there was room for the daughters of the rich merchants of the East; there was room for those clothed in soft garments, who lived in the houses of the king; in fact, there was room for anyone who had a coin to give the innkeeper; but there was no room for Him Who came to be the Inn of every homeless heart in the world. When finally the scrolls of history are completed down to the last words in time, the saddest line of all will be: "There was no room in the inn."

Out to the hillside to a stable cave, where shepherds sometimes drove their flocks in time of storm, Joseph and Mary went at last for shelter. There, in a place of peace in the lonely abandonment of a cold windswept cave; there, under the floor of the world, He Who is born without a mother in heaven, is born without a father on earth.

Of every other child that is born into the world, friends can say that it resembles his mother. This was the first instance in time that anyone could say that the mother resembled the Child. This is the beautiful paradox of the Child Who made His mother; the mother, too, was only a child. It was also the first time in the history of the world that anyone could ever think of heaven as being anywhere else than "somewhere up there"; when the Child was in her arms, Mary now looked down to Heaven.

In the filthiest place in the world, a stable, Purity was born. He, Who was later to be slaughtered by men acting as beasts, was born among beasts. He, Who would call Himself the "living Bread descended from Heaven," was laid in a manger, literally, a place to eat. Centuries before, the Jews had worshiped the golden calf, and the Greeks, the ass. Men bowed down before them as before God. The ox and the ass now were present to make their innocent reparation, bowing down before their God.

There was no room in the inn, but there was room in the stable. The inn is the gathering place of public opinion, the focal point of the world's moods, the rendezvous of the worldly, the rallying place of the popular and the successful. But the stable is a place for the outcasts, the ignored, the forgotten. The world might have expected the Son of God to be born—if He was to be born at all—in an inn. A stable would be the last place in the world where one would have looked for Him. *Divinity is always where one least expects to find it.*

No worldly mind would ever have suspected that He Who could make the sun warm the earth would one day have need of an ox and an ass to warm Him with their breath; that He Who, in the language of Scriptures, could stop the turning about of Arcturus would have His birthplace dictated by an imperial census; that He, Who clothed the fields with grass, would Himself be naked; that He, from Whose hands came planets and worlds, would one day have tiny arms that were not long enough to touch the huge heads of the cattle; that the feet which trod the everlasting hills would one day be too weak to walk; that the Eternal Word would be dumb; that Omnipotence would be wrapped in swaddling clothes; that Salvation would lie in a manger; that the bird which built the nest would be hatched therein—no one would ever have suspected that God coming to this earth would ever be so helpless. And that is precisely why so many miss Him. *Divinity is always where one least expects to find it.*

If the artist is at home in his studio because the paintings are the creation of his own mind; if the sculptor is at home among his statues because they are the work of his own hands; if the husbandman is at home among his vines because he planted them; and if the father is at home among his children because they are his own, then surely, argues the world, He Who made the world should be at home in it. He should come into it as an artist into his studio, and as a father into his home; but, for the Creator to come among His creatures and be ignored by them; for God to come among His own and not be received by His own; for God to be homeless at home—that could only mean one thing to the worldly mind; the Babe could not have been

God at all. And that is just why it missed Him. *Divinity is always where one least expects to find it.*

The Son of God made man was invited to enter His own world through a back door. Exiled from the earth, He was born under the earth, in a sense, the first Cave Man in recorded history. There He shook the earth to its very foundations. Because He was born in a cave, all who wish to see Him must stoop. To stoop is the mark of humility. The proud refuse to stoop and, therefore, they miss Divinity. Those, however, who bend their egos and enter, find that they are not in a cave at all, but in a new universe where sits a Babe on His mother's lap, with the world poised on His fingers.

The manger and the Cross thus stand at the two extremities of the Savior's life! He accepted the manger because there was no room in the inn. He accepted the cross because men said, "We will not have this Man for our king." Disowned upon entering, rejected upon leaving, He was laid in a stranger's stable at the beginning, and a stranger's grave at the end. An ox and an ass surrounded His crib at Bethlehem; two thieves were to flank His Cross on Calvary. He was wrapped in swaddling bands in His birthplace, He was again laid in swaddling clothes in His tomb—clothes symbolic of the limitations imposed on His Divinity when He took a human form.

The shepherds watching their flocks nearby were told by the angels:

> This is the sign by which you are to know Him;
>   You will find a Child still in swaddling clothes,
> Lying in a manger.
>
> *Luke 2:12*

He was already bearing His Cross—the only cross a Babe could bear, a cross of poverty, exile and limitation. His sacrificial intent already shone forth in the message the angels sang in the hills of Bethlehem:

> This day, in the city of David,
>   A Savior has been born for you,
> The Lord Christ Himself.
>
> *Luke 2:11*

Covetousness was already being challenged by His poverty, while pride was confronted with the humiliation of a stable. The swathing of Divine power, which needs to accept no bounds, is often too great a tax upon minds which think only of power. They cannot grasp the idea of Divine condescension, or of the "rich man becoming poor that through His poverty, we might be rich." Men shall have no greater sign of Divinity than the absence of power as they expect it—the spectacle of a Babe Who said He would come in the clouds of heaven, now being wrapped in the cloths of earth.

He, Whom the angels call the "Son of the most High," descended into the red dust from which we all were born, to be one with weak, fallen man in all things, save sin. And it is the swaddling clothes which constitute His "sign." If He Who is Omnipotence had come with thunderbolts, there would have been no sign. There is no sign unless something happens contrary to nature. The brightness of the sun is no sign, but an eclipse is. He said that on the last day, His coming would be heralded by "signs in the sun," perhaps an extinction of light. At Bethlehem the Divine Son went into an eclipse, so that only the humble of spirit might recognize Him.

Only two classes of people found the Babe: the shepherds and the Wise Men; the simple and the learned; those who knew that they knew nothing, and those who knew that they did not know everything. He is never seen by the man of one book; never by the man who thinks he knows. Not even God can tell the proud anything! Only the humble can find God!

As Caryll Houselander put it, "Bethlehem is the inscape of Calvary, just as the snowflake is the inscape of the universe." This same idea was expressed by the poet who said that if he knew the flower in a crannied wall in all its details, he would know "what God and man is." Scientists tell us that the atom comprehends within itself the mystery of the solar system.

It was not so much that His birth cast a shadow on His life, and thus led to His death; it was rather that the Cross was there from the beginning, and it cast its shadow backward to His birth. Ordinary mortals go from the known to the unknown submitting themselves to forces beyond their control; hence we can speak of their "tragedies." But He went from the known to the known, from the reason for His coming, namely, to be "Jesus" or "Savior," to the fulfillment of His coming, namely, the death on the Cross. Hence, there was no tragedy in His life; for, tragedy implies the unforeseeable, the uncontrollable, and the fatalistic. Modern life is tragic when there is spiritual darkness and unredeemable guilt. But for the Christ Child there were no uncontrollable forces; no submission to fatalistic chains from which there could be no escape; but there was an "inscape"—the microcosmic manger summarizing, like an atom, the macrocosmic Cross on Golgotha.

In His First Advent, He took the name of Jesus, or "Savior"; it will only be in His Second Advent that He will take the name of "Judge." Jesus was not a name He had before He assumed a human nature; it properly refers to that which was united to His Divinity, not that which existed from all eternity. Some say "Jesus taught" as they would say "Plato taught," never once thinking that His name means "Savior from sin." Once he received this name, Calvary became completely a part of Him. The Shadow of the Cross that fell on His cradle also covered His naming. This was "His Father's business"; everything else would be incidental to it.

PREHISTORY NOW HISTORY

"The Word became Flesh." The Divine Nature, which was pure and holy, entered as a renovating principle into the corrupted line of Adam's race, without being affected by corruption. Through the Virgin Birth, Jesus Christ became operative in human history without being subject to the evil in it.

> And the Word was made flesh,
>   And came to dwell among us;
> And we had sight of His glory,
>   Glory such as belongs to
> The Father's only-begotten Son,
>   Full of grace and truth.

John 1:14

299

Bethlehem became a link between heaven and earth; God and man met here and looked each other in the face. In the taking of human flesh, the Father prepared it, the Spirit formed it, and the Son assumed it. He Who had an eternal generation in the bosom of the Father now had a temporal generation in time. He Who had His birth in Bethlehem came to be born in the hearts of men. For, what would profit if He was born a thousand times in Bethlehem unless He was born again in man?

> But all those who did welcome Him,
> He empowered to become the children of God.
>
> *John 1:12*

No man can love anything unless he can get his arms around it, and the cosmos is too big and too bulky. But once God became a Babe and was wrapped in swaddling clothes and laid in a manger, men could say, "This is Emmanuel, this is God with us." By His reaching down to frail human nature and lifting it up to the incomparable prerogative of union with Himself, human nature became dignified. So real was this union that all of His acts and words, all of His agonies and tears, all of His thoughts and reasonings, resolves and emotions, while being properly human, were at the same time the acts and words, agonies and tears, thoughts and reasonings, resolves and emotions of the Eternal Son of God.

What men call the Incarnation is but the union of two natures, the Divine and the human in a single Person Who governs both. This is not difficult to understand; for what is man but a sample, at an immeasuraby lower level, of a union of two totally different substances, one material and the other immaterial, one to the body, the other the soul, under the regency of a single human personality? What is more remote from one another than powers and capacities of flesh and spirit? Antecedent to their unity, how difficult it would be ever to conceive of a moment when body and soul would be united in a single personality. That they are so united is an experience clear to every mortal. And yet it is an experience at which man does not marvel because of its familiarity.

God, Who brings together body and soul into one human personality, notwithstanding their difference of nature, could surely bring about the union of a human body and a human soul with His Divinity under the control of His Eternal Person. This is what is meant by the verse:

> And the Word was made flesh,
> And came to dwell among us.
>
> *John 1:14*

The Person which assumed human nature was not created, as is the case of all other persons. His Person was the pre-existent Word or *Logos*. His human nature, on the other hand, was derived from the miraculous conception by Mary, in which the Divine overshadowing of the Spirit and the human *Fiat* or the consent of a woman, were most beautifully blended. This is the beginning of a new humanity out of the material of the fallen race. When the Word became flesh, it did not mean that any change took place in the Divine Word. The Word of God preceeding forth did not leave the Father's side. What happened was not so much the conversion of the Godhead into flesh, as the taking of a manhood into God.

There was continuity with the fallen race of man through the manhood taken from Mary; there is discontinuity through the fact that the second Adam, the Man through whom the human race starts all over. His teaching centered on the incorporation of human natures to Him, after the manner in which the human nature that He took from Mary was united to the Eternal Word.

It is hard for a human being to understand the humility that was involved in the Word becoming flesh. Imagine, if it were possible, a human person divesting himself of his body, and then sending his soul into the body of a serpent. A double humiliation would follow; first, accepting the limitations of a serpentine organism, knowing all the while his mind was superior, and that fangs could not adequately articulate thoughts no serpent ever possessed. The second humiliation would be to be forced as a result of this "emptying of self" to live in the companionship of serpents. But all this is nothing compared to the emptying of God, by which He took on the form of man and accepted the limitations of humanity, such as hunger and persecution; not trivial either was it for the

Wisdom of God to condemn Himself to association with poor fishermen who knew so little. But this humiliation which began in Bethlehem when He was conceived in the Virgin Mary was only the first of many to counteract the pride of man, until the final humiliation of death on the Cross. If there were no Cross, there would have been no crib; if there had been no nails, there would have been no straw. But He could not *teach* the lesson of the Cross as payment for sin; He had to *take* it. God the Father did not spare His Son — so much did He love mankind. That was the secret wrapped in the swaddling bands.

THE NAME "JESUS"

The name "Jesus" was a fairly common one among the Jews. In the original Hebrew, it was "Josue." The angel told Joseph that Mary would:

> Bear a son, whom thou shalt call Jesus,
> For He is to save His people from their sins.
> *Matthew 1:21*

This first indication of the nature of His mission on earth does not mention His teaching; for the teaching would be ineffective, unless there was first salvation.

He was given another name at the same time, the name "Emmanuel."

> Behold, the virgin shall be with child,
> And shall bear a son,
> And they shall call Him Emmanuel,
> (which means God with us).
> *Matthew 1:23*

This name was taken from the prophecy of Isaias and it assured something besides a Divine presence; together with the name "Jesus," it meant a Divine presence which delivers and saves. The angel also told Mary: "And behold, thou shalt conceive in thy womb, And shalt bear a son, and shalt call Him Jesus. He shall be great, and men will know Him for the Son of the Most High: The Lord God will give Him the throne of His Father David, And He shall reign over the house of Jacob eternally; His kingdom shall never have an end. *Luke 1:31-33*

The title "Son of the Most High" was the very one that was given to the Redeemer by the evil spirit which possessed the youth in the land of the Gerasenes. The fallen angel thus confessed Him to be what the unfallen angel said He was:

> Why does thou meddle with me, Jesus
> Son of the Most High God?
> *Mark 5:7*

The salvation that is promised by the name "Jesus" is not a social salvation, but rather a spiritual one. He would not save people necessarily from their poverty, but he would save them from their sins. To destroy sin is to uproot the first causes of poverty. The name "Jesus" brought back the memory of their great leader, who had brought them out of Israel to rest in the promised land. The fact that He was pre-figured by Josue indicates that He had the soldierly qualities necessary for the final victory over evil, which would come from the glad acceptance of suffering, unwavering courage, resoluteness of will and unshakable devotion to the Father's mandate.

The people enslaved under the Roman yoke were seeing deliverance; hence they felt that any prophetic fulfillment of the ancient Josue would have something to do with politics. Later on, the people would ask Him when He was going to deliver them from the power of Caesar. But here, at the very beginning of His life, the Divine Soldier affirmed through an angel that He had come to conquer a greater enemy than Caesar. They must still render to Caesar the things that were Caesar's; His mission was to deliver them from a far greater bondage, namely, that of sin. All through His life people would continue to materialize the concept of salvation, thinking that deliverance was to be interpreted only in terms of the political. The name "Jesus" or Savior was not given to Him after He had wrought salvation, but at the very moment He was conceived in the womb of His mother. The foundation of His salvation was from eternity and not from time.

"FIRSTBORN"

> She brought forth a Son, her firstborn.
> *Luke 2:7*

The term "firstborn" did not mean that Our Lady was to bear other children according to the flesh. There was always a position of honor assigned in law to the firstborn, even if there were not any other children. It could very well be that Luke employs the term here in view of the account which he later on is to give of the Blessed Mother presenting her Child in the temple "as the firstborn Son." The other brethren of Our Lord mentioned by Luke were not sons of Mary; they were either half brothers, sons of Joseph by a possible former marriage, or else His cousins. Mary had no other children in the flesh. But "firstborn" could mean Our Lady's relation to other children she would have according to the Spirit. In this sense, her Divine Son called John her "son" at the foot of the Cross. Spiritually, John was her "second son." St. Paul later on used the term "firstborn" in time to parallel Our Lord's Eternal Generation as the Only Begotten of the Father. It was only to His Divine Son that God said:

> Thou art My Son,
>> I have begotten Thee this day.
> And, again, He shall find in Me a Father,
>> And I in Him a Son.
> Why, when the time comes
>> For bringing His firstborn into the world anew,
> Then He says,
>> Let all the angels of God worship before Him.
>> *Hebrews 1:5-6*

CHRIST'S FAMILY TREE

Though His Divine nature was from eternity, His human nature had a Jewish background. The blood that flowed in His veins was from the royal house of David through His mother who, though poor, belonged to the lineage of the great king. His contemporaries called Him the "Son of David." The people would never have consented to regard as a Messias any pretender who did not fulfill this indispensable condition. Nor did Our Blessed Lord Himself ever deny His Davidic origin. He only affirmed that His Davidic affiliation did not explain the relations which He possessed with the Father in His divine Personality.

The opening words of the Gospel of Matthew suggest the Genesis of Our Lord. The Old Testament begins with the Genesis of heaven and earth through God making all things. The New Testament had another kind of Genesis, in the sense that it describes the making of all things new. The genealogy that is given implies that Christ was "A Second Man," and not merely one of the many that had sprung from Adam. Luke, who directed his Gospel to the Gentiles, traced Our Lord's descent back to the first man, but Matthew, who directed his Gospel to the Jews, set Him forth as "Son of David and Son of Abraham." The difference in the genealogy between Luke and Matthew is due to the fact that Luke, writing for the Gentiles, was careful to give a natural descent; while Matthew, writing for the Jews, verged from the natural after the time of David, in order to make it clear to the Jews that Our Lord was the Heir to the Kingdom of David.

Luke is concerned about the Son of Man; Matthew about the King of Israel. Hence Matthew opens his Gospel:

A record of the ancestry from which Jesus Christ
The Son of David, Son of Abraham, was born.
Matthew 1:1

Matthew pictures the generations from Abraham to Our Lord as having passed through three cycles of fourteen each. This does not, however, represent a complete genealogy. Fourteen are mentioned from Abraham to David, fourteen from David to the Babylonian captivity, and fourteen from the Babylonian captivity to Our Blessed Lord. The genealogy goes beyond the Hebrew background to include a few non-Jews. There may have been a very good reason for this, as well as for the inclusion of others who had not the best reputations in the world. One was Rahab, who was a foreigner and a sinner; another was Ruth, a foreigner though received into the nation; a third was the sinner Bethsabee whose sin with David cast shame upon the royal line. Why should there be blots on the royal escutcheon, such as Bethsabee, whose womanly purity was tainted; and Ruth who, though morally good, was an introducer of alien blood into the stream? Possibly it was in order to indicate Christ's relationship to the stained and to the sinful, to harlots and sinners, and even to the Gentiles who were included in His Message and Redemption.

In some translations of Scripture, the word that is used to describe the genealogy is the word "begot"; for example, "Abraham begot Isaac, Isaac begot Jacob"; in other translations there is the expression "was the father of"; for example, "Jechonias was the father of Salathiel." The translation is unimportant; what stands out is that this monotonous expression is used throughout forty-one generations. But it is omitted when the forty-second generation is reached. Why? Because of the Virgin Birth of Jesus.

> And Jacob was the father of Joseph
> The husband of Mary;
> It was of her that Jesus was born who was called Christ.
> *Matthew 1:16*

Matthew, drawing up the genealogy, knew that Our Lord was not the Son of Joseph. Hence on the very first pages of the Gospel, Our Lord is presented as connected with the race which nevertheless did not wholly produce Him. That He came into it, was obvious; yet He was distinct from it.

If there was a suggestion of the Virgin Birth in the genealogy of Matthew, so there was a suggestion of it in the genealogy of Luke. In Matthew, Joseph is not described as having begotten Our Lord, and in Luke, Our Lord is called:

> By repute, the Son of Joseph.
> *Luke 3:23*

He meant that Our Lord was popularly supposed to be the Son of Joseph. Combining the two genealogies; in Matthew, Our Lord is the Son of David and of Abraham; He is, in Luke, the Son of Adam and the seed of the woman God promised would crush the head of the serpent. Men who are not moral, by God's Providence, are made the instruments of His policy; David, who murdered Urias, nevertheless is the channel through which the blood of Abraham floods into the blood of Mary. There were sinners in the family tree, and He would *seem* to be the greatest sinner of all when He would hang upon the family tree of the Cross, making men adopted sons of the

Heavenly Father.

CIRCUMCISION

> When eight days had passed, and
>   The boy must be circumcised,
> He was called Jesus, the name which
>   The angel had given Him before
> Ever He was conceived in the womb.
>
> *Luke 2:21*

Circumcision was the symbol of the covenant between God and Abraham and his seed, and took place on the eighth day. Circumcision presumed that the person circumcised was a sinner. The Babe was now taking the sinner's place — something He was to do all through His life. Circumcision was a sign and token of membership in the body of Israel. Mere human birth did not bring a child into the body of God's chosen people. Another rite was required, as recorded in the Book of Genesis:

> Then God said to Abraham, thou too
>   Shalt observe this covenant of Mine,
> Thou and the race that shall follow thee,
>   Generation after generation.
> This is the covenant you shall keep with Me,
>   Thou and thine; every male child
> Of yours shall be circumcised.
>
> *Genesis 17:9-11*

Circumcision in the Old Testament was a prefiguring of Baptism in the New Testament. Both symbolize a renunciation of the flesh with its sins. The first was done by wounding of the body; the second, by cleansing the soul. The first incorporated the child into the body of Israel; the second incorporates the child into the body of the new Israel or the Church. The term "Circumcision" was later used in the Scriptures to reveal the spiritual significance of applying the Cross to the flesh through self-discipline. Moses, in the Book of Deuteronomy clearly spoke of circumcising the heart. Jeremias also used the same expression. St. Stephen, in his last address before being killed, told his hearers that they were uncircumcised in

307

heart and ears. By submitting to this rite, which He need not have done because He was sinless, the Son of God made man satisfy the demands of His nation, just as He was to keep all the other Hebrew regulations. He kept the Passover; He observed the Sabbath; He went up to the Feasts; He obeyed the Old Law until the time came for Him to fulfill it by realizing and spiritualizing its shadowy prefigurements of God's dispensation.

In the Circumcision of the Divine Child there was a dim suggestion and hint of Calvary, in the precocious surrendering of blood. The shadow of the Cross was already hanging over a Child eight days old. He would have seven bloodsheddings of which this was the first, the others being the Agony in the Garden, the Scourging, the Crowning with Thorns, the Way of the Cross, the Crucifixion, and the Piercing of His Heart. But whenever there was an indication of Calvary, there was also some sign of glory; and it was at this moment when He was anticipating Calvary by shedding His blood that the name of Jesus was bestowed on Him.

A Child only eight days old was already beginning the bloodshedding that would fulfill His perfect manhood. The cradle was tinged with crimson, a token of calvary. The Precious Blood was beginning its long pilgrimage. Within an octave of His birth, Christ obeyed a law of which He Himself was the Author, a law which was to find its last application to Him. There had been sin in human blood — and now blood was already being poured out to do away with sin. As the East catches at sunset the colors of the West, so does the Circumcision reflect Calvary.

Must He begin redeeming all at once? Cannot the Cross wait? There will be plenty of time for it. Coming straight from the Father's arms to the arms of His earthly mother, He is carried in her arms to His first Calvary. Many years later He will be taken from her arms again, after the bruising of the flesh on the Cross, when the Father's work is done.

PRESENTATION IN THE TEMPLE

At Bethlehem He had been an exile; at the Circumcision, an anticipated Savior; now at the Presentation, He became a sign to be contradicted. As Jesus was circumcised, so Mary was purified though He needed not the first because He was God, and she needed not the second because she was conceived without sin.

> And when the time had come for
> Purification according to the law of Moses,
> They brought Him up to Jerusalem,
> to present Him before the Lord there.
>
> *Luke 2:22*

The fact of sin in human nature is underlined not only by the necessity of enduring pain to expiate for it in circumcision, but also by the need for purification. Ever since Israel had been delivered from the bondage of the Egyptians, after the firstborn of the Egyptians had been slain, the firstborn of the Jews had always been looked upon as one dedicated to God. Forty days after His birth, which was the appointed time for a male child according to the Law, Jesus was brought to the temple. Exodus decreed that the firstborn belonged to God. In the Book of Numbers, the tribe of Levi was set apart for the priestly function, and this priestly dedication was understood as a substitute for the sacrifice of the firstborn, a rite which was never practiced. But when the Divine Child was taken to the temple by Mary, the law of the consecration of the firstborn was observed in its fullness; for this Child's dedication to the Father was absolute, and would lead Him to the Cross.

We find here another instance of how God in the form of man shared the poverty of mankind. The traditional offerings for purification were a lamb and a turtledove if the parents were rich, and two doves or two pigeons if they were poor. Thus the mother who brought the Lamb of God into the world had no lamb to offer — except the Lamb of God. God was presented in the temple at the age of forty days. About thirty years later He would claim the temple and use it as the symbol of His Body in which dwelt the fullness of Divinity. Here it was not the Firstborn of Mary alone Who was presented, but the Firstborn of the Eternal Father. As the Only Begotten of the Father, He was not presented as the Firstborn of a restored humanity. A new race began in Him.

The character of the man in the temple whose name was Simeon and who received the Child, is described as simple as:

> An upright man of careful observance
>> Who waited patiently for comfort to
> Be brought to Israel.
>> *Luke 2:25*

It was revealed to him by the Holy Spirit:

> That he was not to meet death, until he
>> Had seen that Christ Whom the Lord had anointed.
>> *Luke 2:26*

His words seem to imply that as soon as one sees Christ, the sting of death departs. The old man, taking the Child in his arms, exclaimed with joy:

> Ruler of all, now dost Thou let thy servant go in peace,
>> According to thy word; for my own eyes
> Have seen that saving power of thine which Thou
>> Has prepared in the sight of all nations.
> This is the Light which shall give revelation
>> To the Gentiles, this is the glory
> Of thy people Israel.
>> *Luke 2:29-33*

Simeon was like a sentinel whom God had sent to watch for the Light. When the Light finally appeared, he was ready to sing his *Nunc Dimittis.* In a poor Child brought by poor people making a poor offering, Simeon discovered the riches of the world. As this old man held the Child in his arms, he was not like the aged of whom Horace speaks. He did not look back, but forward, and not only to the future of all the Gentiles of all the tribes and nations of the earth. An old man at the sunset of his own life spoke of the sunrise of the world; in the evening of life he told of the promise of a new day. He had seen the Messias before by faith; now his eyes could close, for there was nothing more beautiful to look upon. Some flowers open only in the evening. What he had seen now was "Salvation" — not salvation from poverty, but salvation from sin.

Simeon's hymn was an act of adoration. There are three acts of adoration described in the early life of the Divine Child. The shepherds adored; Simeon, and Anna the prophetess, adored; and the heathen Magi adored. The song of Simeon was like a sunset in which a shadow heralds a substance. It was the first hymn by men in the life of Christ. Simeon, though addressing Mary and Joseph, did not address the Child. It would not have been fitting to give his blessing to the Son of the Highest. He blessed them; but did not bless the Child.

After his hymn of praise he addressed himself only to the mother; Simeon knew that she, and not Joseph, was related to the Babe in his arms. He saw furthermore that there were sorrows in store for her, not for Joseph. Simeon said:

> Behold, this Child is destined for the fall
> And for the rise of many in Israel,
> And for a sign that shall be contradicted.
>
> *Luke 2:34*

It was as if the whole history of the Divine Child were passing before the eyes of the old man. Every detail of that prophecy was to be fulfilled within the lifetime of the Babe. Here was a hard fact of the Cross, affirmed even before the tiny arms of the Babe could stretch themselves out straight enough to make the form of a cross. The Child would create terrible strife between good and evil, stripping the masks from each, thus provoking a terrible hatred. He would be at once a stumbling block, a sword that would divide evil from good, and a touchstone that would reveal the motives and dispositions of human hearts. Men would no longer be the same once they had heard His name and learned of His life. They would be compelled either to accept Him, or reject Him. About Him there would be no such thing as compromise: only acceptance or rejection, resurrection or death. He would, by His very nature, make men reveal their secret attitudes toward God. His mission would be not to put souls on trial, but to redeem them; and yet, because their souls were sinful, some men would detest His coming.

It would henceforth be His fate to encounter fanatical opposition from mankind even unto death itself, and this would involve Mary in cruel distress. The angel had told her, "Blessed art thou among women," and Simeon was now telling her that in her blessedness she would be the *Mater*

Dolorosa. One of the penalties of original sin was that a woman should bring forth her child in sorrow; Simeon was saying that she would continue to live in the sorrow of her Child. If He was to be the Man of Sorrows, she would be the Mother of Sorrows. An unsuffering Madonna to the suffering Christ would be a loveless Madonna. Since Christ loved mankind so much that He wanted to die to expiate its guilt, then He would also will that His mother should be wrapped in the swaddling bands of His own grief.

From the moment she heard Simeon's words, she would never again lift the Child's hands without seeing a shadow of nails on them; every sunset would be a blood-red image of His Passion. Simeon was throwing away the sheath that hid the future from human eyes, and letting the blade of the world's sorrow flash in front of her eyes. Every pulse that she would feel in the tiny wrist would be like an echo of an oncoming hammer. If He was dedicated to salvation through suffering, so was she. No sooner was this young life launched than Simeon, like an old mariner, talked of shipwreck. No cup of the Father's bitterness had yet come to the lips of the Babe, and yet a sword was shown to His mother.

The nearer Christ comes to a heart, the more it becomes conscious of its guilt; it will then either ask for His mercy and find peace, or else it will turn against Him because it is not yet ready to give up its sinfulness. Thus He will separate the good from the bad, the wheat from the chaff. Man's reaction to this Divine Presence will be the test: either it will call out all the opposition of egotistic natures, or else galvanize them into a regeneration and a resurrection.

Simeon was practically calling Him the "Divine Disturber," Who would provoke human hearts either to good or evil. Once confronted with Him, they must subscribe either to light or darkness. Before everyone else they can be "broadminded"; but His Presence reveals their hearts to be either fertile ground or hard rock. He cannot come to hearts without clarifying them and dividing them; once in His Presence, a heart discovers both its own thoughts about goodness and its own thoughts about God.

This could never be so if He was just a humanitarian teacher. Simeon knew this well, and he told Our Lord's mother that her Son must suffer because His life would be so much opposed to the complacent maxims by which most men govern their lives. He would act on one soul in one way, and on another in another way, as the sun shines on wax and softens it, and shines on mud and hardens it. There is no difference in the sun, only in the objects on which it shines. As the Light of the World, He would be a joy to the good and the lovers of light; but He would be like a probing searchlight to those who were evil and preferred to live in darkness. The seed is the same, but the soil is different, and each soil will be judged by the way it reacts to the seed. The will of Christ to save is limited by the free reaction of each soul either to accept or reject. That was what Simeon meant by saying:

> And so the thoughts of many hearts shall be made manifest.
>
> *Luke 2:35*

An Eastern fable tells of a magic mirror that remained clear when the good looked upon it, and became sullied when the impure gazed at it. Thus the owner could always tell the character of those who used it. Simeon was telling His mother that her Son would be like this mirror; men would either love or hate Him, according to their own reflections. A light falling on a sensitive photographic plate registers a chemical change that cannot be effaced. Simeon was saying that the Light of the Babe falling on Jew and Gentile would stamp on each the ineffaceable vestige of its presence.

Simeon also said that the Babe would disclose the true inner dispositions of men. He would test the thoughts of all who were to encounter Him. Pilate would temporize and then weaken; Herod would mock, Judas would lean to a kind of greedy social security; Nicodemus would sneak in darkness to find the Light; tax collectors would become honest; prostitutes, pure; rich young men would reject His poverty; prodigals would return home; Peter would repent; an Apostle would hang himself. From that day to this, He continues to be a sign to be contradicted. It was fitting, therefore, that He should die on a piece of wood in which one bar contradicted the other. The vertical bar of God's will is negated by the horizontal bar of the contradicting human will. As the Circumcision pointed to the shedding of blood, so the Purification foretold His Crucifixion.

After saying that He was a sign to be contradicted, Simeon turned to the mother, adding:

> As for thy own soul, it shall have a
> Sword to pierce it.
>
> *Luke 2:35*

She was told that He would be rejected by the world, and with His Crucifixion there would be her transfixion. As the Child willed the Cross for Himself, so He willed the Sword of Sorrow for her. If he chose to be a Man of Sorrows, He also chose her to be a Mother of Sorrows! God does not always spare the good from grief. The Father spared not the Son, and the Son spared not the mother, With His Passion there must be her compassion. An unsuffering Christ Who did not freely pay the debt of human guilt would be reduced to the level of an ethical guide; and a mother who did not share in His sufferings would be unworthy of her great role.

Simeon not only unsheathed a sword; he also told her where Providence had destined it to be driven. Later on, the Child would say, "I came to bring the sword." Simeon told her that she would feel it in her heart while her Son was hanging on the sign of contradiction and she was standing beneath it transfixed in grief. The spear that would physically pierce His heart would mystically be run into her own heart. The Babe came to die, not to live, for His name was "Savior."

MAGI AND THE SLAUGHTER OF THE INNOCENTS

Simeon had foretold that the Divine Babe would be a Light to the Gentiles. They were already on the march. At His birth there were the Magi, or the scientists of the East; at His death, there would be the Greeks, or the philosophers of the West. The Psalmist had foretold that the kings of the East would come to do homage to Emmanuel. Following a star, they came to Jerusalem to ask Herod where the King had been born.

And thereupon certain wise men came out of the
    East to Jerusalem, who asked,
Where is He that has been born,
    The king of the Jews?
We have seen His star out in the east,
    And we have come to worship Him.
Matthew 2:1-2

It was a star that led them. God spoke to the Gentiles through
nature and philosophers; to the Jews, through prophecies. The
time was ripe for the coming of the Messias and the whole world
knew it. Though they were astrologers, the slight vestige of
truth in their knowledge of the stars led them to the Star out
of Jacob, as the "Unknown God" of the Athenians later on
would be the occasion for Paul preaching to them the God
Whom they knew not, but dimly desired. Though coming from
a land that worshiped stars, they surrendered that religion as
they fell down and worshiped Him Who made the stars. The
Gentiles in fulfillment of the prophecies of Isaias and Jeremias
"Came to Him from the ends of the earth." The Star, which
disappeared during the interrogation of Herod, reappeared and
finally stood over the place where the Child was born.

They, when they saw the star,
    Were glad beyond measure;
And so, going into the dwelling, they
    Found the Child there, with his mother Mary,
And fell down to worship Him; and,
    Opening their store of treasures,
They offered Him gifts, of gold and frankincense and
    myrrh.
Matthew 2:10-11

Isaias had prophesied:

A stream of camels thronging about thee,
    Dromedaries from Madian and Epha,
Bringing all the men of Saba with their gifts
    Of gold and incense,
Their cry of praise to the Lord!
Isaias 60:6

They brought three gifts; gold to honor His Kingship, frankincense to honor His Divinity, and myrrh to honor His Humanity which was destined for death. Myrrh was used at His burial. The crib and the Cross are related again, for there is myrrh at both.

When the Magi came from the East bringing gifts for the Babe, Herod the Great knew that the time had come for the birth of the King announced clearly to the Jews, and apprehended dimly in the aspirations of the Gentiles. But like all carnal-minded men, he lacked a spiritual sense, and therefore felt certain that the King would be a political one. He made inquiries as to where Christ was to be born. The chief priests and learned men told him, "At Bethlehem in Judea, for so it has been written by the prophet." Herod said that he wanted to worship the Babe. But his actions proved that he really meant, "If this is the Messias, I must kill Him."

> Meanwhile, when he found that the wise men
> Had played him false, Herod was angry
> Beyond measure; he sent and made away with all
> The male children in Bethlehem.
>
> *Matthew 2:16*

Herod will forever be the model of those who make inquiries about religion, but who never act rightly on the knowledge they receive. Like train announcers, they know all the stations, but never travel. Head knowledge is worthless, unless accompanied by submission of the will and right action.

Totalitarians are fond of saying that Christianity is the enemy of the State — a euphemistic way of saying an enemy of themselves. Herod was the first totalitarian to sense this; he found Christ to be his enemy before He was two years old. Could a Babe born under the earth in a cave shake potentates and kings? Could He, Who as yet had no *demos* or people following Him, be a dangerous enemy of the *demos-cratos* or democracy, the rule of the people? No mere human baby could ever provoke such violence by a State. The Czar did not fear Stalin, the son of a cobbler, when he was two years old; he did not drive the cobbler's son and his mother into exile for fear that he would one day be a menace to the world. Similarly, no swords hung over the head of the infant Hitler, nor did the government move against Mao Tse-tung while he was still in swaddling clothes because it feared that he would some day deliver China to the murderous sickle. Why then were the soldiers summoned against this Infant? It must surely have been because those who possess the spirit of the world conceal an instinctive hatred and jealousy of God Who reigns over human hearts. The hatred the second Herod would show Christ at His death had its prologue in the hatred of his father, Herod the Great, for Christ as a Babe.

Herod was fearful that He Who came to bring a heavenly crown would steal away his own tinsel one. He pretended that he wanted to bring gifts, but the only gift he wanted to bring was death. Wicked men sometimes hide their evil designs under an appearance of religion: "I am a religious man, but . . . ." Men can make inquiries about Christ for two reasons, either to worship or to harm. Some would even make use of religion for their evil designs, as Herod made use of the Wise Men. Inquiries about religion do not produce the same results in all hearts. *What* men ask about Divinity is never as important as *why* they ask it.

Before Christ was two years of age, there was a shedding of blood for His sake. It was the first attempt on His life. A sword for the Babe; stones for the Man; the Cross at the end. That was how His own received Him. Bethlehem was the dawn of Calvary. The law of sacrifice that would wind itself around Him and His apostles, and around so many of His followers for centuries to come, began its work by snatching these young lives which are so happily commemorated in the Feast of the Holy Innocents. An upended cross for Peter, a push from a steeple for James, a knife for Bartholomew, a cauldron of oil followed by long waiting for John, a sword for Paul, and many swords for the innocent babies of Bethlehem. "The world will hate you," Christ promised all those who were signed with His seal. These Innocents died for the King Whom they had never known. Like little lambs, they died for the sake of the Lamb, the prototypes of a long procession of martyrs — these children who never struggled, but were crowned. In the Circumcision He shed His own Blood; now His coming heralds the shedding of the blood of others for His sake. As circumcision was the

317

mark of the Old Law, so persecution would be the mark of the New Law. "For My name's sake," He told His Apostles they would be hated. All things around Him speak of His death, for that was the purpose of His coming. The very entrance door over the stable where He was born was marked with blood, as was the threshold of the Jews in Egypt. Innocent lambs in the Passover bled for Him in centuries past; now innocent children without spot, little human lambs, bled for Him.

> But God warned the Wise Men not to return to Herod,
>   So they returned to their own country
>   By a different way.
>> *Matthew 2:12*

No one who ever meets Christ with a good will returns the same way as he came. Baffled in his design to kill the Divine, the enraged tyrant ordered the indiscriminate slaughter of all male children under two years of age. There are more ways than one of practicing birth control.

Mary was already prepared for a Cross in the life of her Babe, but Joseph, moving on a lower level of awareness, needed the revelation of an angel, telling him to take the Child and His mother into Egypt.

> Rise up, take with thee the Child
>   And His mother, and flee to Egypt;
> There remain, until I give thee word.
>   For Herod will soon be making search for the child,
> To destroy Him.
>   He rose up, therefore,
> While it was still night, and took the child
>   And His mother with Him,
> And withdrew into Egypt, where he
>   Remained until the death of Herod.
> > *Matthew 2:13*

Exile was to be the lot of the Savior, otherwise the millions of exiles from persecuted lands would be without a God Who understood the agony of homelessness and frantic flight. By His Presence in Egypt, the Infant Savior consecrated a land that had been the traditional enemy of His own people, and

thus gave hope to other lands which would later reject Him.
The Exodus was reversed, as the Divine Child made Egypt His
temporary home. Mary now sang as Miriam had done, while a
second Joseph guarded the Living Bread for which human hearts
were starving. The murder of the Innocents by Herod recalls
Pharaoh's slaughter of the Hebrew children; and what happened
when Herod died recalled the original Exodus. When Herod
the Great died, an angel charted the course of Joseph, bidding
him to return to Galilee. He came and settled there in fulfillment of what had been said by the prophets, "He shall be a
Nazarene."

> And now when all had been done that the
> Law of the Lord required,
> They returned to Galilee, and to their
> Own town of Nazareth.
>
> *Luke 2:39*

The term "Nazarene" signified contempt. The little village
was of ` the main roads at the foot of the mountains; nestling
in a cup of hills, it was out of reach of the merchants of Greece,
the legions of Rome, and the journeys of the sophisticated. It
is not mentioned in ancient geographies. It deserved its name,
for it was just a "netzer," a sprout that grows on the stump of
a tree. Centuries before, Isaias had foretold that a "branch,"
or "sprout," or "netzer," would grow out of the roots of the
country; it would seem to be of little value and many would
despise it, but it would ultimately have dominion over the
earth. The fact that Christ took up His residence in a despised
village was a prefigurement of the obscurity and ignominy that
would ever plague Him and His followers. The name "Nazareth"
would be nailed over His Head on the "sign of contradiction"
as a scornful repudiation of His claims. Before that, when Philip
told Nathanael:

> We have discovered who it was Moses wrote of in his Law,
> And the prophet too;
> It is Jesus, the Son of Joseph, from Nazareth.
>
> *John 1:45*

319

Nathanael would retort:

Can anything good come from Nazareth?
John 1:46

The big cities are sometimes thought to contain all the
wisdom, while the little towns are looked upon as backward
and unprogressive, Christ chose the insignificant Bethlehem
for the glory of His birth; the ridiculed Nazareth for His youth;
but the glorious, cosmopolitan Jerusalem for the ignominy of
His death. "Can anything good come out of Nazareth?" is but
the prelude to "Can anything redemptive come from a man
who dies on a cross?"

Nazareth would be a place of humiliation for Him, a training
ground for Golgotha. Nazareth was in Galilee, and the whole of
Galilee was a despised region in the eyes of the more cultured
people of Judea. Galilean speech was supposed to be crude and
rude, so much so that when Peter denied Our Lord, the maid-
servant reminded him that his speech betrayed him; he had been
with the Galilean. No one would ever look to Galilee, therefore,
for a teacher; and yet the Light of the World was the Galilean.
God chooses the foolish things of the world to confound the
self-wise and proud. Nathanael merely gave expression in an
evil prejudice probably as old as humanity itself; people and
their power to teach are judged by the places whence they
come. Worldly wisdom comes from where we expect it, in the
best-sellers, the "standard brands" and universities. Divine
Wisdom comes from the unsuspected quarters, which the world
holds in derision. The ignominy of Nazareth would hang about
Him later on. His hearers would taunt:

How does this man know how to read?
He has never studied.
John 7:15

While this was a reluctant tribute to His learning, it was also
a sneer at His "backwoods" village . . . . How did He know?
They did not suspect the true answer; namely, that in addition
to the knowledge of His human intellect, He had a Wisdom that
was not school-taught, nor self-taught, nor even God-taught,
in the sense in which the prophets were God-taught. He
learned from His mother and the village synagogue; but the

320

secrets of His knowledge must be found in His oneness with the Heavenly Father.

1 'What Child Is This?" John Cardinal Wright.

2"Christmas Discovery." Thomas Merton. *Commonweal,* Dec. 27, 1968.©1968 by Commonweal Publishing Co., Inc.

3"Mother Means Love." Fulton J. Sheen. *Life is Worth Living.* ©1953 by the McGraw-Hill Book Co.

4"The Cave of Bethlehem." Denis O'Shea. *The First Christmas.* ©1952. Bruce Publishing Co.

5"The Virgin Birth." Denis O'Shea. *The First Christmas,* ©1952. Bruce Publishing Co.

6"Why in a Cave?" Giuseppe Ricciotti. *Life of Christ.* ©1947. Bruce Publishing Co., Translated by Alba I. Zizzamia.

7"Through the Speech of Angels." Henri Daniel-Rops. *The Life of Our Lord.* ©1964. Hawthorn Books, Inc.

8"Shepherds of Bethlehem." Richard Murphy, O.P. *The Bible Today.* ©1964 by the Liturgical Press.

9"The Star the Magi Saw." Kay Sullivan.

10"When Our Lord Was a Boy." Francis L. Filas, S.J. *The Family for Families.* ©1951 J. S. Paluch Co., Inc.

11"The Infant Warrior." R. L. Bruckberger. *The History of Jesus Christ.* ©1965 by R. L. Bruckberger, Viking Press.

12"Why We Have a Saviour." Sister Eugene, S.C.

13"The Family in the Parking Lot." Norman Spray. *Guideposts Magazine,* Dec. 1969.©1969 by Guideposts Associates, Inc.

14"Oatmeal for Christmas." John J. Marquardt. *Glenmary's Challenge.* Christmas 1963. Official organ of the Glenmary Home Missioners.

15"Sleep in Heavenly Peace." Father John Reedy, C.S.C. *U. S. Catholic.* ©1975 by Claretian Publications.

16"Joe's Christmas Gifts." Vincent Argondezzi.

17 "The Day After Christmas." Paul C. O'Connor, *S. J. Alaska*. Dec. 1970. © 1970 by Alaska Northwest Publishing Co.

18 "A Contemporary Christmas Carol." Marvin R. O'Connell. *Catholic Bulletin*. Dec. 19, 1969. © 1969 by Catholic Bulletin Publishing Co.

19 "Christmas Stocking." Bob Considine. *Bob Considine's Christmas Stocking*. © under International and Pan-American Copyright Conventions © 1958 by Hawthorn Books, Inc.

20 "My Christmas Story." Leon Williams.

21 "When Christmas Came Again." Dina Donohue. *Guideposts*, Dec. 1969. © 1968 by Guidepost Associates, Inc.

22 "Grandfather's Christmas Story." Nova M. Lee. *Good Old Days*, Dec. 1971. © 1971 by Good Old Days.

23 "The Christmas After Alice Died." Harold Melowski.

24 "No Room at the Motel." C. W. Chambers. *Detroit News*, Dec. 1, 1974. © 1974 by the Detroit News.

25 "The Twelve Days of Christmas." Ralph Reppert. *The Sunday Sun*. Dec. 20, 1971, © 1971 by the A. S. Abell Co.

26 "Christmas Grows On Many Trees." Harold Dunn.

27 "The Christmas We Hunted Henry James." Richard W. O'Donnell.

28 "Christmas Kidnaping." Maurice S. Sheehy (U.S.N.R.)

29 "Christmas Cards Are Clues to Character." Diana Serra Cary.

30 "My Christmas Tree Angel." Miriam Lynch.

31 "My First American Christmas." Louise Sottosanti.

32 "In a Little Methodist Church on Christmas." Joseph O'Donnell. *Glenmary's Challenge*. Dec. 1967. © 1967 by Glenmary Home Missioners.

33 "I Remember Handel's 'Messiah'". Joseph Sittler. *The Christian Century*, Dec. 22, 1965. ©1965 by Christian Century Foundation.

34 "The Choir from Little Hell." Robert Hardy Andrews. *A Corner of Chicago*, ©1963 by Robert Hardy Andrews, Little, Brown & Co.

35 "The Angel Song." Janos Varkonyi.

36 "On Christmas Eve." James Wolfgram. *Family Horizons.* Winter 1971-72. ©1972 by the Cuna Mutual Insurance Society.

37 "An Old-time Christmas." Doran Hurley. *Information.* Jan. 1958. ©1958 by Missionary Society of St. Paul the Apostle.

38 "Helping Out — My Two Weeks of Christmas Masses." Alcantara Gracias, S.F.X.

39 "First Christmas in the New World." June A. Grimble.

40 "Mexican Magi." Martha Murray.

41 "My Christmas in Rome." Francis R. Moeslein. *North Carolina Catholic.* Dec. 21, 1956. ©1956 by North Carolina Catholic.

42 "Holy Night." James E. Walsh. *The Young Ones.* 1958 by The Maryknoll Fathers, Farrar, Straus & Cudahy.

43 "One Holy Night in Japan." Tats Blain. *Mother-Sir!* Hawthorn Books, Inc. ©1951, 1953, Mary D. Blain.

44 "Christmas in North Dakota." Helen C. Califano. *Ave Maria,* Dec. 23, 1944.

45 "The Donkey's Ears." June A. Grimble

46 "The Fox at the Manger." P. L. Travers. *Town & Country,* December 1949.

47 "The Birthplace of Santa Claus." Marcus Brooke.

48"Silent Night." By Hertha Pauli. Condensed from the book © 1943 by Alfred A. Knopf, NYC

49"The Poetry of Christmas." John Druska. *Commonweal.* Dec. 20, 1974. © 1974 by Commonweal Publishing Co., Inc.

50"The Burning Babe." Francis Howard. *Catholic Herald Citizen.* Dec. 14, 1968. © 1968 by Milwaukee Catholic Press Apostolate.

51"Anniversary of a Guitar Mass." Dan Madden.

52"Merry Christmas Cooking." Florence S. Berger. *Cooking for Christ,* 1949. National Catholic Life Conference.

53"Blessed Are the Christmas Shoppers." Daniel Durken, O.S.B. *Sisters Today.* Dec. 1974. © 1974 by Sisters Today.

54"Give a Gift of Time." Peg Kehret. *Christian Herald.* August, 1972. © 1972 by Christian Herald.

55"Christmas in Stamps." M. W. Martin. *Tropical Stamp Collecting.* © 1975 by M. W. Martin. Avco Publishing Co., Inc.

56"The Early Life of Christ on Earth." Fulton J. Sheen. © 1958 by Fulton J. Sheen. McGraw-Hill Book Co., Inc.

325